CRITICAL PERSPECTIVES
IN INTERNATIONAL STUDIES

CRITICAL PERSPECTIVES IN INTERNATIONAL STUDIES

Edited by

Frank P. Harvey and Michael Brecher

Ann Arbor

THE UNIVERSITY OF MICHIGAN PRESS

Copyright © by the University of Michigan 2002
All rights reserved
Published in the United States of America by
The University of Michigan Press
Manufactured in the United States of America
∞ Printed on acid-free paper

2005   2004   2003   2002   4   3   2   1

A CIP catalog record for this book is available from
the British Library.

Library of Congress Cataloging-in-Publication Data applied for
ISBN 0-472-08862-9

ACKNOWLEDGMENTS

The editors would like to thank the distinguished scholars who contributed to this project for their gracious response to our demands over an extended period. We are very grateful to Jeremy Shine, political science editor of the University of Michigan Press, for his encouragement and support; to the International Studies Association for the opportunity to organize the millennial reflections panels at the Los Angeles conference in March 2000; to Ann Griffiths and Graham Walker for their excellent editorial assistance; to Kevin Rennells, of the University of Michigan Press, and to Impressions Book and Journal Services, for steering this multivolume project to publication with skill and empathy; and to Sarah Lemann for valuable word-processing assistance in the preparation of the typescript.

Frank Harvey would like to thank Michael Brecher for the privilege of serving as ISA program chair in 1999–2000 and for his truly outstanding contribution to the intellectual quality of the final manuscript, the Social Sciences and Humanities Research Council of Canada, the Centre for Foreign Policy Studies (Dalhousie University), and the Security and Defence Forum (Directorate of Public Policy, Department of National Defence, Canada) for supporting various stages of the project. Michael Brecher wishes to thank Frank Harvey for his selfless and invaluable role as coeditor of the Millennial Reflections Project. He also appreciates the reduced teaching load accorded by McGill University for the autumn term of 1999, which facilitated the organization of the millennial reflections panels and, more generally, the ISA's Los Angeles conference in March 2000.

Contents

THE ESSENCE OF MILLENNIAL REFLECTIONS ON INTERNATIONAL STUDIES

Critical Perspectives

Michael Brecher and Frank P. Harvey

When Michael Brecher was introduced to international relations (IR) at Yale in 1946, the field comprised international politics, international law and organization, international economics, international (diplomatic) history, and a regional specialization. The hegemonic paradigm was realism, as expressed in the work of E. H. Carr, Arnold Wolfers, Nicholas Spykman, W. T. R. Fox, Hans Morgenthau, Bernard Brodie, and others.[1] The unquestioned focus of attention was interstate war and peace.

By the time the other editor of this collection, Frank Harvey, was initiated into international relations at McGill in the late 1980s, the preeminent paradigm was neorealism,[2] but there were several competing claimants to the "true path": institutional theory,[3] cognitive psychology,[4] and postmodernism.[5] And by the time he received his doctoral degree, other competitors had emerged, notably, critical theory,[6] constructivism,[7] and feminism.[8]

The consequence, at the dawn of the new millennium, was a vigorous, still inconclusive, debate about the optimal path to knowledge about international studies (IS), most clearly expressed in the views that it is a discipline—international relations (IR) or world politics—like economics, sociology, anthropology, history, or that it is a multidisciplinary field of study; the "big tent" conception of the premier organization, the International Studies Association (ISA).

It was in this context that the Millennial Reflections Project was conceived. The origin and rationale of the idea may be found in the central theme of Michael Brecher's presidential address to the ISA conference in Washington in February 1999: "International Studies in the Twentieth Century and Beyond: Flawed Dichotomies, Synthesis, Cumulation." The next stage was the creation of a set of ten millennial reflections theme-panels by Michael Brecher, then ISA president, and Frank Harvey, the program chair for ISA 2000: these panels served as the highly successful centerpiece of the Los Angeles conference in March 2000. Soon after, we enlisted the enthusiastic support of the University of Michigan Press for the idea of publishing revised and enlarged versions of these conference papers. Most of the participants in the Los Angeles panels readily agreed to revise and enlarge their papers. A few other papers were invited. The result is this volume and the accompanying set of four shorter, segment-focused volumes, prepared for the benefit of teachers and students of IS in colleges and universities everywhere.

Whether a discipline or a multidisciplinary field of study, IS has developed over the last half century with diverse philosophical underpinnings, frameworks of analysis, methodologies, and foci of attention. This diversity is evident in the papers that were presented at the panels at the 2000 Los Angeles conference and revised for publication in this state-of-the-art collection of essays on international studies at the dawn of the new millennium.

In an attempt to capture the range, diversity, and complexity of IS, we decided to organize the forty-four "think piece" essays into eight clusters. The mainstream paradigms of realism and institutionalism constitute the first two concentrations; critical perspectives (including critical theory, postmodernism, and constructivism); feminism and gender perspectives; methodology (including quantitative, formal modeling, and qualitative); foreign policy analysis; international security, peace, and war; and international political economy make up the remaining six.

The raison d'être of the Millennial Reflections Project was set out in the theme statement of the Los Angeles conference, titled "Reflection, Integration, Cumulation: International Studies Past and Future." As we noted in that statement, the number and size of subfields and sections has grown steadily since the founding of the International Studies Association in 1959. This diversity, while enriching, has made increasingly difficult the crucial task of identifying intrasubfield, let alone intersubfield, consensus about important theoretical and empirical insights. Aside from focusing on a cluster of shared research questions related, for example, to globalization, gender and international relations, critical theory, political economy, international institutions, global development, democracy and peace, foreign and security policy, and so on, there are still few clear signs of cumulation.

If the maturity of an academic discipline is based not only on its capacity to expand but also on its capacity to select, the lack of agreement *within* these communities is particularly disquieting. Realists, for instance, cannot fully agree on their paradigm's core assumptions, central postulates, or the lessons learned from empirical research. Similarly, feminist epistemologies encompass an array of research programs and findings that are not easily grouped into a common set of beliefs, theories, or conclusions. If those who share common interests and perspectives have difficulty agreeing on what they have accomplished to date or do not concern themselves with the question of what has been achieved so far, how can they establish clear targets to facilitate creative dialogue across these diverse perspectives and subfields?

With this in mind, our objective was to challenge proponents of specific paradigms, theories, approaches, and substantive issue areas to confront their own limitations by engaging in self-critical reflection within epistemologies and perspectives. The objective was to stimulate debates about successes and failures but to do so by avoiding the tendency to define accomplishments with reference to the failures and weaknesses of other perspectives.

It is important to note that our call to assess the state of the art of international studies was not meant as a reaffirmation of the standard proposition that a rigorous process of theoretical cumulation is both possible and necessary. Not all perspectives and subfields of IS are directed to accomplishing cumulation in this sense. Some participants found the use of such words as *synthesis* and *progress* suspect, declaring in their original papers that they could not, or were not prepared to, address these social science–type questions. We nevertheless encouraged these individuals to define what they considered to be fair measures of success and failure in regard to their subfield, and we asked them to assess the extent to which core objectives (whatever they may be) have or have not been met, and why.

Our intention obviously was not to tie individuals to a particular set of methodological tenets, standards, assumptions, or constraints.

We simply wanted to encourage self-reflective discussion and debate about significant achievements and failures. Even where critiques of mainstream theory and methodology are part of a subfield's raison d'être, the lack of consensus is still apparent and relevant.

As a community of scholars, we are rarely challenged to address the larger question of *success* and *progress* (however one chooses to define these terms), perhaps because there is so little agreement on the methods and standards we should use to identify and integrate important observations, arguments, and findings.

To prevent intellectual diversity descending into intellectual anarchy, the editors set out "guidelines" for the contributors, in the form of six theme questions, or tasks. The panelists were requested to address one or more of these tasks in their essays:

1. Engage in self-critical, state-of-the-art reflection on accomplishments and failures, especially since the creation of the ISA more than forty years ago.
2. Assess where we stand on unresolved debates and why we have failed to resolve them.
3. Evaluate the intrasubfield standards we should use to assess the significance of theoretical insights.
4. Explore ways to achieve fruitful synthesis of approaches, both in terms of core research questions and appropriate methodologies.
5. Address the broader question of progress in international studies.
6. Select an agenda of topics and research questions that should guide the subfield during the coming decades.

The result, as is evident in the pages to follow, is an array of thought-provoking think pieces that indicate shortcomings as well as achievements and specify the unfinished business of IS as a scholarly field in the next decade or more, with wide-ranging policy implications in the shared quest for world order. Readers will no doubt derive different conclusions from the various contributions. Some will observe that divisions within and across subfields of international studies are so entrenched that constructive dialogue is virtually impossible. Others will conclude that there is much more consensus than might have been imagined. In either case, the need for self-critical assessment among IS scholars is imperative as we enter the new millennium.

Alternative and Critical Perspectives

A diverse group of critical perspectives on international studies is represented in this segment: an overview (Steve Smith); critical theory (Robert W. Cox); radical theory (Michael Cox); constructivism (Ernst B. Haas and Peter M. Haas); postmodernism (Yosef Lapid, R. J. Walker); system change (James N. Rosenau); and a cluster of feminist gender perspectives (Ling, Peterson, Pettman, Sylvester, Tickner, and Zalewski).

Smith

The rationale of Steve Smith's "Alternative and Critical Perspectives" is the need to defend the legitimacy and affirm the importance of "nonmainstream theoretical work within IR." This takes the form of an unremitting critique of the U.S.–centered, social science–oriented mainstream of international relations (realism and liberalism).

The pervasive tone of this millennial reflections paper is evident in Smith's lengthy response to the editors' request for a "self-critical, state-of-the-art reflection on accomplishments and failures" in one's own field: it takes the form of a blunt attack on "the incredible power of the critiques of a number of writers who claim that alternative approaches are not part of the social science enterprise" and engage in "the delegitimization of reflectivist approaches." Those cited are Katzenstein, Keohane, and Krasner in the 1998 special issue of *International Organization*; Keohane's presidential address to the ISA in 1988; and Steve Walt.

The attack continues: "This does not mean that there have been no [nonmainstream] successes, only that these successes have never changed the nature of the mainstream. . . . Why is this? . . . [because] the mainstream has tended to reconsolidate itself so as to continue the U.S. social science project"; and, in that context, he accuses Keohane and the others of co-opting the Wendt version of social constructivism.

Smith notes that critical perspectives reject the "four main tenets of U.S. social science"—the fact/value distinction, empiricism as the optimal epistemology, naturalism as possible, and the goal of uncovering regularities in the social world. He acknowledges the failure to establish an alternative epistemology: this he attributes partly to disagreement among themselves; and "secondly, the grip on the discipline of positivism U.S.-style is so great as to close down any space for alternatives. This is the nub of the issue." He also quotes, approvingly, Ole Waever's criticism in the 1998 *IO* special issue of "the internal intellectual structure of American IR . . . [its] disciplinary elite . . . [and the claim that] American IR alone generates an apex that therefore comes to serve as the global core of the discipline."

On the second theme of the Millennial Reflections Project—assess where we stand on key debates and why we have failed to resolve them—Smith rejects the two underlying assumptions: first, "that the key debates are debates open to all . . . [and] second, that they can be resolved. . . . I do not think that the mainstream is willing to assess 'alternative' perspectives on any terms other than its own . . . [and the notion of "resolved"] is based on a positivist view of inquiry."

Smith's fundamental rejection of mainstream IR thought is also apparent in his response to the third theme—that is, evaluate what intrasubfield standards we should use to evaluate the significance of theoretical insights. He responds: "The 'alternative and critical' approaches tend to resist any attempt to make the kinds of assessments about 'progress' or 'success'. . . . The reason is obvious: the language of 'assessment,' 'progress,' 'success' smack of a modernist notion of knowledge . . . [and they are] not . . . willing to buy into this model of assessment." As for "the broader question of progress," "frankly, I do not see much progress in IR."

In a more subdued tone, he concludes by expressing the "hope that theoretical work, of whatever persuasion, should be informed by, and in turn inform, empirical material . . . [and that] the discipline will foster intellectual pluralism and open rather than close down analytical space."

Cox (Robert)

Robert Cox introduced critical theory to international studies in the early 1980s and has been its most prolific and influential advocate since then. His paper, "Universality in International Studies: A Historicist Approach," is much narrower in scope than Smith's overview of critical perspectives and is very different in tone: it focuses on "the issue of universality versus relativism (which includes the issue of positivism versus historicism)."

The critical theory approach is framed in terms of three questions: "(1) What is critical theory and how has it come into international studies? (2) What is the core philosophical issue inherent to critical theory? (3) What ontology can the critical approach propose as a framework for inquiry and action?"

For Cox, critical theory is synonymous with problem-solving theory. "The existing world is a given (datum). . . . The analyst is concerned with dysfunctions, with homeostasis, and the restoration of equilibrium. . . . Critical theory takes a diachronic perspective, one of history informed by sociological theory. . . . The analyst, the historically oriented social scientist, goes through a double process of historical thinking . . . self-consciousness of one's own historical time and place . . . [and] the effort to understand the historical dynamics that brought about the conditions in which these questions arise."

The issue of universality relates to norms and knowledge. Cox rejects the European Enlightenment consensus that both were universal in time and space, in favor of the "dissident perspective" of Vico, Kant, and, later, Dilthey, Croce, Collingwood, Heidegger, and Gramsci, who viewed the study of history as basically different from physical science. Cox claims that the gap between positivist natural science and intersubjective social science has narrowed as a result of a growing recognition in physics that its laws are more relative than absolute.

Cox extends this line of argument to prehistorical biological evolution and concludes that humanity is "a product of the very *longue durée* [Braudel's term for early modern history] of biological history," which will end through self-destruction or a long evolution, a theme for which he discerns support in Carl Jung's concept of the collective unconscious. He also notes his preference for Weber's notion of an ethic of responsibility rather than an ethic of ultimate ends.

Cox concludes his reflections by framing the critical research program in terms of his view of the primary purpose of international studies: it is "to prepare the ground for a pluralist world of diversity in social organization and ethical norms"—not dissimilar from Smith's call for pluralism in IS. Thus his IS research program would include "the study of civilizations, civil society and its complex context including the covert world, the maintenance of the biosphere, and the problem of social cohesion for the maintenance of collective entities and their institutions." As with Smith, this is a very different conception than mainstream IR, both in the realism and institutionalism versions.

Cox (Michael)

Michael Cox begins his wide-ranging survey of radical, mostly Marxist—traditional, neo–, Gramscian and other—literature on IR, "The Continuing Story of Another Death Foretold: Radical Theory and the New International Relations," with a scathing criticism of IR: "by any measure [notably its proven ability to anticipate future global trends] it has to be judged to have been one of the more dismal of the social sciences." Among the "major academic trends" in IR, the one that "has suffered the greatest damage . . . as a result of what happened in 1989 [is] that loosely defined, deeply divided and heterogeneous current . . . known rather vaguely as 'radical.'" Cox, however, suggests that "just as with realism, it might still be a little premature to declare it dead altogether."

He defines his task as summarizing "a large, very uneven, and deeply schismatic literature"—radical IR—focusing on four themes: how radicals came to terms with the death of socialism in the Soviet bloc and the end of the cold war; their intellectual response to globalization; the development of a radical theory of crisis; and how they cope with American hegemony, as well as with a "new" world that displays "as much, if not more, suffering than at any point over the last fifty years."

Radical analysts, notes Cox, have finessed the issue of the fall of official socialism in several ways: denying that the Soviet Union and Eastern European regimes were genuinely socialist; claiming that socialism's demise was not inevitable but, rather, that it was due to Gorbachev's "ill-fated reforms"; or attributing it to external factors, notably the Reagan-era arms expenditure by the United States that Moscow could not match. Moreover, radicals tried to compensate for their problem of coming to terms with the fall of the Soviet Union by dismissing the "new" world order as nothing new at all. Some even argued that the end of communism created space for a social democratic "third way."

On the concept of "globalization," Cox notes four "quite reasonable questions" posed by radicals, each with dissenting answers. First, "what exactly is so new about the idea?" The response is *nothing* — that is, Marx, Lenin, Trotsky, and the theorists of dependency had acknowledged economic interdependence; for Cox, "it was only a recycled version of a very old idea." Second, is globalization "an accurate description of the world economy in the late twentieth century"? Here too, radicals dissent; they assert that the state and politicians can still make a difference. A third criticism of globalization is "its appalling human consequences. . . . [It] has led to the most extreme forms of inequality and economic polarization." Finally, while acknowledging that major-power war is unlikely, radicals anticipate much more intense economic competition than do advocates of globalization.

In the tradition of Hobson and classical Marxism, radical analysts are profoundly skeptical about the long-term stability of world capitalism. One part of their theory of crisis is a belief in a "fundamental contradiction between the world economy's capacity to produce and the people's ability to consume." Further, they contend that world capitalism is now dominated by finance capital, which is disinterested in full employment. And, finally, they argue that the end of the cold war has reduced the need and rationale for persistent large-scale military spending that sustained capitalist economies for almost half a century.

Three aspects of the U.S. behemoth have attracted the attention of radical IR: the use of American power; U.S. post–cold war foreign policy; and American hegemony in the global system. Most radical writings criticized U.S. intervention in Iraq in 1991. However, its intervention in ex-Yugoslavia created a dilemma: visceral antagonism to any U.S. involvement in Europe, indeed anywhere, and the awareness that only U.S. power would end the genocide in Bosnia and, later, Kosovo. The U.S. policy of "promoting democracy," by contrast, has evoked unanimous criticism as "a sham or . . . a device designed to obscure America's economic objectives in the larger capitalist system." The third aspect—is the United States in decline?— has evoked varying radical views, with reluctant acceptance that "the twenty-first century will be American." Finally, radicals accept that prospects for political renewal on the Left are dim, at best, confined to resistance to globalization, promoting democracy, and moving environmental issues to the center of the international political agenda.

Haas and Haas

The main thrust of Ernst Haas and Peter Haas's millennial reflections paper, a forthright dissent from the "scientific realism" espoused by leading figures in institutional theory such as Keohane and Nye, of whom Ernst Haas was an early mentor, is captured by its unusual title, "How We Learned to Escape Physics Envy and to

Love Pluralism and Complexity." Their objectives are "to frame a pragmatic-constructivist approach for the study of international institutions, and of IR more generally . . . [and] to sidestep the philosophical chasms now dividing the discipline"—ideographic versus nomothetic studies, explanation versus understanding, and positivism versus reflectivism, "procrustean constraints on inquiry."

Much of their paper focuses on their view of the fundamental difference between the natural and social sciences regarding truth, positivism, progress, knowledge, and cumulation. They appear to adopt a middle ground on truth: it "is neither as absolute as positivists and scientific realists demand nor as biased, subject to someone's domination, or hegemonic as relativists proclaim." However, their "consensus theory of truth" posits that "a given solution [is] true . . . only temporarily and for a restricted purpose."

The Haas and Haas espousal of constructivism is also evident in their discussion of positivism: while acknowledging its "very impressive achievements" in the natural sciences, they term its procedures "appropriate in the social sciences [only] when and where their epistemological requirements do not clash with the social construction of reality. . . . More often [than not] . . . social science inquiry is outside the positivist domain." Moreover, "In the social sciences nothing is 'discovered.' Our understanding of social reality is subject to the reflexivity of our minds." Similarly, they reject the claim to universal validity of findings: "It is difficult to formulate universal claims over time and across cultures because of the mutable nature of institutions and the potential role of free will."

In a lengthy discussion of progress, they ask: "Is there something wrong with the very notion of progress as applied to international studies? . . . Yes and no. . . . A theoretical contribution may be considered progressive if it changes the way most scholars think about the problem or puzzle . . . at a level *below that of grand theory.*"

On the foundations of their philosophical disposition, they declare, "Pragmatists, including ourselves, . . . differ from positivists because we eschew any crisp notion of causality." Further, "the world is not immediately accessible to actors. . . . Willful actors, through intersubjective activities, construct the world. Institutions are thus causes and effects of this process."

Haas and Haas distinguish three types of knowledge: brute facts, the traditional domain of natural science; hybrid facts, "much more common in the study of international institutions"; and social facts, "which exist ultimately by definition and have no meaning independently of the social world in which they exist."

"Knowledge cumulation is a social activity conducted by communities of scholars rather than by individuals working in isolation. . . . Pragmatists hold that truth is provisional. They prefer to think in terms of complex relations among variables, not simply 'A is explained by B'. . . . Progress can be had if we lower our ambitions. There will be no consensual grand theory for us."

They conclude with a call for tolerance of a plurality of approaches—tolerance being "an inevitable by-product of the double hermeneutic in which we, as pragmatist-constructivists, are stuck"—and, with that, a denigration of knowledge cumulation: "any cumulating that may be achieved is temporally and spatially limited. . . . But a few puzzles get solved along the way."

Lapid

"En Route to Knowledge: Is There a 'Third Path' (in the Third Debate)?" presents Yosef Lapid's reflections on achievements and failures in the domain of IS critical perspectives. This is done "through the related concepts of *pluralism, dialogue, and reflexivity* . . . [the] common denominators . . . in the change-oriented disciplinary transition known as the third debate." His objective is "to highlight, in particular, the wisdom of exploring more fully the promise of possible, but currently still submerged, 'third way/middle ground' positions."

"My main argument," he declares, "is based on the premise (and hope) that this polarized situation [between mainstream and critical IR perspectives] may be finally changing now." His method is to offer an update on the three responses by early advocates of critical IR—*despair, celebration,* and *reconstruction*—noted in his seminal 1989 article on the "third debate," and then to try to demonstrate how IR can benefit from *via media,* middle-ground solutions to the perennial problem of generating and employing knowledge.

Although all three critical responses are visible a decade later, they have undergone change. Despair has diminished somewhat because "the recent spectacular rise of constructivism" has made the IR mainstream "far less suspicious or paranoid about third debate–minted ideas"; but Lapid hastens to add that the mood of despair has not vanished. Lapid himself does not share this mood: "Ten years into the third debate, IR's journey to the land of better knowledge continues."

The celebratory response, by contrast, "has been constantly losing altitude": its two agenda items, the achievement of "a more open, diverse, and interdisciplinary theoretical enterprise" and "the hope for a more dialogically oriented and communicatively engaged scholarly enterprise," remain unfulfilled, in the view of its adherents, though Lapid discerns "significant and, most likely, irreversible achievements" in the first item.

The most vibrant of the critical responses at the dawn of the new millennium, in Lapid's view, is reconstruction, that is, a widespread "call . . . for 'bridge building' across the paradigmatic divides, 'dialogue' and 'interaction' among contending schools." He, too, cautiously favors the "third way" as a means of "reconfiguring pluralism, dialogue, and reflexivity in the IR domain," but he sees "little evidence of a plausible and imaginative architectural design . . . [for] such a critical disciplinary project."

Lapid's highest-priority goal is to foster pluralism, but of what kind? Here he follows Zerubavel's profile of three intellectual mindsets and their corresponding pluralist type: the rigid, leading to "fortresslike" pluralism; the fuzzy, which generates "flabby" pluralism; and the flexible mind-set, which produces a *via media* pluralism—the clear preference of Lapid, who quotes Zerubavel approvingly: "an intellectual environment that would allow for both order and creativity, structure and openmindedess, focus and change."

Such an environment would also be conducive to dialogue, a means of reconciling differences in approach to knowledge, as well as generating understanding, empathy, and, possibly, collaboration between mainstream and critical perspectives. And pluralism and dialogue, together, can facilitate reflexivity in IR.

Lapid concludes by reaffirming the central theme of his millennial reflections paper, the desirability and feasibility of energizing his third path in the third debate, so that "coalitions of the willing" (to use Ruggie's phrase) would engage in more "conversations" and fewer "great debates," to the benefit of all the diverse theoretical, epistemological, and ontological strands in international studies.

Walker (R. B. J.)

The R. B. J. Walker millennial reflections paper, "Alternative, Critical, Political," centers on "four among many possible areas of convergence among the heterogeneous literatures that are currently identified, and disciplined, as alternative and critical." However, he begins with the "primary argument" that these literatures "are interesting primarily as attempts to politicize practices that have been profoundly depoliticized." His "secondary argument" is that they "lead to engagements with the constitutive practices of a specifically modern politics, especially with the practices of sovereign authorization," a pivotal concept in his paper. In that context, he reiterates his oft-expressed view that "one way of understanding many of the problems of contemporary politics is to think of the difficulties of imagining an outside to a politics that is already constituted as a structure of insides and outsides." And he reaffirms the view of all advocates of critical IR perspectives that there is no subfield or community that can be identified as alternative or critical.

He dwells at some length on the Kantian distinction between the critical and the dogmatic, which he regards as "an unavoidable point of orientation . . . crucial, even if difficult." Surprisingly, he claims that the questions addressed by Hobbes, Machiavelli, Rousseau, Kant, and others are closer to those posed by critical theorists than to those addressed by the IR mainstream. And, in a gesture of tolerance and all-inclusiveness, he acknowledges that noncritical perspectives, including those from the mainstream, along with literary, cultural, and ecological theory, "also have much to say."

Turning to the main focus of his paper, Walker specifies "a shared concern [among alternative and critical perspectives] with four core themes. First, the tendency to interrogate the received assumptions about what the world is taken to be; . . . Second, the tendency to engage with sovereignty as an enormously complicated site of political practice, . . . Third, the tendency to get very annoyed when told that difficult questions about ontology and sovereignty ought to be adjudicated on the ground of epistemology and method. And fourth, the insistence that there are interesting parallels . . . between . . . [notions of IR] as a discipline . . . and . . . what it means to have alternative or critical perspectives on that discipline."

Walker devotes the rest of his paper to an elaboration of these themes. Although he acknowledges that "each of these four themes can be made to seem highly arcane, trivial, philosophical, and so on . . . [they] seem to get at political practices that are of considerable practical importance." He challenges the priority given to epistemology and method among mainstream theorists on two grounds: that epistemology depends on ontology and that the mainstream priorities "served to mask a sustained silence about the ontological categories and assumptions that are thereby reified." He adds, to clarify his view, "questions about how we know what we claim to know are dependent on what we assume we are trying to know." Yet "epistemology remains crucially important." But on social science: "Critique trumps social science, not the other way around. Or rather, there is no social or any other kind of science without critique." He is also critical of social constructivism, "a term that makes little sense to me unless taken as some vintage opposition to a claim to nature, to essence, or a methodological injunction to reify." And he concludes: "it is this fourth set of convergences that seems to me to be the most significant. . . . the problem of authorization (the Hobbesian *problem* of sovereignty . . .) [is crucial; but IR theory, like political theory, has refused] to take the problem of sovereignty seriously"; "there is certainly a lot of work to be done."

Rosenau

In his reflections on the state of international relations, James Rosenau expresses "mixed feelings": he has "no doubt" there has been "enormous growth and progress" in concepts and methodology since the 1950s; "on the other hand, . . . [he has] doubts about the field's capacity for adapting to the transformations at work in the world today."

The central thesis of "The Globalization of Globalization" is that "the preoccupation with the dynamics of globalization, both good and bad, has undergone globalization," although in his view, political science and IR lag far behind other social sciences in this regard.

His "out-of-the-mainstream perspectives" are articulated in terms of four major dimensions of globalization. The first is change—"a major conceptual challenge . . . how do we know change when we see it? How do we differentiate between evolutionary and breakpoint change?" He finds our conceptual ability to assess the durability of change or its early indicators rudimentary, at best. The second dimension is "fragmegration," a concept Rosenau introduced in 1983 that merges forces for centralization and integration with decentralization and fragmentation. For Rosenau, the contemporary era is one of fragmegration, not simply globalization. There are many sources of this hybrid process—the "skill revolution"; authority crises; bifurcation of global structures; the organizational explosion; mobility upheaval; microelectronic technologies; the weakening of territoriality, states, and sovereignty; and the globalization of economies; all of which Rosenau discusses at four levels of aggregation—micro, macro, macro-macro, micro-macro, a concept similar to, but not quite the same as, systemism as elucidated by James in his paper on realism. The third dimension is micro-macro links—Rosenau deplores the lack of a viable theory in this domain and the indifference of IR scholars to the puzzles raised by these links. The last dimension is methodology—he deems conventional linear methods inadequate and urges reliance on nonlinear procedures made possible by advances in computer technology, although these are not specified except for a reference to computer simulation.

His hope for future advances in the IR field rests with the training of students in these hitherto ignored or underused methodologies now available to the IR community.

Feminist Theory and Gender Perspectives

Ling

In "The Fish and the Turtle: Multiple Worlds as Method," L. H. M. Ling uses a Vietnamese folktale to assert "the central problematique facing our discipline . . . today: multiple worlds and how to know them." After many traditional-type questions from the fish, to which the turtle replies simply, "No," causing the fish to swim away in anger, the turtle sighs, "How can one know something *new* when one's questions are based on the prejudices of the *old*?"

Ling's bête noire is realism: "In the case of IR, the fish is more like a whale . . . [who] rules the seas. . . . For too long, the whale of IR . . . has subjected our discipline to an illusory universalism propagated through notions of power and the state. . . . Feminists and other critical theorists have led the charge against such realist one-worldism . . . [which] is but one representation of the world. . . . Feminists have pointed out that what . . . [realism] has passed off as 'universal' or 'human' . . . really are the experiences, practices, norms, and institutions of a particularly small segment of the world's population: propertied, white males."

For Ling, the challenge facing IR feminists is, therefore, "further explorations into *other worlds and their ways of world making*."

Those worlds, other than the dominant one of "men, masculinity, and patriarchy," are "a second, hidden one of women, femininity, and matriarchy ... [and] a 'queer,' third world of blurred pairings between men/women, masculinity/femininity, patriarchy/matriarchy."

In that context, she criticizes liberal, white, Western feminist IR: by proclaiming "global sisterhood," it "presumes that gender supersedes race, class, and culture, thereby allocating one categorical patriarchy to rule over all. Doing so effectively upholds a de facto hegemonic identity that is white, heterosexual, and North American/western European. . . . This pluralist logic . . . returns Third World women to a center/periphery dichotomy . . . [and] hegemonic self-involvement [by liberal feminists] prohibits learning about who and what *we* are."

How, then, to know the multiple worlds? asks Ling. She responds in terms of her initial folktale: "we need the fish and the turtle [realism and feminism], first and foremost, to continue their mutual inquiry [begun through an exchange of articles between Robert Keohane and Ann Tickner in 1997 and 1998]. But the turtle needs to speak up . . . to show the fish/whale how to 'see' the other, unfamiliar world through its relationship to the familiar one. . . . The fish/whale, in turn, should listen, patiently and openly, while developing a method or hermeneutic of asking questions. . . . [It] has a vested interest in forgoing age-old hierarchies of anarchy/order, center/periphery, Self/Other, or masculinity/femininity. . . . [It] must learn, finally, to forsake the illusion of power and control in exchange for substantive growth and learning."

Peterson

The two interrelated themes of V. Spike Peterson's "On the Cut(ting) Edge" are the strengths and "failures" of feminist IR scholarship—"what renders it 'cutting edge' . . . [and] what renders it 'cut'—in relation to mainstream IR."

Like all feminist contributors to the Millennial Reflections Project, she emphasizes the "wide spectrum of analytical and political positions [in feminism] . . . a continuum that spans positivist and 'alternative' (postpositivist, poststructuralist) orientations"; further, she writes, "gender is not simply an empirical category . . . but an *analytical* category, pervasively shaping how we conceptualize, think, and 'know.'"

The first of Peterson's two main theses, namely, that feminism is at the cutting edge analytically and politically is clearly articulated: "the study of gender requires and produces transdisciplinary orientations. . . . [these] stretch or transgress familiar and often constraining boundaries"; ergo feminism is more open than mainstream IR to multiple methods and interdisciplinary debates. The result is that it "generates more wide-ranging and encompassing analyses of social relations." She concludes a lengthy discussion of why feminisms are cutting edge, analytically, as follows: "in part because they are transdisciplinary, translevel, and multidimensional, in part because they pioneered studies of identity, and in part because they address complexity through innovative and relational analytics." And, in this context, she notes her "alternative analytical framing, or 'triad analytics' . . . [which] posits identities, social practices/institutions, and meaning systems as three co-constituting dimensions of social reality," a conception that can be related to some mainstream IR concerns.

Feminism does not confine its attention to critical scholarship, writes Peterson. Rather, it has normative and political commitments, for several reasons: first, feminists are committed to improving the conditions of women everywhere and in every respect; second, feminists must be political to survive, let alone prosper, in the academy; third, their diversity in outlook compels critical reflection on the meaning of feminism; and fourth, cutting edge theory and practice are inextricably linked, a linkage that "also informs and enacts emancipatory political practice," which Peterson regards as "progress."

Peterson's second thesis derives inescapably from that progress: "what renders feminisms analytically cutting edge effectively cuts them out of the picture framed by dominant starting points in IR. . . . [They are] cut down as suspicious and inappropriate by a mainstream that claims its knowledge is apolitical, its privilege is either irrelevant or unproblematic, and its desire for change is limited." Nevertheless, in her conclusion on "what is to be done," she favors continuing to ask feminist questions in IR for two reasons: it is important to build on the differences/progress feminism has already made in IR, however limited they may be; and feminism has resources that can contribute much to enhancing IR's "analytical contributions to our understanding of the world(s) we live in . . . [for example, its] glaring failure to take racism (and other structural oppressions) seriously."

Pettman

"Bringing It All Back Home?" begins with some reflections, or "claims," by Jan Jindy Pettman on feminism in international studies: first, it was effectively excluded until the late 1980s—on the assumption that IS was "gender neutral . . . or that [IS] was . . . men's business"; second, it is still on the periphery, measured in terms of courses, articles, and textbook references, but it has "a remarkably robust, diverse, and productive presence in and around IS"; third, the "visibility of women and feminist-informed critique in the 'real world'" is greater than in academe and the discipline of IS; and fourth, while women are frequently noticed in the Western media, they tend to be portrayed as "victims or as symbols of the costs of world politics" or as survivor-witnesses, as in the case of Japanese military sexual slavery during World War II.

There is no single feminist view on IS, notes Pettman, as do all the other feminist contributors; but she discerns a wide-ranging impact on the field. Specifically, feminist scholars "(1) radically expand the kinds of topics, issues, and content in IS . . . [that] unsettle the discipline. They suggest new ways of thinking about core issues, including power, security, and the state, and introduce new ones"; "(2) ask different kinds of questions"; "(3) reveal the masculinist assumptions, investments, and strategies of mainstream IS"; "(4) in the process, widen definitions of the political in the international too"; "(5) disrupt or transgress disciplinary boundaries"; "(6) internationalize the account—raising questions about the identity of the discipline, too"; "(7) gender the account. . . . the constitutive role of gender in world politics is now the subject of keen interrogation"; "(8) sex the account . . . identifying the roles that sex and sexuality, and heterosexism, play in international politics"; and "(9) [provide] the possibility of an embodied IS. . . . feminist writings . . . identify particular kinds of bodies in different international engagements and the privilege or penalty that can flow from being identified as male or female, inside or outside, exotic or 'normal.'"

Pettman cites two illustrations of feminist approaches to IS. Referring to war, feminism provides "more, and more useful, ways of interrogating the kinds of relations that make organized large-scale violence possible . . . [and] whether certain kinds of masculinity are more violent than others." So too does a feminist lens shed light on the shifting sands of Asian "triumphalism" and its 1997 crisis. The former "claimed a newly dynamic, successful Asia had recovered from its colonial emasculation . . . [while] 'the West' was seen to be faltering, losing [its] manly qualities . . . [and] becoming decadent, immoral, obsessed with consumption and pleasure—in short, feminized." And the 1997 Asian crisis "ushered in new configurations in gender representations of state power, national identity, and international relations. . . . Both Asian miracle and crisis were culturalized."

She concludes on an ambivalent note: "feminism is now well into critical mass in IS. Clearly, however, feminists are (not yet?) at home in IS. . . . Like the real world, it is messy, jumpy, sometimes cumulative, sometimes contradictory or doubling back." As for prescription, "it is not possible . . . to propose a future research agenda." Her own goal is "to internationalize the agenda, to generate more feminist accounts from outside the usual centers of power."

Sylvester

Most of Christine Sylvester's millennial reflections paper, "'Progress' as Feminist International Relations," addresses one of the project's six theme questions. Her introductory remarks set the tone: "'Progress' is an odd thing. It twists my head around. . . . Much of IR tries to reach 'it' cumulatively, using the right methods harnessed to the right research programs. . . . Indeed, progress is a cre(a)p and a leap, a jump, and a crawl. It strives for and against, thrusts, moves, makes a crumble, flows. It is a fact, a sorrow, a make-believe, a virtuality, a compromise, a cynicism. Progress advances. It stands us still. It writhes. It invites nostalgia. It is at once a common notion, easily grasped by the modern mind, and something difficult to understand, make happen, or repudiate. Progressive deterioration even bespeaks of progress. . . . The term eludes definitional clarity."

She hails two feminist scholars, Jean Bethke Elshtain and Cynthia Enloe, as "innovators inclined toward framing questions of international relations around feminist concerns rather than around IR agendas," in *Women and War* and *Bananas, Bases, and Beaches: Making Feminist Sense of International Relations*, respectively. But Sylvester notes that not all feminists adhere to that path, citing Ann Tickner [another contributor to the Millennial Reflections Project] among those who prefer to bring to "a recognizable IR topic . . . new gender-highlighting questions, which lately telescope feminist angles on international political economy, foreign policy, war, peace, globalization, the state, nationalism, trade, and so forth."

In this context, Sylvester lays bare the fundamental contrast in the approaches of feminism and traditional IR: "Feminists begin with gender, bodies, sexuality, difference, voice, patriarchy, subjectivity, representation, and/or travel theory. . . . conventional IR typically begins with states, war, trade, regimes, anarchy, and/or rationality. It maps relations of force, power, decision, threat, and agreement."

The conventional subject matter of IR is inadequate in Sylvester's view: "I recommend forays into novels, choreography, drama, poetry, music, and visual arts. These places of fiction, expression, and emotion assist those of us trained in IR to escape narrow vision in order to see other international actors, interactions, products, exchanges, and dramatizations." She is also skeptical of the search for patterns, as in Enloe's work on militarism. And she wonders whether building feminist IR theory is archaic or perhaps premature. She also displays a touch of criticism in her distinctive phrasing: "Feminist IR, impressive as it is, has not capitalized sufficiently on its progressive tendencies by theorizing the connective tissues that bind the genre." At the same time, she is emphatic in asserting once more the difference between (her view of) feminism and IR: "Theory need not be lawlike. It need not be problem solving."

Tickner

In "Feminist Theory and Gender Studies: Reflections for the Millennium," J. Ann Tickner presents a survey of part of the burgeoning literature on this long-neglected segment of international studies, along with an assessment of its contribution to the field.

The dominant theme of her reflections—as of all feminist papers in the Millennial Reflections Project—is the "great divide" between feminist and mainstream thought in IR: the questions they pose, their methods, their conception of theory, cumulation, and the primary purpose of inquiry.

Referring to the six theme questions that millennial reflections contributors were asked to address, Tickner speaks for all feminists with her skeptical rejection: "these questions are not ones that many feminists would ask when engaging in self-evaluation"; by contrast, "the choice of questions we ask is never neutral." Moreover, such terms as *state of the art* and *cumulation* "are in tension with an approach that 'celebrates diversity' in terms of its subject matters, normative focus, and methodologies."

Tickner notes a variety of IR feminist approaches—"liberal, radical, psychoanalytic, socialist, postmodern, and postcolonial"—but only the first employs mainstream empiricist methodology. Most feminist scholars "do not use social scientific methodologies, preferring instead methodologies more compatible with hermeneutic, interpretive epistemological traditions"; in fact, "their methodologies tend to be eclectic."

With regard to theory, she notes Zalewski's three types as a means of conveying the "great divide": "a tool for understanding the world; theory as critique, or understanding how the world got to be as it is so that it can be changed; and theory as practice in . . . everyday life." The first of these conceptions of theory is positivist and mainstream, unacceptable to feminism in IR. The second and third are more congenial.

The reason is closely tied to their basic difference on the purpose of IR research: "For many feminist theorists, knowledge construction is explicitly linked to emancipatory political practice, primarily that of transforming unequal power relationships between women and men." This in turn explains why "it is unlikely that feminists would use 'scientific' criteria, such as integration and cumulation, to evaluate them."

A consequence of this multifaceted "great divide," reinforced by the definition of gender "as a social construction of inequality," is to make difficult an assessment of feminist IR scholarship in terms of "explanatory power." Nonetheless, Tickner does reflect on its achievements and limitations. In general, "the most significant accomplishments have been the enormous productivity of a relatively small group of scholars and their success in creating a supportive space within the ISA." Specifically, she evaluates feminist progress through the McIntosh lens of five stages, in ascending order: "a womanless world"; the absence of women, except for the "famous few" (e.g., Thatcher); women as victims; "women as valid human beings whose various life experiences have shaped the world in which we live"; and at the apex, stage five, the inclusion in IR subject matter of "the experiences of all individuals regardless of race, culture, class, and gender." IR scholarship, in Tickner's view, remains at stages one and two, while feminist IR has moved on to three and four.

In the rest of her paper Tickner surveys briefly several feminist writings other than Zalewski's three types of theory and McIntosh's five stages of progress: Moon on military prostitution; Chin on the important supportive economic role of domestic workers in Malay-

sia, using the method of narrativity; Mansbridge on feminist research
questions; and Enloe on the relevance of women's roles to international politics. At the same time, she acknowledges the legitimacy
of feminist research conducted from a social scientific perspective
and urges an engagement "across these theoretical divides."

Zalewski

Marysia Zalewski's reflections are presented in the form of two "stories": "Feminism and/in International Relations: An Exhausted Conversation? OR Feminists Doing International Relations: The
Cut(ting) Edge of Contemporary Critical Theory and Practice?" She
begins by explaining why the Millennial Reflections Project's guide-
line questions are "problematic": first, "a critical approach such as
feminism will have an alternative sense of what counts as 'reasonable' in the realm of the intellectual"; second, feminist work is diverse, even contradictory, making generalizations very difficult; and
third, conventional-type IR questions could make "vulnerable" any
critical perspective that challenges the status quo.

The "conversation" between feminism and IR is "exhausted," in
Zalewski's view, because the latter resists "a radical restructuring
of many of IR's epistemological, ontological, and political beliefs,"
that is, separating them from power. Stated differently, feminism
and conventional IR are "mismatched."

Her second story is told in the form of a response to two questions
that Zalewski poses: what did IR feminists expect to happen, and
what does feminist theory contribute to IR? In the early days of "euphoric optimism" feminists expected "a more equitable inclusion of
women" in the real world of international politics and in the academy,
as well as legitimacy in the discipline. The first was partly achieved,
but few women have risen to a high level in the hierarchies.

At the same time, Zalewski notes several achievements. One is
in the realm of teaching—students are keenly interested in feminism. Moreover, feminist studies are "cutting edge" because they
"alter the very subject of knowledge by calling into question what
is considered knowledge in any discipline." And by "opening the
doors for other deconstructive theories and practices such as critical
theory," feminism upsets the conventional fabric of IR. She is also
proud of the new *International Feminist Journal of Politics* and the
publication of "backpack" books on feminism, reaching a larger audience than university students.

As for what feminist theory does and its impact, its role is, in large part, "blurring disciplinary boundaries," which leads to "incremental resistance" by those who dominate the discipline. The dialogue between feminism and IR, Zalewski acknowledges, does not work well; and feminist work is still underrepresented in journals and textbooks. Moreover, feminist scholarship has not yet attained legitimacy, using standards of conventional IR. Nor has an "intrasubfield consensus" been reached by the feminist community—but she does not lament the failure to do so, for diversity and differences are of the essence of feminism. In short, the record of "progress" has been mixed.

As for the future, Zalewski calls for a new "conversation," centering on the feminist IR community, rather than as in the past an attempt at dialogue between two separate communities, feminism *and* IR.

Notes

1. E. H. Carr, *The Twenty Years' Crisis, 1919–1939: An Introduction to the Study of International Relations* (London: Macmillan, 1939); E. H. Carr, *Conditions of Peace* (London: Macmillan, 1942); Arnold Wolfers, *Britain and France between Two Wars: Conflicting Strategies of Peace since Versailles* (New York: Harcourt, Brace, 1940); Arnold Wolfers, *Discord and Collaboration: Essays on International Politics* (Baltimore: Johns Hopkins University Press, 1962); Nicholas J. Spykman, *America's Strategy in World Politics: The United States and the Balance of Power* (New York: Harcourt, Brace, 1941); W. T. R. Fox, *The Super-Powers: The United States, Britain, and the Soviet Union—Their Responsibility for Peace* (New York: Harcourt, Brace, 1944); Hans Morgenthau, *Scientific Man versus Power Politics* (Chicago: University of Chicago Press, 1946); Hans Morgenthau, *Politics among Nations: The Struggle for Power and Peace* (New York: Knopf, 1948); Bernard Brodie, ed., *The Absolute Weapon: Atomic Power and World Order* (New York: Harcourt, Brace, 1946).
2. Kenneth N. Waltz, *Theory of International Politics* (Reading, Mass.: Addison-Wesley, 1979); Robert Gilpin, *War and Change in World Politics* (Cambridge: Cambridge University Press, 1981).
3. E. B. Haas, *The Uniting of Europe* (Stanford, Calif.: Stanford University Press, 1958); E. B. Haas, *Beyond the Nation-State: Functionalism and International Organization* (Stanford, Calif.: Stanford University Press, 1964); Robert O. Keohane and Joseph S. Nye Jr., *Power and Interdependence: World Politics in Transition* (Boston: Little, Brown, 1977).
4. Robert Jervis, *Perception and Misperception in International Politics* (Princeton, N.J.: Princeton University Press, 1976); Robert Jervis, Richard Ned Lebow, and Janice Gross Stein, *Psychology and Deterrence* (Baltimore: Johns Hopkins University Press, 1985).

5. Richard K. Ashley, "The Poverty of Neorealism," *International Organization* 38, no. 2 (1984): 225–86.

6. Robert W. Cox, "Social Forces, States, and World Orders: Beyond International Relations Theory," *Millennium* 10, no. 2 (1981): 126–55; Robert W. Cox, *Production, Power, and World Order: Social Forces in the Making of History* (New York: Columbia University Press, 1987).

7. Alexander Wendt, "The Agent-Structure Problem in International Relations Theory," *International Organization* 41, no. 3 (1987): 335–70; F. V. Kratochwil, *Rules, Norms, and Decisions: On the Conditions of Practical and Legal Reasoning in International Relations and Domestic Affairs* (Cambridge: Cambridge University Press, 1989).

8. Jean B. Elshtain, *Women and War* (New York: Basic Books, 1987); Cynthia Enloe, *Bananas, Beaches, and Bases: Making Feminist Sense of International Politics* (Berkeley: University of California Press, 1990); V. Spike Peterson, ed., *Gendered States: (Re)Visions of International Relations Theory* (Boulder, Colo.: Lynne Rienner, 1992); J. Ann Tickner, *Gender in International Relations: Feminist Perspectives on Achieving Global Security* (Minneapolis: University of Minnesota Press, 1992).

ALTERNATIVE AND CRITICAL PERSPECTIVES

ALTERNATIVE AND CRITICAL PERSPECTIVES

Steve Smith

This chapter is a rewritten version of the paper originally presented on one of the millennial reflections panels, but the basic argument and structure of the paper remain the same. I have kept the argument and structure largely because I was one of the few who wrote my paper in exactly the format requested by the organizers; that is, I wrote a paper that addressed each of the six questions the panel organizers asked. My fellow panelists interpreted the invitation in different, and equally legitimate, ways, but none of them answered the precise exam paper they had been sent! At the panel, one of them, Yosef Lapid, responded in detail to the text of my (precirculated) paper, and he clearly had important disagreements with the way I had characterized the current state of the discipline. The other participants raised important points about the problems of characterizing, compressing, labeling, and representing "alternative and critical perspectives." In rewriting my paper for publication, I have decided to retain my main arguments and claims, mainly because it was clear that some of the other participants would want to disagree with or dissent from my paper when they came to write up their own. Thus, what follows is an extended version of the paper as presented, and this will hopefully allow the other participants to continue their disagreements with me in print. It would have been scarcely ethical for me to change my arguments, when I knew that some of them wished to take those arguments as their starting points! Tempting, but unethical!

Like all participants on the panel I was asked to focus on six tasks, all designed to get me to "confront [my] own limitations, stimulate debate about their most significant accomplishments and shortcomings, and discuss research paths for the years ahead." I interpreted this as an invitation to assess where alternative and critical perspectives stand at the start of the new millennium. Aside from the obvious fact that these approaches involve a variety of different (and sometimes contradictory) positions since there are few assumptions that they share, I was also troubled by the expectation of offering a definitive statement of how things stood. Thus, what follows is a very partial and personal account of the development of these approaches. My other initial health warning is simply that I was not really sure what "alternative and critical perspectives" included. But from the lineups of the other panels I deduced that the panel should focus on critical theory and postmodernist accounts of international relations (IR).

But within that general label, there is a real problem over gender and feminist work. Although one panel dealt solely with feminist and gender scholarship, it struck me as interesting, to say the least, that those scholars were not involved in the panel on which I had been invited to participate. My presumption was that the organizers saw this as a way of giving feminist/gender work its own platform, rightly signifying the importance of the work in this area of the discipline. Yet, paradoxically, this decision seemed to backfire, as it was widely seen as a way of marginalizing feminist/gender work into its own ghetto. But probably more important than this was that the division of work into feminist/gender on the one hand and alternative and critical on the other created the unfortunate implication that feminist/gender work was not alternative or critical. This is *not* a statement about the motives of the organizers, but it evidently did impart a dynamic to the alternative/critical panel and certainly made me feel decidedly uncomfortable about the absence of women on the panel. I said this in my presentation but nonetheless got criticized for taking part in an all-male panel (dealing with, of all things, alternative and critical work) given the enormously important role that female scholars have played in the development of these parts of the discipline.

With this proviso about the implied content of the terms *alternative* and *critical,* my paper will concentrate on what is usually defined as nonmainstream theoretical work within IR. The very move of delineating what is and is not alternative and critical work within the discipline of IR has enormous political and professional consequences, especially if those who define what counts as alternative and critical perspectives are mainstream scholars. Let me be clear, I am not so much concerned with the precise boundaries that are drawn between mainstream and alternative scholarship, nor about the boundary between alternative and feminist work; rather I want to stress the enormous implications of being able to define X (whatever X is) as "an alternative" or as "critical." Think of the implications of such a move: the very notion of an alternative carries with it a set of connotations, as does the label *critical* (though note that the term *critical* is the chosen description of a school of thinking that self-consciously wants to challenge conventional ways of interpreting and explaining the social world). It may not have been the organizers' intention, but the label does imply that these approaches are not "normal," and it even implies a certain stigma of being more than a little fashionable and wacky, providing alternatives or being merely critical.

I now turn to the six set tasks, in the order that they were presented to me.

1. Engage in self-critical, state-of-the-art reflection on accomplishments and failures, especially since the creation of the ISA more than forty years ago. My first comment is that it is far too easy to overemphasize the achievements of what can broadly be called alternative approaches to IR. I think that alternative perspectives have not really made significant inroads into the mainstream of the discipline, for one simple reason: they do not share the epistemological and methodological assumptions of that mainstream. I think this is the key issue. Many discussions of alternative perspectives focus on their different ontological assumptions, and thus have argued that their alternative status derives from the fact that they look at nonmainstream issues. Such was evidently the case with peace research and environmental approaches; more recently a similar response has been made to feminist work within IR. But I think this is not the main judgment that is at work. Rather, I think that the alternative perspectives are seen as such because they do not work within the model of social science that dominates the U.S. IR academic community (and thus the world community of IR scholars). Hence the incredible power of the critiques of a number of writers who claim that alternative approaches are not part of the social sci-

ence enterprise. Let me note three examples: the first is that of Keohane, Krasner, and Katzenstein in their 1998 *International Organization* paper,[1] when they argue that postmodern work in IR is not
really social science and therefore cannot be assessed by the usual
academic standards. They argue that the journal has published little
postmodern IR work "since *IO* [*International Organization*] has
been committed to an enterprise that postmodernism denies: the use
of evidence to adjudicate between truth claims. In contrast to conventional and critical constructivism, postmodernism falls clearly
outside of the social science enterprise, and in IR research it risks
becoming self-referential and disengaged from the world, protests to
the contrary notwithstanding."[2]

A second example is the now famous claim made by Robert Keohane in his 1988 address as president of the International Studies
Association (ISA). Noting that reflectivist approaches had important
criticisms to make about rationalism, he nonetheless noted that
their greatest weakness was "the lack of a clear reflective research
program. . . . Until the reflective scholars or others sympathetic to
their arguments have delineated such a research program and shown
in particular studies that it can illuminate important issues in world
politics, they will remain on the margins of the field, largely invisible
to the preponderance of empirical researchers, most of whom explicitly or implicitly accept one or another version of rationalistic
premises."[3] Reflectivist scholars needed to develop "testable theories" without which "it will be impossible to evaluate their research
program."[4] The most significant point about this challenge was that
it was, not surprisingly, made on the epistemological terrain of rationalism: it is frankly impossible to see just how reflectivist accounts could conceivably provide answers that Keohane would accept given the gap between their epistemological starting points.

The final example of this delegitimization of reflectivist approaches comes in Stephen Walt's review of the state of international
relations theory.[5] Although Walt notes that the central debate in IR
theory remains that between realism and liberalism, he notes that
there is an alternative, but this is not reflectivism or any of its components; rather it is constructivism. His only discussion of any reflectivist work is the following reference to the "deconstruction"
approach: "because these scholars focused initially on criticizing the
mainstream paradigms but did not offer positive alternatives to
them, they remained a self-consciously dissident minority for most
of the 1980s."[6] Even constructivism comes out of this survey badly.

He lists its "unit of analysis" as "individuals" and its "main instruments" as "ideas and discourse." Its "post–cold war prediction" is "agnostic because it cannot predict the content of ideas," and its "main limitation" is that it is "better at describing the past than anticipating the future." Not only are alternative and critical approaches ignored in his overview, but constructivism receives the following disciplining of its role: "The 'compleat diplomat' of the future should remain cognizant of realism's emphasis on the inescapable role of power, keep liberalism's awareness of domestic forces in mind, and occasionally reflect on constructivism's vision of change."[7]

These claims have enormous professional consequences for anyone working in the alternative perspectives. They immediately delegitimize such scholars' work as not serious research, and one can only guess at the implications of this for their careers. In short, I do not think that the alternative perspectives have achieved much in the way of challenging the mainstream of the discipline for the simple reason that they are dismissed as outside the standards of social science. Such is the political power of assumptions about epistemology.

This does not mean that there have been no successes, only that those successes have never changed the nature of the mainstream. Taken together, the works of the writers such as those who appeared on the panel with me have made it impossible for the discipline to pretend that there are no criticisms of the dominant assumptions. The work of Cox, Walker, Ashley, and Lapid, along with that of Shapiro, Der Derian, Campbell, Linklater, Sylvester, Enloe, Tickner, and many more, has offered a sustained critique of the assumptions of the mainstream literature and has thus opened up major avenues for research. But, to repeat, this does not mean that this research has been accepted as relevant or legitimate by the mainstream. It certainly means that much of the work in the leading graduate schools is informed by the work of these writers, but this has yet to have a significant impact on the everyday politics, psychology, and sociology of the profession.

Why is this? In my view it is not that the work carried out in alternative perspectives is less academic or less thorough; rather it is that the mainstream has tended to reconsolidate itself so as to continue the U.S. social science project. The classic case has been the fate of neorealism since Waltz's 1979 book *Theory of International Politics* was published. Despite the critiques of it, and despite the rather inconvenient fact that the structure of the international system changed in a way unforeseen by the theory, neorealism has remained a central part of the mainstream and now constitutes one of two main poles of that mainstream, the other being neoliberalism. A similar and very significant development is occurring with social constructivism. What I find amazingly important is the way that (a particular version of) social constructivism is becoming part of the developing mainstream. Note how Wendt in his new book[8] places himself firmly on the side of IR as social science: "Epistemologically, I have sided with positivists. . . . our best hope is social science."[9] He is, he states, "a strong believer in science. . . . I am a positivist."[10] This position is, presumably, one opposed to "Parisian social theory."[11] Similarly, note the co-opting noises made by Keohane, Krasner, and Katzenstein, and by Stephen Walt, in their reviews noted previously. By these moves the mainstream can say that it deals with the ontological questions raised by the alternative perspectives, but that it does so within the canons of U.S.-style social science.

I have written about the dominance of the discipline by the U.S. IR academic community for the last twenty years,[12] but in an important sense for a long time I missed the point. I tended to see the reason for this as the importance of the United States in world politics and the effect of this on how the discipline has evolved. Whilst I would not want to ignore that point, I now see the impact of the U.S. model of social science as absolutely critical in explaining the lack of impact of alternative perspectives. They simply do not seem to fit within what the discipline defines as the right way to carry out academic study; together they question the four main tenets of U.S. social science—that there is a distinction between facts and values, that empiricism is the appropriate epistemology, that naturalism is possible, and that the task of the researcher is to uncover regularities in the social world. What is of central importance in all this is that these assumptions are not incompatible with studying identity, perceptions, culture, or normative concerns: it is only that they are to be studied from a social science perspective. It is in this way that the concerns of the alternative perspectives can be dealt with by the mainstream, and in a way that fits comfortably within the pressing and powerful norms of social science U.S.-style.

In this light the main failure of the alternative perspectives is that whilst they have done much to undermine the epistemological assumptions of the mainstream, they have not succeeded in establishing an alternative epistemology. This is not surprising for two main reasons: first they disagree amongst themselves over questions of epistemology (look at the differences between, say, Robert Cox and Rick Ashley or Rob Walker to take an example from the other panel participants). Second, the grip on the discipline of positivism U.S.-style is so great as to close down any space for alternatives. This is the nub of the issue, since I genuinely do not think that any alternative perspective can replace the mainstream if it does not fit within positivism, and here of course is the problem: alternative perspectives cannot fit because they are not based on positivism. This has considerable influence on the development of the discipline in the rest of the world, where IR communities have to deal with not only the ontological and policy commitments of U.S. IR but also the dominance of a particular view of social science.

This situation has been brilliantly analyzed by Ole Waever in a recent paper.[13] As Waever notes: "The internal intellectual structure of American IR explains both the recurring great debates and why American IR generates global leadership. It has a hierarchy centered on theoretical journals, and scholars must compete for access to these. This they have not had to do in Europe, where power historically rested either in sub-fields or in local universities, not in a disciplinary elite. American IR alone generates an apex that therefore comes to serve as the global core of the discipline."[14] Waever argues persuasively that in the future there will be a parting of the ways between the work going on in the U.S. IR community and that of the other main IR communities, especially those in Europe. The U.S. IR community will tend toward "national professionalization," with the mainstream concentrating on rational choice theory. These methods will not "travel well" to IR communities such as Germany, France, and the United Kingdom, and those communities will both develop their own national identities and, at the same time, combine more to form a European IR community. These trends will result in "a slow shift from a pattern with only one professional and coherent national market—the United States, and the rest of the world more or less peripheral or disconnected—toward a relative American abdication and larger academic communities forming around their own independent cores in Europe."[15] These, then, are some of the main issues at the start of the new millennium concerning the politics of international politics, and the social relations of international relations.

2. *Assess where we stand on key debates and why we have failed to resolve them.* My answer to this question follows directly from what I have already argued. The key debates are defined as those

within the mainstream of the discipline, and any debate with alternative perspectives is axiomatically defined as impossible because the alternatives do not adhere to the same forms of scholarship as are found in the mainstream. In my view the mainstream has been very successful both in setting out the Kuhnian normal science puzzles and in stating the ways in which these kinds of questions should be answered. I view the neo-neo synthesis to be an extraordinarily powerful boundary-making and boundary-enforcing exercise for defining and assessing the key debates. Alternative perspectives do not fit within these boundaries. Similarly, note the way in which the Wendtian arm of social constructivism is now setting out the terrain of the next key debate with the neoliberalist arm of the neo-neo synthesis as one of the ways in which ideas construct and influence policy choices. I can easily see this becoming the key debate, and all within the U.S. model of social science.[16]

In short, I would argue that the key debates have been very largely solved within the mainstream. I think that the neo-neo debate does involve some genuinely important and complex questions, mainly those to do with whether anarchy can be mitigated by institutions and whether state actors pursue relative or absolute gains. The social constructivism/neoliberal institutionalism debate will likewise focus on the important issue of the role of ideas in international relations; but there is much more to international relations than this, and I can see no easy way in which the alternative perspectives can enter into any debate with the mainstream if the standards for scholarship are so positivistic and so fixed.

Within the alternative camp, there is some debate between rival perspectives, but frankly there is little agreement on epistemological matters. Thus critical theory requires exactly the kind of foundational epistemology that postmodernism denies is possible, just as standpoint feminism stands in contrast to postmodern feminism. Alternative may be a good catchall term, but any term that includes work inspired by writers with as distinctive positions as Gramsci, Habermas, Butler, Spivak, Virilio, and Foucault hides more than it reveals. Within each of the alternative perspectives there is lively debate around a series of research questions, but these cannot be expected to add up to *one* alternative perspective to challenge the mainstream. Just as it is naive to ask for *the* feminist perspective on an issue, so is it misguided to ask for the alternative perspective on an issue. But do note how politically powerful it is to ask for that answer and then to consign the "well, it all depends on which alternative you are talking about" response to outside the walls of the academy, to the land of nonserious research and a (regretful) overlap between the explanatory and the normative.

In summary, the question assumes two things: first, that the key debates are debates open to all; second, that they can be resolved. The first assumption is false because I do not think that the mainstream is willing to assess alternative perspectives on any terms other than its own, which, by definition, they do not accept. The second assumption is false because it is itself an assumption based on a positivist view of inquiry. Maybe the key debates cannot be resolved because there are no answers, if by answers one means the kind of social scientific answer that positivism assumes. Maybe, the key debates revolve around not questions of explanation but questions of understanding, or even possibly questions of ethics or morality. Resolving requires giving an answer, but what if there is no one answer? What if the answers are ultimately dependent on which "facts" one selects and what one sees as the main issues in the debate? Think for a second about the concept of globalization: how might one resolve a debate about its impact on world politics if one cannot agree on who is the relevant unit for assessing this impact, or if one sees it as having both positive and negative effects? Resolving the debates may simply not be possible; indeed the belief that it should be is itself just one example of how deeply ingrained are the assumptions of positivistic social science in the U.S. academic community.

3. *Evaluate what intrasubfield standards we should use to evaluate the significance of theoretical insights.* This is an important question because a common version of the problems of the alternative perspectives is that they have no standards for demarcating good academic work from bad. This is especially the charge leveled at postmodern work, with the usual version of the charge being that since for postmodernism anything goes, there can be no standards for deciding between good and bad scholarship. This was clearly a major issue on the panel, as it indeed is with any attempt to bring together mainstream and alternative approaches and then discuss them in terms of standards of assessment. The alternative and critical approaches tend to resist any attempt to make the kinds of assessments about "progress" or "success" that characterize mainstream assessments of the field. The reason is obvious: the language of "assessment," "progress," and "success" smacks of a modernist notion of knowledge, whereby we are all involved in a process of

learning more and more, with a hint of an increasing ability to use this knowledge in the world of policy and politics. The organizers have tried to be open in their guidelines for participants to write up these chapters, stressing that they do not expect conformity to one model of social science: instead we have been asked to "at least define what you consider to be a fair measure of success/failure in [sic] regard to your own subfield, and then assess the extent to which core objectives (whatever they may be) have or have not been met, and why." The problem here for alternative and critical approaches is the familiar one of not being willing to buy into this model of assessment. This is clearly a fundamental difference between the mainstream and the alternative and critical literatures, and I see no easy way to bridge it. My own view, for what it is worth, is that the acid test for the success of alternative and critical approaches is the extent to which they have led to empirically grounded work that explores the range and variety of world politics. My "core objective" has been to create space for thinking and for politics, and to refuse attempts to determine what counts as scholarship on the basis of a culturally and historically specific notion of social science. My concern is not so much to push a particular view of what counts as knowledge but to examine the (often hidden) assumptions of those approaches that claim to have solid epistemological foundations, so as to show that these foundations are far less secure than those who propound them like to think.

With regard to the criteria used to assess alternative and critical work, I have not found that there is an absence of standards for distinguishing between good and poor scholarship. This is simply not the case in my experience. I would like to make my point by referring to my own direct experience of this matter. I edit the Cambridge University Press series Studies in International Relations. It is a big series, with more than seventy-five books published or under contract, and in excess of 150,000 copies sold since it published its first volume in 1988. In that time the series has had more than 750 submissions, with a success rate of about one in ten. In the 1990s we have attracted a lot of work from what would be considered the alternative perspectives. Now, in all that time, I have never felt that there was anything particularly problematic about intrasubfield standards in alternative perspectives. Referees have seemed to have no problems in making tough judgments as to the scholarly standing of manuscripts, and since the usual practice has been to have two or three referees for each submission, it is important to note that there has been no noticeable difference between the pattern of referees' reactions in the alternative perspectives and those found in the mainstream. I think this is a very important point: of course there are gatekeepers and inflexible scholars working in the alternative perspectives, but there are certainly no more of them than one would find in, say, social constructivism or neorealism. It does not appear any more difficult to determine intrasubfield standards in the alternative perspectives than in any other area. Of course, there can and should be debate over what these are, and it is obviously the case that those working within the alternative perspectives do not appeal to the relatively straightforward (if demanding) standards of positivist scholarship. But there does appear to be roughly the same degree of agreement among, say, feminist scholars over what constitutes scholarship in their field as one finds in the mainstream. These standards tend to revolve around the categories of coherence, tight argumentation, knowledge of the relevant literature, the use of empirical evidence, persuasiveness of the major analytical moves, innovative scholarship, and the standard of writing and expression. To put it bluntly, I have sent out quite a few manuscripts for review and have had back very tough and ultimately negative reports from individuals working precisely in that part of the alternative and critical perspectives. It is *not* the case that referees support proposals because they work in the same area. However comforting it might be for those who deride this work as not being in accordance with the canons of social scientific inquiry to say that adherents to a given alternative perspective promote the work of others in that area, that is simply not the case in my experience. The problem is not one of intrasubfield standards; the problem is one of intersubfield standards, and here the situation is that the standards of the mainstream skew the situation. They become *the* standards for assessing work and are never seen as themselves open to critique or question. They are presented as if they were beyond reproach, beyond debate, and beyond the realm of politics. They are the standards of the academy, and that is that. In my view, of course, they are the place where the discipline needs to begin its self-examination at the start of this millennium.

   4. *Explore ways to achieve fruitful synthesis of approaches, both in terms of core research questions and appropriate methodologies.* As can be deduced from the foregoing comments, I have problems with this question. The obvious reason is that any answer I give to it will end up disciplining, by definition, the content of the discipline

of IR, and I do not want to do that. Rather than cut down the area
of study, rather than prescribe what should be the research questions
and the appropriate methodologies, I want instead to insist on a pluralism about research questions and methods. I am interested in supporting the best scholarship within any of the approaches. Another
personal experience might be relevant: when Cambridge University
Press (recently voted the number-one publisher in political science
and IR by the American Political Science Association) undertook its
latest five-yearly review of the series I have edited since 1986, the
press asked a lot of academics what they thought of the list. The
most interesting feature of the U.S. responses (as opposed to the responses from other parts of the world) was the perception that the
series lacked an identity, a position on what to study and how to
study it. This was seen as a weakness: the series needed to have an
identity and a common approach. That was never the idea behind
the series: as far as I was concerned the whole point of it was to
publish the best scholarship across the entire gamut of approaches
to IR. This was the first statement in the initial proposal to Cambridge University Press, and I think it remains as relevant today as
it was then. I think that this says a lot about the difference between
what can broadly be termed U.S. and European/Australasian IR.

Accordingly, I think the way forward is to insist only on research
being carried out to the highest standards possible as defined in the
research area. I want the series to publish the best postmodern feminist work, the best neorealist work, the best quantitative work, and
so on. I think this is the right way to answer the question of what
are the core research questions and the appropriate methodologies.
Any other route, say by defining the core questions according to the
policy interests of the United States, or in accordance with the views
of the dominant approaches in the discipline, results in a closing
down of space for scholarship. As I mentioned, my interest is in
opening it up and trying as far as possible to assess scholarly standards by reference to the best standards in each perspective.

Let me end this answer with two further personal experiences: in
1993 Martin Hollis and I submitted an article on the agent-structure
debate to a leading U.S. journal, arguing that there were always at
least two stories to tell about the social world (explaining and understanding). We noted that there could be no common standard for
evaluating the rival stories, since the epistemologies and methodologies behind each were so very different. Specifically we noted that
quantitative data could not be used to solve the debate. Well, the

article was refereed and given a revise and resubmit, with the main requirement being the use of quantitative empirical evidence to demarcate between the two sets of claims. We sent it to the leading U.K. journal, which, after getting three referees' reports, accepted it as it stood. Note, I am not claiming that the U.S. journal should have accepted it, only that its standards were based on an overarching view of scholarship that precluded almost by definition work that was not explanatory social science.

The second example is that in 1995 Ken Booth and I published the edited book *International Relations Theory Today*.[17] It has sold well (including several thousand copies in its U.S. imprint) and has been well reviewed. But our U.K. publisher initially discussed the book with one of the two or three leading U.S. presses, and that press had it refereed. The interesting thing is that the press liked the book but asked us to rewrite it so that it had a clear theme and argued for a specific view of international theory. Our point in editing the book, of course, was to bring together a variety of different approaches. Now, it may be that the book wasn't good enough for the press and that its reason was a nice way of rejecting our work, or it may be the case that the themes were not well integrated, but my honest view is that the press simply didn't like the idea of a set of essays arguing for different interpretations of IR. I know of the dangers of arguing from one's own experiences, but I do think that these are interesting reflections of the dominance of a particular view of how research should be undertaken and what it should be studying—as is the above task when it speaks of synthesis as the way forward. Epistemological assumptions lie deep, and they affect far more than how we study: in practice they end up determining what we can study, how we assess our studies, and how they should be related together (as compatible parts of one social world that exhibits regularities and is "knowable" from the outside).

  5. *Address the broader question of progress in international studies.* Frankly, I do not see much progress in IR. This is because I remain convinced that the discipline has remained wedded to a particular view of the world throughout the period of the ISA's history. Broadly speaking, I accept John Vasquez's view of the "power of power politics," the "colouring it Morgenthau" thesis.[18] I think that the ontological assumptions of contemporary mainstream IR theory are little changed from the assumptions that dominated the discipline when the ISA was founded. I see the history of IR since the war as one of a continuing debate between realist and liberal worldviews,

and it is particularly interesting to note how the two of them have come together in the neo-neo synthesis. The U.S. study of IR has always had its liberal and its realist wings (as Brian Schmidt has convincingly shown in his recent book),[19] and I see the differences between these two positions as relatively minor when compared with the wider political spectrum, or the world of social theory. Think of the similarities between the current phase of mainstream IR theory and that of the late 1950s and early 1960s, or that of the early 1970s: in all cases the "debate" in the discipline was between broadly liberal (integration studies, the nonstate actor literature respectively) and a dominant realist account. The mainstream has, in other words, remained relatively unchanged over the last half century. Of course, this is not the dominant self-image of the U.S. IR community, which presents the story as one of progress in terms of the refinement of specific models and theories of IR.

The liberal peace theory and neoliberal institutionalism are two such "progressive" research paradigms. But in my view, they are not so much progressive as political views of IR: they define a set of parameters as given and then examine behavior within those parameters, never looking at what aspects of world politics are excluded from the analysis. These debates take place within a powerful framework that defines the political in a very specific way, and which excludes a whole set of "politics" (defining these as "not political" or as "private" or as "domestic politics"). Thus economic power is separate from political power, and even the dominant international political economy work in the United States can end up presenting economics and politics as two separate things that need to be combined. Thus, the liberal peace theory defines both peace and democracy in a very U.S. way, and neoliberal institutionalism deals with the role of ideas in constituting actors' identities and interests in an equally specific (and normative) way.

In this light, IR presents itself as a discipline that explains (and I use the word deliberately) international politics. Its progress comes, it is said, from its growing sophistication and explanatory power. My view is that IR does far more than this; specifically I see IR theory as partly constituting the practice of international relations, and therefore I see its progress as more instrumental than emancipatory. Ultimately, IR is unavoidably normative, both in the narrow sense that by choosing to study some subjects rather than others it normalizes and naturalizes the world, and in the more general sense that it is overwhelmingly focused on explaining that world. I maintain that explanation is not the name of the game in the social world, and to argue that it is leads to a view of the social world that is ultimately limiting and normative in its choice of what to study and how to study it. This is not to deny that there have been significant developments in IR theory since the ISA was founded, only that these developments have all taken place within a very restricted view of the political, the international, and the social.

6. *Select an agenda of topics and research questions that should guide the subfield during the coming decades.* I am not going to pronounce on the topics and questions for all the perspectives presumably included under the label *alternative,* although my general view is that the issues that will be studied by the profession at large will continue to be informally dominated by the policy agenda of the United States, and these will be studies in an essentially positivistic way (although one significantly influenced by the Wendtian form of social constructivism). Referring to the work in the alternative perspectives, in my view it is for those who work in each of those areas to study those aspects of IR that they want to study. I decidedly do not want to prescribe what should be studied or how it should be studied. I have my own intellectual biases and views on these questions, but that is all they are—judgments and opinions, fallible, hopefully humble, and always provisional. Just as it would be entirely wrong for me as editor of a series (or as journal referee) to reject a book proposal (or article) because of the topic or the approach or to try and stop a scholar being appointed to my own or any other department because of his or her approach, so it should decidedly not be down to me or to anyone else to lay out the agenda for others to study; more important, even, I do not think that a commitment to studying certain issues in a given way should become a view that *only* that issue or that way is legitimate. My views of what might be studied, then, argue a case; they do not seek to delegitimize other views.

Having said which, what I do want to do under this heading is to make three points. First, I hope that theoretical work, of whatever persuasion, should be informed by, and in turn inform, empirical material. There is nothing as practical as a good theory, and I find the most valuable work to be that which is empirically grounded. There will be some work dealing with metatheoretical issues, but I do think that this has its place. I write as someone who has spent much of the last decade dealing with metatheoretical issues, but during that time I have also published a lot of empirically grounded material. Indeed, my publication list to date splits almost equally between metatheory and empirical work. Interestingly, I got heavily involved in metatheory only because my empirical work on arms control and foreign policy seemed to run into some rather serious theoretical problems. Second, I hope that the discipline will foster intellectual pluralism and open rather than close down analytical space. I would like to see work evaluated by the standards of its own perspective rather than by pretending that there is one undisputed metatheoretical standard of scholarship for all approaches, especially when that approach takes such a dogmatic, and blinkered, position on what constitutes a social science.

Finally, I want to return to the notion of alternative perspectives. The simple and beguiling move of classifying perspectives as alternative is in my view an act that disciplines the discipline. However well-meaning and however much it is intended to give a voice to those perspectives that might otherwise be ignored, my worry is that the simple act of defining perspectives as alternative reinforces that definition and their standing in the profession. Presumably they are alternatives to the dominant or mainstream: they are not "normal"; they are not "standard"; they are not the most important perspectives. A genuine attempt to be pluralistic may end up reinforcing the very marginality of the perspectives. My worry is that the very act of defining perspectives as alternative and critical performs an important gatekeeping task.

My hope is that these comments stimulate discussion and debate on the current state of the discipline. Despite the thrust of some of the foregoing comments, I am in fact quite heartened by the developing pluralism in areas of the discipline. Whether one focuses on journals or on the panels at conferences, one sees a variety of perspectives in the discipline, and I feel that this is a sign of a vigorous and healthy discipline. However, I remain concerned that this pluralism does not extend into the heartland of the discipline in the United States. I wait to see significant numbers of leading alternative and critical scholars appointed to the most prestigious departments in the United States. I remain to be convinced that one historically and culturally specific model of social science is not the touchstone for judgments about academic quality, be that about the fate of Ph.D.'s or about the fate of job applicants.

In conclusion, I am worried about two main features of the discipline at the turn of the millennium. The first is the sheer dominance of the U.S. IR community. A good example was provided by the simple mathematics of the millennium panels. Although I know that the organizers were trying to ensure that a variety of voices were heard, those were overwhelmingly North American, male, and white voices. There were ten panels on the program, with two ("alternatives" and "gender") dealing with the nonmainstream. Interestingly, there was no place for social constructivism. But in terms of who spoke for the discipline, I noted that according to the list of confirmed participants, of the forty-nine speakers only six were from outside North America, and four of those six appeared on the feminist theory panel (the other two were myself and Mick Cox, who appeared on the "editors" panel). In terms of male/female, only twelve of the forty-nine speakers were women, and five of those twelve were on the feminist theory panel. Indeed, had it not been for the feminist theory panel, there would have been only two non–North Americans and seven women out of the forty-four speakers! I am much less certain when it comes to identity in terms of color, but I could only readily identify one nonwhite participant from the list. I think these figures tell us a lot about the kind of IR that dominates the discipline at the start of the millennium. My second concern is even more fundamental and influential, and it is the main theme running through this paper and indeed my work over the last decade. I need to say little more about it at this juncture, except to reiterate it: it concerns the continuing dominance in IR of a very specific definition of social science. It is this dominance that makes alternative perspectives alternative, that links the discipline of IR to the practice of international relations, and that, by naturalizing the social world, has constituted the hidden politics of the profession of IR since, as well as before, the founding of the ISA.

Notes

1. Peter Katzenstein, Robert Keohane, and Stephen Krasner, "*International Organization* and the Study of World Politics," *International Organization* 52 (1998): 645–85.
2. Ibid., 678.
3. Robert O. Keohane, *International Institutions and State Power: Essays in International Relations Theory* (Boulder, Colo.: Westview, 1989), 173.
4. Ibid., 173–74.
5. Stephen Walt, "International Relations: One World, Many Theories," *Foreign Policy*, no. 110 (1998): 29–46.
6. Ibid., 32.
7. Ibid., 44.

8. Alexander Wendt, *Social Theory of International Politics* (Cambridge: Cambridge University Press, 1999).
9. Ibid., 90.
10. Ibid., 39.
11. Ronald Jepperson, Alexander Wendt, and Peter Katzenstein, "Norms, Identity, and Culture in National Security," in *The Culture of National Security: Norms and Identity in World Politics,* ed. Peter Katzenstein (New York: Columbia University Press, 1996), 34.
12. See Steve Smith, ed., *International Relations: British and American Perspectives* (Oxford: Blackwell, 1985); Steve Smith, "The Development of International Relations as a Social Science," *Millennium: Journal of International Studies* 16 (1987): 189–206; Steve Smith, "Hegemonic Power, Hegemonic Discipline? The Superpower Status of the American Study of International Relations," in *Global Voices: Dialogues in International Relations,* ed. James Rosenau (Boulder, Colo.: Westview, 1993), 55–82; Steve Smith, "Foreign Policy Theory and the New Europe," in *European Foreign Policy: The EC and Changing Perspectives in Europe,* ed. Walter Carlsnaes and Steve Smith (London: Sage, 1994), 1–20; Steve Smith, "The Self-Images of a Discipline: A Genealogy of International Relations Theory," in *International Relations Theory Today,* ed. Ken Booth and Steve Smith (Cambridge, England: Polity Press, 1995), 1–37; Steve Smith, "Positivism and Beyond," in *International Theory: Positivism and Beyond,* ed. Steve Smith, Ken Booth, and Marysia Zalewski (Cambridge: Cambridge University Press, 1996), 11–44.
13. Ole Waever, "The Sociology of a Not So International Discipline: American and European Developments in International Relations," *International Organization* 52 (1998): 687–727.
14. Ibid., 726.
15. Ibid., 726.
16. See Steve Smith, "Wendt's World," *Review of International Studies* 26 (2000): 151–63.
17. Booth and Smith, *International Relations Theory Today.*
18. John Vasquez, *The Power of Power Politics: A Critique* (London: Frances Pinter, 1983); see new edition published as *The Power of Power Politics: From Classical Realism to Neotraditionalism* (Cambridge: Cambridge University Press, 1998).
19. Brian Schmidt, *The Political Discourse of Anarchy: A Disciplinary History of International Relations* (Albany: State University of New York Press, 1998).

Universality in International Studies

A Historicist Approach

Robert W. Cox

One of the problems in participating on a panel entitled Alternative and Critical Perspectives is that the very nature of "alternative" is diversity and nonconformity. There can be no single alternative perspective nor any alternative school. Nor can I think of alternative as a "subfield." Alternative is a residual category for all who are not considered to be "mainstream." It has a clearer exclusionary meaning for those who consider themselves to be mainstream than it does for those who are so excluded. As a participant in an alternative panel, I can only write about the intellectual problems that confront me in my own work. I cannot discuss alternative perspectives in general.

"Critical" is a different matter. It describes an approach toward understanding and action. So far as I am concerned, there is no "critical school," no orthodoxy of criticism. It is, however, possible to distinguish a critical approach to a topic from other approaches that express different purposes—description, explanation, restoration, reconstruction, promotion, for example—and to ask what the critical approach consists of, how the critical theorist approaches the subject.

In this brief paper I focus on one theme that I found important in my own work: the issue of universality versus relativism (which includes the issue of positivism versus historicism). Among the tasks assigned to the panel members by the conveners, what I have to say probably relates most of all to item four—synthesis of approaches and appropriate methodologies—and item six—agenda of topics and research questions.[1] I approach the theme mentioned from the standpoint of critical theory, and I ask where it leads me toward a research program.

Critical theorists have been accused of not having a substantive research program. In my perspective (and I speak only, of course, for myself) the question of a research program follows from the nature of the critical approach itself. I would outline this approach through three questions:

1. What is critical theory and how has it come into international studies?
2. What is the core philosophical issue inherent to critical theory?
3. What ontology can the critical approach propose as a framework for inquiry and action?

Critical and Problem-Solving Theory

Problem-solving theory takes the existing world as its framework and considers how things work within that framework and how disturbances or dysfunctions may be remedied. It is essentially synchronic in its way of conceiving reality. The existing world is a given (datum), a set of supposedly stable relationships that may be disturbed. The analyst is concerned with dysfunctions, with homeostasis, and with the restoration of equilibrium.

Critical theory addresses itself to the frameworks for action, how these frameworks came into being, what are the conflicts or contradictions that call them into question, and what directions of change in frameworks are possible and desirable.[2] Economics and political science have been primarily problem solving in their approaches—dealing with the issues that concern them respectively within the assumed or "given" frameworks of markets and of existing sets of political institutions. Critical theory takes a diachronic perspective, one of history informed by sociological theory. It deals with facts, that is, "mades," rather than data or "givens," and, as Giambattista Vico argued, facts are to be understood through the minds of their (individual or collective) makers, that is, as products of history.[3] The analyst, the historically oriented social scientist, goes through a double process of historical thinking. The first phase is self-consciousness of one's own historical time and place, which determines the questions that claim attention. The second phase is the effort to understand the historical dynamics that brought about the conditions in which these questions arise.

Critical theory in recent decades has entered international studies through the revival of international political economy (IPE), although, of course, some earlier writers such as E. H. Carr were critical scholars. Initially, IPE was a branch of political science addressing the politics of economic policy.[4] It evolved, however, into the study of structural change in the world economy—that is, the focus came to be on changes in the organization of the economy and the changes in social and political structures and in cultural values associated with economic change.

While primacy was given to the economic as what is to be explained, other factors in change came to have comparable weight, depending upon the topic and the theorist. IPE remained a convenient name but would be a misnomer if it were to obscure the attention required in an examination of structural change to demography, migration, gender, race relations, cultural differences, and humanity's place in the biosphere. IPE opened the way to a comprehensive critical inquiry into structural change and also to the infusion of a normative concern, whether for maintenance of the status quo or for emancipatory action, as the purpose of inquiry.

The Core Philosophical Issue: Universality

The issue of universality arises in two ways: about norms and about knowledge. Are there universal norms, for instance about human rights? Can there be a universally knowable definitive, final, complete form of human knowledge about anything? These questions take us to assumptions about human nature and the human mind that are the basis for considering both forms of universality.

We can start our inquiry with the broad consensus of the European Enlightenment that human nature was universal and unchanging in time and space (e.g., in both Hobbes and Rousseau) and that political truths could be deduced from this construction. The Enlightenment, by and large, had a low opinion of history as an inferior, imprecise kind of knowledge. The natural sciences were the model in which scientists were observers of physical phenomena whose regularities could be demonstrated to be universal laws. The assumption of a universal human nature opened the way to explore the possibility that human activity in history and society could be treated like the phenomena of physical nature by social scientists who would assume the position of external observers and catalogue human activities in search of universal laws.

Already in the eighteenth century a dissident strand of European philosophy challenged the hegemony of the Enlightenment. In this dissident perspective the study of history and society was fundamentally different from physical science. Kant, of course, made the distinction between the phenomena that were the object of scientific observation and the "thing-in-itself" that could not be known. Giambattista Vico, before Kant, reversed the Enlightenment view about the supremacy of natural science over what we would now call social science by affirming that a thing could only be truly known by its maker. For Vico, the physical universe could only be known truly in the mind of God, its maker, whereas human history was intelligible to the minds of human beings who are the makers of history.

Nineteenth- and twentieth-century theorists like Wilhelm Dilthey, Benedetto Croce, R. G. Collingwood, and Martin Heidegger pursued the analysis of historical thought as a distinct tradition. This led initially to the sense of a dichotomy between the world as nature and the world as history. The same distinction between positivism and historicism emerged within Marxism in the thought of Antonio Gramsci.

Following Vico, human nature could no longer be regarded as universal. Human nature was a creation of history, made and remade by human beings, and therefore changeable over time (albeit very slowly) and diverse in space. The key point here is that, for Vico, there was enough similarity among human minds for one mind to be able empathetically to reproduce the mental processes of another so as to be able to understand minds differently shaped by history. Today, a more extreme position would deny that possibility, affirming that human natures have no common foundation, that they are distinct products of historical development, which in effect denies any possibility of historical or social knowledge that is not particularistic.[5]

In the late twentieth century, the classic distinction between an "objective" positivist natural science and a subjective (or better, intersubjective) historical and social science has been narrowed from the natural science side. The second law of thermodynamics and entropy, the relativity of space and time, Heisenberg's principle of uncertainty, the introduction of reflexivity recognizing that the scientist is part of the experiment and not just an external observer, complexity in cybernetic systems, and chaos theory (recognizing that there is an order in chaos) have all meant that chance gains over predictable determinism.[6]

Contemplation of the infinitely big and the infinitely small, the cosmos and the atomic particle, has made the conventional laws of physics less absolute, more relative. The gap between the natural and social sciences has been reduced. Notions of universality in the natural sciences have been weakened so that the recognition of reflexivity in historical and social knowledge no longer need seem so inferior as it did to the Enlightenment philosophers.

The *subjects* of knowledge, actual human beings, the concrete instances of the species Homo sapiens, are products of a long evolution. *Homo sapiens* has existed for somewhere between fifty thousand and one hundred thousand years, having evolved out of hominids during a passage of some four million years. Some people have speculated upon a biological evolution beyond *Homo sapiens*, involving a significant increase in brain cells, trading in the "end of history" (of *Homo sapiens*) for a "posthuman" world, which according to some such speculations, could lead to a self-organizing network of beings not needing formal institutions. The future is open and unpredictable. The speculation does, however, underline that our humanity is itself a product of the very *longue durée* of biological history that, having had a beginning, will by implication come to its end through either self-destruction or a long biological evolution.[7]

Our capacity for reasoning is, for practical purposes, stuck with the condition of *Homo sapiens*. And this reason we know is not a means of access to knowledge about Kant's noumenal world. It is a practical tool for making the best of the particular predicaments in which various specimens of *Homo sapiens* find themselves. Reason is colored by the circumstances that give rise to our use of it. Knowledge is reflexive—it knows itself in relation to its specific historical experience. Accordingly, several kinds of knowledge coexist as the intersubjective truths of different groups of people. This brings us back to Vico's challenge: can a person participating intersubjectively in one kind of truth, in one perception of reality, painstakingly reproduce the intersubjective meanings of another group and its truth.

Carl Jung has suggested a possible answer in defining three levels of consciousness and unconsciousness:

- First is personal consciousness, which is the common awareness we have of our perceptions and reasoning. This consciousness can be reflexive, that is, self-aware of the conditions in
  which it is being applied.
- The second level is the personal unconscious, which includes
  the occulted influences that affect our conscious awareness and
  may bias our perceptions and evaluations.
- The deepest level is the collective unconscious consisting of
  archetypes, that is, myths or forms that have a variety of different contents among different peoples and different eras but, as
  archetypes, are common to all humanity beyond time and
  space. This third and deepest level is the closest thing to universality in Jung's thinking. It could be the basis, the common
  foundation, upon which rests the possibility of penetrating the
  minds of others constituted differently by history. Jung's
  method is indeed reminiscent of Vico's in tracing myths and
  symbols common to the different "nations."[8]

Even this third level, the closest to universality, would only be
universal for the era of *Homo sapiens*, the longest *durée*. And the
implication that common archetypes have been given different content in the stories and myths of different peoples suggests that what
is universal as a starting point has become diverse in time and space
while at the same time retaining its common base in the human
psyche. It should therefore be possible to retrace the development of
diverse mentalities because of this common foundation.

What, then, is to be done?

In recognizing that values are products of history for particular peoples and particular times, does this thereby undermine those values?
That is what relativism sometimes is held to mean. The dilemma was
confronted by Isaiah Berlin when he wrote (quoting Schumpeter, I
believe, but without attribution): "To realize the relative validity of
one's convictions and yet stand for them unflinchingly is what distinguishes a civilized man from a barbarian." And Berlin went on: "To
demand more than this is perhaps a deep and incurable metaphysical
need; but to allow it to guide one's practice is a symptom of an equally
deep, and far more dangerous, moral and political immaturity."[9]

The difficulty is that there is more than one way of becoming
civilized, and each way has its barbarians to cope with. As between
different civilized values, active pretensions to universality are ultimately reducible to power. Moreover, the context in which abso-

lute values are advanced is always complex. Absolutist claims obscure other motives of an economic, geopolitical, or institutional kind. There are no absolutely pure motives as there are no just wars.

In such a context of divergence or conflict in values, we are led to Max Weber's distinction between an ethic of ultimate ends and an ethic of responsibility.[10] The ethic of ultimate ends makes absolutist claims and brooks no compromises. The ethic of responsibility looks to the likely consequences of action eschewing absolutist claims.

Ontology and a Research Program

An ontology for critical research (the specification of the key issues and foci of study) depends upon purpose—whether to maintain existing values and structures or to transform them, whether to conceive the future world as homogeneous or pluralistic. In a purpose geared to restoration and maintenance, it may be appropriate to focus on specific institutions or practices that have become dysfunctional, assuming stability in the whole. Where the purpose is for change and transformation and where homogeneity is abandoned in recognition of pluralism, the ontology has to be broadened to include all those factors that will have a bearing upon the fixing of goals for societies and the processes of transformation.

In the latter perspective, states and markets remain key institutions, but they function within a broader framework. Popular forces have become suspicious of both states and markets. In the established democracies large segments of the public have become alienated or nonparticipant in formal political processes; and under authoritarian regimes public participation is repressed. In both cases, efforts at self-organization articulate dissent in a new kind of politics.

The "battle in Seattle" of December 1999 when civil society groups from North America and many other parts of the world confronted what they saw as the alliance of state and corporate powers in the World Trade Organization illustrated both the breadth and the diversity of dissent at both national and transnational levels. Similar confrontations have followed with other high-level meetings of managers of world and regional economies.

A focus on *civil society* gives an indication of the issues and the forces for change. The concept of civil society itself requires reformulation. It no longer has the connotation it had for Hegel or Adam Smith as the realm of private interests distinct from the public in-

terest realm of the state. That eighteenth-century notion of civil society was equated with the bourgeoisie. Today's civil society distinguishes itself from both the state and economic power and seeks to
bring both under social control.

Encompassing the totality of activities in state, markets, and
civil society is the *common sense* of an era and of a community, or
the set of intersubjective meanings that give people a sense of reality and enable them to communicate meaningfully with one another. I would equate this with *civilization*, and since there are
coexisting forms of common sense, there are coexisting civilizations. Civilizations exist in people's minds, but they are formed in
the practices and institutions through which people confront their
material conditions of existence. The understanding of civilizations is to be approached through the interaction between common
sense ideas and materially conditioned practices.[11] Understanding
civilizations enables one to understand how people whose common
sense is differently formed by history perceive and interpret events
differently. Civilizations are not, however, a methodological a
priori. They are shaped by the development of civil society in the
longue durée. There is a reciprocal relationship or dialectic between
civil society and civilization in which states and markets may be
mediating factors. Civil society is a terrain of conflict among social
forces. Exclusionary as well as inclusionary forces compete; right-
wing populism and fascism are probably stronger now than at any
time since the 1930s.[12]

Covert forces—organized crime, intelligence services, money-
laundering banks, the drug and arms trades, people smuggling, mer-
cenary military forces, even hermetic religious cults—influence sur-
reptitiously the outcomes of overt political and economic processes.
One hypothesis is that the weaker civil society is, the greater space
there is for the influence of the covert world. A more developed civil
society enhances transparency and accountability.

The totality of human activity takes place within the *biosphere*
within which humanity is interdependent with other forms of life
and life-sustaining substances. The future of humanity depends
upon evolving ways of living that maintain the biosphere, and this
imposes a categorical constraint upon ecologically destructive practices and is an injunction to collective change in lifestyles. This in
turn raises the ethical issue of who is to make the changes and of
equity in sharing the burden and benefits of change.

Finally, there is the matter of social cohesion. This is ignored by methodological individualism but has been one of the oldest questions of political philosophy. Ibn Khaldun called the quality required to make a state *'asabiya,* a group consciousness generated in the warrior band. Machiavelli called the quality *virtú.* He thought his own contemporaries were too corrupt to possess it and looked to a prince to embody it. Gramsci sought for it in the political party (the modern prince).[13] Today we may look for it in the revival of civil society.

If you accept that a primary purpose for international studies is to prepare the ground for a pluralist world of diversity in social organization and ethical norms, then a research program toward this end would give emphasis to the study of civilizations, civil society and its complex context including the covert world, the maintenance of the biosphere, and the problem of social cohesion for the maintenance of collective entities and their institutions. These constitute the framework for understanding and coping with the more immediate issues of poverty, racism, discrimination, and violence. In this approach, "universality" has a different meaning from that bequeathed by the Enlightenment. In the Enlightenment meaning universal meant true for all time and space—the perspective of a homogeneous reality. In the approach just sketched, universality means comprehending and respecting diversity in an ever-changing world.

Notes

1. I have discussed some of these points in "Social Cleavages and the Way Ahead: Towards a New Ontology of World Order," in *Critical Theory and World Politics,* ed. Richard Wyn Jones (Boulder, Colo.: Lynne Rienner, 2001).
2. I have discussed problem-solving and critical theory in "Social Forces, States, and World Orders: Beyond International Relations Theory," in Robert Cox with Timothy J. Sinclair, *Approaches to World Order* (Cambridge: Cambridge University Press, 1996), 87–91.
3. Giambattista Vico, *The New Science of Giambattista Vico,* trans. from the 3d ed. (1744) by Thomas Goddard Bergin and Max Harold Fisch (Ithaca, N.Y.: Cornell University Press, 1970).
4. For example, in the textbook by Joan Spero, *The Politics of International Economic Relations,* 1st ed. (New York: St. Martin's, 1977). Earlier, Susan Strange in "International Economics and International Relations: A Case of Mutual Neglect" (*International Affairs* 46, no. 2 [1970]: 304–15) had appealed for a rapprochement of the two disciplines. Strange

later articulated in *States and Markets* (London: Pinter, 1988) a structural view of political economy that contributed to a critical approach.

5. Richard Rorty, as I read him, affirms that there is no core human nature, no residue once the creations of history have been peeled off such as Vico thought, and that only the experience of pain is common to human beings (and to animals). In *Contingency, Irony, and Solidarity* (Cambridge: Cambridge University Press, 1989), Rorty sees no common nature in the past but the possibility of creating one in the future.

6. Among the earliest exponents of this approach to the natural sciences was Jacques Monod, *Le hasard et la nécessité* (Paris: Seuil, 1970). His thinking was extended with implications for the social sciences by Edgar Morin, *Science avec conscience* (Paris: Fayard, 1982). An American overview is in M. Mitchell Waldrop, *Complexity: The Emerging Science at the Edge of Order and Chaos* (New York: Touchstone, 1993).

7. See, for example, Edgar Morin, *Le paradigme perdu: La nature humaine* (Paris: Seuil, 1973).

8. Jung wrote: "When I first took this direction I did not know where it would lead. I did not know what lay in the depths of the psyche—that region which I have since called the 'collective unconscious,' and whose contents I designate as 'archetypes.'" *Modern Man in Search of a Soul* (New York: Harcourt Brace, 1933), 241. Compare this with Vico: "To discover the way in which this first human thinking arose in the gentile world, we encountered exasperating difficulties which have cost us the research of a good twenty years. We had to descend from these human and refined natures of ours to those quite wild and savage natures, which we cannot at all imagine and can comprehend only with great effort." *New Science*, para. 338.

    Jung's brief definition is: "We mean by collective unconscious, a certain psychic disposition shaped by the forces of heredity; from it consciousness has developed. In the physical structure of the body we find traces of earlier stages of evolution, and we may expect the human psyche also to conform in its make-up to the law of phylogeny." Jung, *Modern Man in Search of a Soul*, 165.

9. Isaiah Berlin, *Two Concepts of Liberty* (Oxford: Clarendon, 1958), 57. Berlin has also written, referring to Vico and Herder: "In the house of human history there are many mansions: this view may be un-Christian; yet it appears to have been held by both these pious eighteenth-century thinkers." "This doctrine is called pluralism. There are many objective ends, some incompatible with others, pursued by different societies at various times, or by different groups in the same society, by entire classes or churches or races, or by particular individuals within them, any one of which may find itself subject to conflicting claims of incompatible yet equally ultimate and objective ends. Incompatible these ends may be but their variety cannot be unlimited, for the nature of men however various and subject to change, must possess some generic character if it is to be called human at all. This holds, *a fortiori*, of differences between entire cultures." Isaiah Berlin, *The Crooked Timber of Humanity* (London: Fontana, 1991), 79–80.

10. Max Weber, "Politics as a Vocation," in *From Max Weber*, ed. H. H. Gerth and C. Wright Mills (London: Routledge and Kegan Paul, 1948), 118–28.

11. I have tried to develop this idea of civilizations in "Civilizations and the 21st Century: Some Theoretical Considerations," *International Relations of the Asia-Pacific* 1 (2001): 105–30.

12. I have expanded on this point in "Civil Society at the Turn of the Millennium: Prospects for an Alternative World Order," *Review of International Studies* 25, no. 1 (1999): 3–28.

13. In some recent work the quality has been called "social capital," reflecting a market mentality. Robert D. Putnam, "Bowling Alone: America's Declining Social Capital," *Journal of Democracy* 6, no. 1 (January 1995): 65–78.

THE CONTINUING STORY
OF ANOTHER DEATH FORETOLD

Radical Theory and the New International Relations

Michael Cox

Introduction

If international relations is to be judged by its capacity not just to understand the world as it is but by its proven ability to anticipate future global trends—a not unreasonable demand—then by any measure it has to be judged to have been one of the more dismal of the social sciences. The list of its failures is too long to bear repetition here and is possibly best forgotten. Others, however, might not let us forget quite so easily. As a senior editor of a leading foreign policy magazine once reminded us, consider what we, the so-called experts, either managed to get wrong or failed to get right.[1] Who, he asked, called the following? The East Asian crisis? Or the collapse of the Soviet Union? The end of the cold war in Eastern Europe? Yugoslavia's demise or Japan's swift transformation from global economic powerhouse to financial wreck? The answer, he concluded, was no one.[2] Nor, he might have added, did many people get very close to guessing the shape of the post–cold war order either. In fact, so complicated did the world look after 1989 that many writers took refuge in old intellectual certainties—with either dire predictions coming from one section of the international relations community

---

The title is of course a derivative and draws very directly from that used by Stafano Guzzini in his excellent discussion of another premature fatality. See Stafano Guzzini, *Realism in International Relations and International Political Economy: The Continuing Story of a Death Foretold* (London: Routledge, 1998).

about the future looking very much like the past or Kantian optimism emanating from another about a new international system in formation where the pacifying force of democracy, the integrating power of the market, and the stabilizing role of multilateral institutions would combine together to create a world of peace and relative prosperity.[3] But such simplicities could not begin to capture the structural complexity of the new international system. Indeed, so complex did it seem that the term most frequently deployed by writers to describe it—other than the much-disputed notion of globalization and the less-than-original idea of unipolarity—was the prefix *post*. Thus, according to whom you happened to be reading at the time, we were now entering into, or had in fact entered, a post–cold war era whose chief feature was that the cold war happened to be over, a postsocialist order whose main ideological characteristic was that there was no longer any socialism, or a postmodern world where apparently there was no order at all. For the first time in history it appeared that we were trying to make sense of the world around us not in terms of what it was, but rather in terms of what it happened to have superseded. Intellectually, at least, it was all rather depressing.[4]

In spite of the fact that few of the major academic trends can claim very much credit for either predicting the end of the cold war or what followed, one, it would seem, has suffered the greatest damage of all as a result of what happened in 1989: that loosely defined, deeply divided, and heterogeneous current in international relations known rather vaguely as "radical." Since the "fall," realism, it appears, has recovered its nerve.[5] Liberalism has experienced something of a resurgence. And constructivism has done especially well.[6] But radicalism, according to some accounts at least, has virtually disappeared off the intellectual map. This point was made somewhat clearer than the truth by the influential Stephen Walt in a recent survey of the discipline after the cold war. The death of realism, he felt, had "been largely exaggerated"; liberalism meanwhile was experiencing a new lease of life following the "defeat of communism"; while the end of the cold war had played "an important role" in actually "legitimating constructivist theories because realism and liberalism both failed to anticipate the event and had some trouble explaining it." Radicalism, however, had a bleak future. Indeed, in its largely Marxist form, it appeared to have no future at all—and for good reason according to Walt. First, it had failed to provide a serious theory of intercapitalist relations in the modern world. It had then advanced a false theory of dependency that had proven quite unable to explain relations between the North and the South. And finally, it could not really account for what had happened under "actually existing socialism"; in particular, it had no means of explaining the often aggressive and frequently fissiparous nature of communism as a system. For all these reasons (and no doubt others could think of more) radical analysis had lost any appeal it might have once had and held no particular allure for students of international relations in the post–cold war era.[7]

The argument that radical theory in its old historical materialist form has had its day is certainly a popular one. My purpose here, basically, is to suggest that just as with realism, it might still be a little premature to declare it dead altogether. In part this is based on a simple empirical observation: there is still lots of it out there, as any brief skim through the programs of either the British International Studies Association or the International Studies Association annual conferences would quickly reveal. If radical analysis has disappeared from the agenda as Walt, and no doubt many others seem to believe, then nobody appears to have told a sizable number of the profession who continue to do applied research on such subjects as Gramscian theories of hegemony,[8] the geography of the world economy,[9] U.S. foreign policy,[10] capitalism and law,[11] and global governance. If radical theory has suffered a setback since 1989, it is not one that has proved fatal.[12] This brings me to make a second, related point, which in many ways runs directly counter to the commonsense view that the death of communism dealt a body blow to radical theory:[13] whereas the cold war with its focus on the superpower competition and the strategic arms race was never that susceptible to radical materialist theorizing, unfettered capitalism (which is what we've now got) is. As the doyen of liberal American historians has recently pointed out, the irresistible dynamic of our modern form of "unbridled capitalism" makes very fertile ground indeed for radical analysis[14]—a view also endorsed by one of Mrs. Thatcher's onetime academic supporters.[15] Nor should this come as much of a surprise. Marxism after all was a theory of global market relations, not of state conflict, and under modern conditions where the market is geographically dominant, the tools developed by Marx and others like Marx are just as likely to be useful (if not more so) in understanding the modern world as those employed by liberalism, realism, or constructivism. Stanley Hoffmann made much the same point in a useful intervention in the debate in 1995. We have, he suggested, to make a distinction between what existed in countries like the USSR and the analytical categories of historical materialism. The former may have collapsed, but that does not mean the latter is therefore invalidated. Marxism might have given birth to a utopian politics. This does not mean however that it lacks serious analytical power.[16]

In the end of course nothing is given, and the credibility of radical analysis is going to depend more on its scholarship than on its materialist categories or its skepticism toward capitalism. Nothing after all is inevitable, and if radicals fail as badly in their attempts to explain the shape of the post-Soviet world as they did in analyzing the contradictions of the former Soviet Union itself, then they have—and will deserve—no future. It might therefore be useful to see how well the different varieties of radicalism have thus far come to terms with a world they, and nearly everybody else for that matter, never anticipated. In what follows I shall therefore try to summarize a large, very uneven, and deeply schismatic literature. In my brief review I will include many writers who some might not even include within the fold, and others who themselves would not be comfortable being labeled as Marxist. Robert Cox for example is often associated with Marxism, though he himself could hardly be described as orthodox.[17] The same might be said of André Gunder Frank, whose most recent work seems to challenge the whole edifice of Marxist thought on the history of capitalism.[18] Noam Chomsky moreover is no Marxist. On the other hand, his writings on the new international order are highly critical of the status quo. Furthermore, unlike many of the analysts mentioned in this paper, his works have a fairly wide readership, especially outside the narrow confines of the international relations' profession.[19]

I have divided the discussion into four sections. In the first, I look at the way radicals have tried to come to terms with the death of actually existing socialism and the associated international result in the shape of the "end of the cold war." In the second, I examine their efforts to decode the meaning of the term *globalization.* Part three then sees whether radical analysts have developed a theory of crisis. Finally, part four examines the way or ways radicals have tried to come to terms with American power. In the concluding section I explore what is far and away the greatest problem facing radical analysis today (possibly its greatest problem throughout the twentieth century): identifying the source of political regeneration in a world where there is possibly as much, if not more, suffering than at any point over the last fifty years, but little sense that much can be done to alleviate it.

The End of the Cold War

The collapse of Soviet power and with it the end of the cold war was as big a surprise to most radicals as it was to more mainstream analysts, perhaps more so because many on the Western Left had a certain regard for "actually existing socialism": quite a few out of a misplaced sense of political loyalty, some because they just didn't like capitalism, and others because they felt that the Soviet Union (whatever its faults internally) played an internationally progressive role by counterbalancing the power of the United States while underwriting numerous anti-imperialist regimes—especially in the less developed countries of what was then, but is no more, referred to as the Third World.[20]

Lacking a proper political economy of communism (for reasons which would take too long to discuss here) radical analysts have in the main tried to deal with the politically problematic question of the fall of official socialism not by confronting the problem head on but rather by finessing the issue. They have done so in a number of different ways.

The first way, quite simply, has been to deny that the regimes in Eastern Europe or the former Soviet Union were genuinely socialist. Thus what "fell" between 1989 and 1991 was not the real article, but some odd hybrid that had little or nothing to do with what American Marxist Bertell Ollmann once tried to describe as "Marx's vision" of the new society. This inclination to deny the socialist authenticity of the former USSR can in fact be found in the writings of many radicals, though it is perhaps most strongly articulated in the work of Hillel Ticktin, editor of the journal *Critique* and the only Western Marxist to have developed a detailed political economy of the USSR before its disintegration. According to Ticktin (who was one of the few radicals to have ever lived in the USSR for any extended period of time) the Soviet system was not just repressive but economically far less efficient than what existed in the West. For this reason he did not believe that what he termed this "economy of waste" could endure over the long term. This view—first articulated as early as 1973—in turn became the basis of a very specific politics, which meant that Ticktin at least was somewhat less surprised than other Marxists by the Soviet Union's subsequent collapse. Indeed, in his opinion, until the USSR passed from the stage of history, there was little chance of a genuine "new" Left ever emerging in the West.[21]

If Ticktin detected deep and life-threatening economic flaws in the Soviet system, this was not the position of most socialists. Indeed, one of the more obvious ways in which other radicals have tried to come to terms with the fall of the Soviet Union has been to imply that the system did not have to go under at all: and the only reason it did was because of ill-fated attempts to reform the country in the 1980s. Thus one of the better-informed socialist economists has argued that although the Soviet Union had its fair share of problems, it did not face a terminal crisis. What brought it down, in the end, was not its flaws but Gorbachev's contradictory policies.[22] The American radical Anders Stephanson also insists that there was nothing inevitable about the demise of communism in the USSR. In his assessment it was largely the result of what he terms "contingency."[23] Halliday too has suggested that the Soviet system did not (in his words) "collapse," "fail," or "break down."[24] Rather, the Soviet leadership after 1985 decided—albeit for good objective reasons—to rule in a different way: and it did so not because of massive internal difficulties but because the Soviet elite finally realized that the USSR could neither catch up with nor compete with the West. Once this became manifest, the ruling group effectively lost its historical nerve.[25]

The argument that the old Soviet system might not have been suffering incurable economic cancer has also led certain radical writers to the not illogical conclusion that if the system was not doomed because of its internal problems, it was in the end external factors that caused it to implode. This is certainly implicit in the influential work of Halliday, who, significantly, says little about the USSR's domestic weaknesses but a good deal about the impact Western economic performance had upon Soviet elite perceptions. Others have stressed a more direct connection. Thus in the view of the Dutch Marxist Kees van der Pijl, though the final transformation of the Soviet system was the result of several internal factors, one should not underestimate the role played by the United States and its declared objective of quite literally spending "the Soviet Union into bankruptcy."[26] Robert Cox appears to have come to much the same conclusion in his writings. Like van der Pijl, Cox accepts there is no simple explanation of what happened in the former USSR after 1985. Nonetheless he still concludes that "the arms race provoked by the

Reaganite phase of the Cold War was too much for an unreformed Soviet economy to sustain."[27] Michael Ellman has also laid great stress on the importance of U.S. strategy: taken together Reagan's rearmament program, Star Wars, and U.S. support for anticommunist guerillas throughout the world were, in his opinion, "key external factors" in bringing about Soviet economic collapse in 1991.[28]

But if the Left has faced very real problems in coming to terms with the fall of the Soviet Union, it has tried to compensate for this in two very different ways. One has been to understate the impact the communist collapse has actually had upon the "essential" nature of the international system. Hence, in the view of Noam Chomsky, there is nothing "new" at all about the new world order: the rich remain rich, the poor South remains the poor South, and the United States still remains in charge.[29] Robert Cox concurs. The new international system, he thinks, looks very much like the old one. Indeed, in the most basic of ways, the cold war, he argues, has "not ended" at all, and its more basic structures continue "to live in the West" in the shape of high military spending, in the operation of intelligence services, and in the unequal distribution of power among the various states.[30] This also appears to be the position of the doyen of world systems theory, Immanuel Wallerstein. Unfortunately, in his metastructural (and highly abstract) output over many years, one had no real sense that the cold war ever had much meaning at all. Thus its conclusion was unlikely to have a great deal of impact upon a world system that had existed since the sixteenth century, that had been in some fairly unspecified "crisis" since the late 1960s, and that would presumably remain in crisis until it came to an equally unspecified end twenty or thirty years down the historical line.[31]

Finally, if writers such as Wallerstein have tended to minimize the impact of the end of the cold war, others have argued (perhaps rather more convincingly) that its passing has in fact created new political spaces that did not exist before. This is more or less the position adopted by Bogdan Denitch. Starting from the not unreasonable assumption that the division of Europe rested upon an illegitimate form of Soviet domination over the East, and a legitimate form of American hegemony in the West, Denitch concludes that in the new united continent there are now great opportunities. Unlike many politically active Marxists, Denitch is no utopian. Thus in his view the new openings are unlikely to free the workers from the grip of capitalism. Yet 1989 does make possible the deeper integration of Western Europe, and upon this basis Europe—in his opinion—will be able to develop a new social democratic third way between a highly dynamic but politically unacceptable American-style liberal capitalism and a moribund Soviet-style communism. This hardly amounts to the same thing as world revolution. Nonetheless, in a postcommunist world, the possibility of building a new progressive Europe is one that should animate intelligent radicals more than pointless calls to man barricades that nobody wants to build and few want to stand behind.[32]

New World Economic Order: Globalization

Though analysts like Denitch have tried to find some crumbs of comfort from the events of 1989, overall the collapse of planning in Eastern Europe, followed as it was by the adoption of radical market strategies in countries such as Poland and the Czech Republic, had an enormously debilitating political impact on Western radicals. Yet, as I have implied earlier, the pessimism did not last long, and those who managed to survive the baptism by fire began to take intellectual heart somewhere around the mid-1990s. There were two reasons for this. The first, quite simply, was that the much-heralded transition in the former communist countries turned out to be far more problematic than most market triumphalists had originally anticipated. In the case of Russia of course the so-called transition to something better and higher soon turned into a minor tragedy for the Russian people.[33] The other, equally important, reason was the birth of a new world order in which economics assumed center stage. In fact, it almost looks now as if it required a healthy dose of capitalism to reignite radical analysis and provide the intellectual Left with a clear focus. But perhaps we should not be so surprised by this. In an age of geoeconomics where even staid bankers were now prepared to use words like "capitalism," where the former editor of the *London Times* talked menacingly of the "coming depression,"[34] and an American president paid tribute to a book that speculated in almost Leninist terms about the coming economic struggle for dominance between the great powers in the twenty-first century[35]—it was almost inevitable that radicals would begin to take heart! Having been ground under politically since 1989, it looked to some of them at least (and at last) that historical materialism had finally come of age.

Rather than trying to provide a detailed reconstruction here of a single radical or "neo-Marxist" analysis of late-twentieth-century capitalism (one that has yet to be written), it might be more useful to briefly point to some of the issues now being debated in the growing left-wing literature. Not surprisingly, one issue that has been discussed more than most is globalization. While there is no agreed-upon radical view on the subject, four quite reasonable questions have been asked of the concept since it literally exploded onto the academic agenda in the early 1990s.[36]

The first has perhaps been the most challenging: namely, what exactly is so new about the idea? As many on the Left have argued, the apparently novel thesis that national economies have become mere regions of the global economy and that productive forces have expanded far beyond the boundaries of the nation-state is not novel at all.[37] Indeed, one of the first writers to advance the argument was no less than the abused and much-ignored Karl Marx, who in the *Communist Manifesto* made it abundantly clear that the central feature of the capitalist epoch was the "universal interdependence of nations." Moreover, this simple but critical idea ran like a red thread through Marxist thinking thereafter. It was, for instance, repeated by Lenin in his 1916 pamphlet *Imperialism* in an effort to provide a materialist explanation of World War I. Trotsky also deployed very much the same argument in his critique of Stalin's claim that it was possible to build socialism in one country. And later theorists of dependency took it as read that until the less developed countries could break away from the spidery economic web of the world market, they had no chance of overcoming the limits of backwardness.[38] Globalization might have become a fashionable concept in the 1990s amongst those desperately looking for a "relevant" topic now that traditional security questions no longer seemed to be interesting. But like most intellectual fads and fashions it was only a recycled version of a very old idea. In fact, according to Burnham, even the idea itself was not a very good one.[39]

The theme of continuity is also developed in the work of Hirst and Thompson. However, rather than attacking mainstream academics for failing to recognize the radical antecedents of the concept, they question whether globalization is even an accurate description of the world economy in the late twentieth century. In a much-cited study whose underlying purpose is as much political as it is economic, they conclude that the image of globalization has for too long mesmerized analysts.[40] In their opinion the theory can be criticized on at least two grounds. The first is in terms of its descriptive power. In their view the "present highly internationalized economy is not unprecedented" at all; indeed, "in some respects the current international economy is less open and integrated than the regime which prevailed between 1870 and 1914." Moreover, "genuinely transnational companies appear to be relatively rare," while the world economy itself, far from being genuinely "global," is still very much "dominated by the Triad of Europe, Japan and North America." They also question its political implications and suggest that far from being powerless as the theory implies, the state can still make a difference. As they argue, in this less than completely globalized economy, there are still opportunities for the development of governance mechanisms at the level of the international economy that neither undermine national governments nor hinder the creation of national strategies for international control. In other words the world of "markets" remains susceptible to conscious intervention. To this extent, the world economy is not out of control: politics, politicians, and the people—in other words the state under conditions of democracy—can make a difference.[41]

A third line of radical attack has not been to question the reality of globalization so much as to point to its appalling human consequences. In a world where the market is "unbound"—they argue—where there is in effect no alternative to the market, capitalism has assumed an increasingly aggressive posture: and this has led to the most extreme forms of inequality and economic polarization.[42] Nor is this accidental; nor can it be overcome without challenging the foundations of the system itself. Furthermore, if global economic integration has generated what one critic has rather mildly termed "underconsumptionist tendencies," it has tended to do so not only within capitalist countries but also across them.[43] This is why the gap between the have and have-not nations has tended to increase rather than decrease in an era of global capitalism. According to one study, in an unregulated capitalist world economy, the outcome has been that those countries and regions that already possessed abundant resources and power have remained powerful and prosperous, while those that did not have become poorer and even more dependent than before.[44]

Finally, many radical critics have wondered whether some of the advocates of globalization have tended to underestimate the anarchic and competitive character of the world capitalist system. Though accepting the more general thesis about global interdependence, many on the Left do not accept the liberal corollary that we have moved beyond the age of conflict. And though war in the more traditional sense is highly unlikely, this does not rule out intense competition at the other levels. Realist by inclination, radicals have noted several areas in the world today where antagonism rather than cooperation is the norm. America's intense rivalry with France over trade, Germany's attempt to exercise economic hegemony over Europe at the expense of the United Kingdom, and the United States' more recent drive to open up the markets of Asia-Pacific all point to a slightly less benign view of economic reality than that suggested by the "globalists."[45]

Capitalist Contradictions

Perhaps the most serious difference, however, between radicals and their more orthodox peers concerns the long-term stability of world capitalism. Though few but the most orthodox economists would subscribe to a simple theory of global economic equilibrium, there is an underlying assumption amongst most non-Marxists that even though the international economic system might go through periodic booms and busts, these movements are either functional to the system overall (Schumpeter, you will recall, once talked of "creative destruction") or can easily be resolved.[46] Naturally enough radicals do not share this sense of optimism. Nor in one sense can they, given their opposition to the status quo. The problem for the Left of course is that they have too often cried wolf before to be taken seriously now. However, with the onset of the Asian economic crisis it at last seems as if their prediction of economic doom has finally turned out to be true; and inevitably they have drawn some comfort from the fact that the so-called Asia-Pacific miracle has turned into a nightmare—one that has even prompted *The Economist* to ask whether the world as a whole is on the cusp of a new slump.[47]

But long before the collapse of capitalist optimism in Asia, radicals had already begun to articulate a theory of crisis. Basically, this consisted of a number of distinct arguments.

The first part was in essence an updated version of Hobson mediated via Keynes and restated in different forms by radical economists like Sweezy and Magdoff: and what this amounted to in effect was a belief that there was a fundamental contradiction between the world economy's capacity to produce and the people's ability to consume. In other words, there existed what Marx had frequently referred to in his work as a systemic tendency to overproduction—one

that he thought could not be overcome as long as capitalism continued to exist. Though long consigned to the proverbial dustbin of
history, this particular theory has enjoyed something of a revival
over the past few years, and not just amongst radicals but also more
mainstream economists concerned that the great boom of the 1990s
could well easily be followed by the great crash of the early twenty-
first century. Indeed, the thesis itself has been given an enormous
boost with the publication of the evocatively subtitled study by William Greider, *The Manic Logic of Global Capitalism.* Though Greider's underlying argument is not designed to support revolutionary
conclusions, that his study evokes the ghost of Marx (and has become an instant best-seller) would suggest that what one radical re-
viewer has called this "powerful and disturbing book" has touched
a very raw nerve amongst more orthodox analysts.[48]

Greider's pessimism, however, is not just based upon a general
argument about the overproductive character of modern capitalism.
It also flows from a more detailed analysis and awareness of the increasingly integrated and highly open character of the international
economy, which allows billions to be moved, or lost, in a matter of
hours; and where events in one country or set of countries are very
rapidly felt around the world in a domino process that once set in
train becomes very difficult to stop. A good example of this is provided by what happened in Hong Kong in late 1997. Here a 25 percent
fall on the Hong Kong Stock Exchange quickly led to a major decline
in share prices around the world. In the same way, the meltdown in
Indonesia has had a profoundly depressing effect upon the rest of
Asia, while the financial crisis in Japan has sent seismic shocks right
across the Pacific to the United States. And so it will go on according
to radicals until governments either decide to reflate the world economy—which they are scared to do politically—or there is the crash
predicted by Greider.

The argument that the system might well be spinning out of control is further supported in radical analysis by the argument that we
are now living in an era when finance rather than industry—and
finance capital rather than productive capital—has assumed the
dominant role in the world economy.[49] While there may not be anything especially "radical" about that particular empirical observation, there is about some of the conclusions radical theorists tend to
draw from it. First, in their view, the preponderance of finance effectively means that capitalism today has little or no interest in sup-

porting industrial policies that sustain full employment. This therefore means that the system overall is now less able to fulfil at least
one basic human right: the right to work. More generally, the overwhelming power of finance capital introduces enormous instability
into the system as those with money either seek speculative gain
with little concern about the political consequences of their actions
or move their money at very high speed if and when conditions
change. What makes the situation all the more volatile of course is
that there are no national or international means for controlling
these various movements and flows. Consequently, a very dangerous
and apparently unbridgeable gap has opened up between those institutions that are supposed to manage the world economic system in
the general interest and the specific interests of the banks, the large
pension funds, and the insurance companies.

Finally, the tendency to crisis in the post–cold war epoch has been
reinforced it has been argued by the end of the cold war itself.
Though not all radicals adhere to the argument that the cold war
was good for capitalism (there was a powerful current of thought that
suggested the opposite), there are those who maintain that even
though the superpower conflict was costly these costs were more
than offset by the benefits. By the same token, while there has been
obvious economic benefits accruing from the termination of the cold
war, its ending has created major problems for the West as a whole.
First, governments in key capitalist countries like the United States
and the United Kingdom no longer have military spending as a way
of pump priming their economies.[50] Second, there are the unforeseen
but really quite huge costs involved for Germany caused by reuni-
fication—costs that have transformed Germany from being a boom
economy into one of the great underperforming economies of Europe. Third, though the end of the cold war has been followed by
what most radicals see as a temporary boom in the United States,
its passing has fundamentally weakened America's capacity to act
abroad. And without American leadership, the international order in
general and the world capitalist system in particular are bound to
suffer. Working on the good realist assumption that American power
was an essential element in the postwar reconstruction of international capitalism, a number of radicals believe that now that the cold
war is over and America can no longer exercise its hegemony so
effectively, the world system is likely to become a good deal less
stable.[51] Difficult times lie ahead for the last remaining "superpower
without a mission."[52]

Hegemonic Still? The United States

This brings us quite logically to the question of the United States: the source of most radical distaste during the cold war and the cause of much intellectual anguish since now that it has seen off the only power in the world capable of limiting its reach. Though less vilified in the 1990s than it was previously, the United States nonetheless continues to fascinate radicals in ways that no other nation does. The reasons for this are clear. No other country is as powerful, dynamic, or as "exceptional" as the United States of America. Indeed, according to one "European" analyst, even American radicals and Marxists are more interesting and "have been more intellectually productive and innovative" than their comrades across the Atlantic since the late 1960s![53]

Three issues have been of greatest interest to radical critics: one concerns the use of American power; another, the nature of American foreign policy in the post–cold war era; and the third, America's position within the larger international system. Let us deal briefly with each.

The question about American power has been an especially problematic one for the Left in the post–cold war period. Naturally enough, most (but by no means all) radicals opposed American intervention against Iraq in 1991. However, since then, many have found themselves in the somewhat paradoxical position of attacking the United States not for being too interventionist but for not being interventionist enough. The issue that led to this rather odd state of affairs was of course the war in ex-Yugoslavia. Here the Left found itself caught between a rock and a hard place. On the one hand, being radicals they were deeply suspicious of any American involvement on the continent of Europe. On the other hand, it was palpably clear that if the United States did not get involved, the genocide in Bosnia would continue. There was no easy squaring of this particular circle. Some therefore decided to stick to their ideological guns and opposed any American role.[54] Others, however, bit the political bullet and urged Washington on. Indeed, one of the greatest ironies of this particular tragedy was that many radicals who had earlier criticized the United States for having intervened in the Gulf because of oil now pilloried the United States for not intervening in the Balkans because there was no oil. Moreover, having been the strongest critics of the American military before Bosnia, some on the Left at least now became the most bellicose advocates of tough military action against the Serbs.

If radicals seemed to have had serious problems in dealing with U.S. power in the post–cold war world, they appear to have had none at all in attacking America's self-proclaimed goal of promoting democracy. To be fair, they did not oppose the United States because they were against democracy as such, but rather because they thought that its championing of the policy was either a sham or, more obviously, a device designed to obscure America's economic objectives in the larger capitalist system. Chomsky in fact has even argued that the United States has actually deterred democracy,[55] while Furedi in his broadside has attacked all Western talk of making the world a better place as little more than a cover for neocolonialism.[56] Others have been slightly less harsh, or at least more subtle. This is certainly true of the important work undertaken by Gills and Robinson in their analysis of the Third World. In an attempt to move the argument forward, both have proposed the thesis that certain forms of "low intensity democracy" have had an important role to play in both containing popular protest while legitimizing painful economic reforms being advocated by Washington.[57] Robinson indeed has put forward a whole historical argument concerning the complex interplay between social change and elite rule in Latin America. Deploying the much-used and admired Gramsci, he argues that by the 1980s it had become clear to the dominant group that the old repressive methods were no longer workable in an age of globalization; and supported by the United States, they therefore replaced coercive means of social control with consensual ones. Though the policy carried certain risks, in the end it achieved precisely what it had been designed to: namely, to secure political stability in a period of social upheaval caused by Latin America's more complete integration into the world capitalist system.

The third and final "great debate" has turned around the hoary old problem as to whether or not the United States is, ever has been, or will be in decline. Regarded by many in the international relations profession today as a nonissue (though this was not the view between the Vietnam War and the end of the cold war), it continues to inform a large part of the modern radical discussion about the United States. Some like Bernstein and Adler have little doubt that the United States is in decline—and has been so since the late 1960s.[58] Others like Stephen Gill assert that the "declinist" thesis is quite false.[59] Clearly there is no consensus on the issue, and it would be misleading to suggest that there was one. Yet whereas radicals before the collapse of the USSR were more inclined to believe that the United States was on the way down, since 1991 they have tended (along with nearly everybody else) to assume that there is still a good head of steam left in the engine of the American capitalist machine. U.S. success in the cold war, its easy victory over Iraq, the financial crisis in Japan, Europe's inability to resolve the situation in ex-Yugoslavia, and the economic boom in the United States after 1992 have in fact convinced many that American power is still something to be reckoned with. Indeed, according to one study written by a Latin American with impeccable left-wing credentials, Marxists have to face up to the unpalatable fact that the United States is not only *not* in decline but can actually look forward to the future with enormous self-confidence. The prophets of (relative) doom like Paul Kennedy may know their history according to Valladao. However, they are in his view a century or two adrift; and if historical analogies must be drawn then it should be with Rome in triumph after its victory over Carthage, not with Britain in the postwar period, or Spain in the sixteenth century. The twenty-first century will be American.[60]

Changing the World

The issue of American power leads finally to the question of political renewal on the Left. The two are obviously connected. After all, if America is in decline as some on the Left believe, the political possibilities for radicals would seem to be bright. If, on the other hand, we can look forward to continued American hegemony, then capitalism by implication must be secure: and if capitalism is secure, then the possibility of a radical breakthrough is highly unlikely.

This in turn raises the even larger problem of what radicals or Marxists are supposed to do in a world where on the one hand the "socialist alternative" seems to have failed and where on the other the market in spite of its manifest contradictions looks like "it's the only game in town." The intellectual Left has responded to this dilemma in a number of ways. Two deserve special mention here.

The first has been to accept that for the time being there may in fact be no alternative to the market, and the only thing one can do therefore is develop strategies that seek to build areas of opposition and resistance within the larger interstices of "civil society"—either at the national or global level.[61] With this in mind, no doubt, many on the Left have endorsed campaigns to extend the realm of democracy or increase the degree of information available to the public at large. In Britain a good deal of radical energy has also been expended on supporting constitutional change, while in the United States radical activists have been involved in an as yet unsuccessful effort to develop a comprehensive health system. The Left has also engaged in numerous other campaigns covering a range of questions, from women's rights and trade union recognition right through to the increasingly popular issue of the environment—on which there is now a vast academic literature. Indeed, one of the more interesting developments over the past few years has been the marked rise in a radical discourse on major environmental questions. One might even be tempted to suggest that the struggle to save "mother earth" from what some now see as impending environmental catastrophe has taken over from the equally influential movement ten years previously to prevent the collapse of the world into nuclear war.

The second way in which the Left has responded to the current situation has been to explore ways and means by which the dynamics of globalization can either be slowed down or even arrested entirely—a perspective explored with typical intellectual sensitivity by Robert Cox. According to Cox, there is no reason for despair insofar as the dynamics of globalization are bound to throw up various forms of resistance around the world. This will come from many layers affected by the internationalization of production, including groups outside of the production process proper. Resistance to global capitalism, however, is also bound to involve workers themselves who have been placed under unremitting pressure by the logic of a global capitalism constantly seeking to weaken the position of organized labor.[62] According to radical critics, moreover, the proletarian genie is not just a figment of some rabid left-wing imagination. In country after country—from South Korea to France, from Germany to the United States itself—workers have begun to take action to resist attempts to make them mere robots in a world without frontiers, where capital owes no loyalty—except of course to its shareholders.[63] They may not yet have united, but at last the workers are beginning to act.

However, as Cox would be the first to admit, resistance to globalization is not exactly the same thing as a positive or coherent strategy, and until there is such a strategy, there will always remain what he calls "a vacuum to be filled—a challenge to critical thinking on the left." And at the heart of this challenge "is the question of the motive force for change."[64] For if the working class is not the universal class described by Marx, and the vision of a new society has been besmirched by the experience of the USSR, then there is little possibility of major political transformation. Furthermore, even if the world is in crisis, or in what Hobsbawm prefers to call a "state of social breakdown," without a vision of a different society, nothing can fundamentally change.[65] This presents radicals with a major problem. For however sound their analysis, if the world remains the same (or even gets worse) they will simply be left standing where they have been for a very long time: on the sidelines of history. In this sense their greatest challenge perhaps is not so much intellectual as political; and until they can provide a coherent answer to the question of what it is they are for rather than what it is they are against, they will remain what they have been, in effect, for more years than they would care to admit—well-informed rebels without a political cause.

Notes

1. Moises Naim, "Editor's Note," Foreign Policy 110 (spring 1998): 9–11.
2. The admittedly controversial issue of prediction, and predicting the end of the cold war in particular, is dealt with at length in Michael Cox, ed., Rethinking the Soviet Collapse: Sovietology, the Death of Communism, and the New Russia (London: Pinter, 1998).
3. Some of these issues are dealt with in Michael Cox, G. John Ikenberry, and Takashi Inoguchi, eds., American Democracy Promotion: Strategies, Impacts (Oxford: Oxford University Press, 2000).
4. For one attempt to explore the various features of the international system after the "fall" see Michael Cox, Ken Booth, and Tim Dunne, eds., The Interregnum: Controversies in World Politics, 1989–1999 (Cambridge: Cambridge University Press, 1999).
5. On the state of realism see the useful collection of essays in Ethan B. Kapstein and Michael Mastanduno, eds., Unipolar Politics: Realism and State Strategies after the Cold War (New York: Columbia University Press, 1999).
6. Though who is and who is not a "constructivist" these days remains unclear. See the lengthy discussion occasioned by the publication of Alexander Wendt's book Social Theory of International Politics (Cambridge: Cambridge University Press, 1999) in the Review of International Studies 26 (January 2000): 123–80.
7. Stephen Walt, "International Relations: One World, Many Theories," Foreign Policy 100 (spring 1998): 29–46.
8. See Mark Rupert, Producing Hegemony: The Politics of Mass Production and American Global Power (Cambridge: Cambridge University Press, 1995).
9. For a tour through the new radical geography, see Paul Knox and John

Agnew, *The Geography of the World Economy*, 3d ed. (London: Arnold, 1998).

10. See Nicholas Guyatt, *Another American Century? The United States and the World after 2000* (London: Zed Books, 2000).

11. Claire Cutler, "Critical Reflections on the Westphalian Assumption of International Law: A Crisis of Legitimacy," *Review of International Studies* 27 (April 2001): 133–50.

12. For a very useful and comprehensive guide to radical theory in an age of globalization see Steve Hobden and Richard Wyn Jones, "Marxist Theories of International Relations," in *The Globalization of World Politics*, 2d ed., ed. John Baylis and Steve Smith (Oxford: Oxford University Press, 2001).

13. For a more nuanced position, however, see Peter J. Katzenstein, Robert O. Keohane, and Stephen D. Krasner, "*International Organization* and the Study of World Politics," in their *Exploration and Contestation in the Study of World Politics* (Cambridge: MIT Press, 1999), esp. 24–26.

14. See Arthur Schlesinger, "Has Democracy a Future?" *Foreign Affairs* 76 (September–October 1997): 12–22.

15. See John Gray, *False Dawn: The Delusion of Global Capitalism* (London: Granta Books, 1998).

16. See the interview with Stanley Hoffmann, "Democracy and Society," *World Policy Journal* 12 (spring 1995): 35.

17. See Robert Cox, "Social Forces, States, and World Orders: Beyond International Relations Theory," *Millennium* 10, no. 2 (1981): 126–55; and "Gramsci, Hegemony, and International Relations: An Essay in Method," *Millennium* 12, no. 2 (1983): 162–75.

18. See André Gunder Frank and Barry Gills, eds., *The World System: Five Hundred Years or Five Thousand?* (London: Routledge, 1993).

19. See, for example, Noam Chomsky, *World Orders: Old and New* (London: Pluto, 1994).

20. Fred Halliday, *The Making of the Second Cold War* (London: Verso, 1993).

21. See also Hillel Ticktin, *The Origins of the Crisis in the USSR: Essays on the Political Economy of a Disintegrating System* (New York: Sharpe, 1992).

22. See Michael Ellman and Vladimir Kontorovich, eds., *The Disintegration of the Soviet Economic System* (London: Routledge, 1992).

23. See Anders Stephanson, "Rethinking Cold War History," *Review of International Studies* 24 (January 1998): 119–24.

24. See Fred Halliday, *Rethinking International Relations* (London: Macmillan, 1994), esp. 191–215.

25. See Fred Halliday's essay "The End of the Cold War and International Relations," in *International Relations Theory Today*, ed. Ken Booth and Steve Smith (University Park: Pennsylvania State University Press, 1995), pp. 38–61.

26. See Kees van der Pijl, "Soviet Socialism and Passive Revolution," in *Gramsci, Historical Materialism, and International Relations*, ed. Stephen Gill (Cambridge: Cambridge University Press, 1993), 237–58.

27. See Robert Cox with Timothy J. Sinclair, *Approaches to World Order* (Cambridge: Cambridge University Press, 1996), 217.

28. Michael Ellman, "Multiple Causes of the Collapse," *RFE/RL Research Report* 2, no. 23 (1993): 56.

29. See Noam Chomsky, *Deterring Democracy* (New York: Vintage, 1992).

30. Cox with Sinclair, *Approaches to World Order*, 34.

31. See Immanuel Wallerstein, "The Inter-State Structure of the Modern World-System," in *International Theory: Positivism and Beyond*, ed. Steve Smith, Ken Booth, and Marysia Zalewski (Cambridge: Cambridge University Press, 1996). See also Immanuel Wallerstein, ed., *The Capitalist World-Economy* (Cambridge: Cambridge University Press, 1979).

32. Bogdan Denitch, *The End of the Cold War: European Unity, Socialism, and the Shift in Global Power* (London: Verso, 1990), 3–14.

33. See the essays by Stephen Cohen, Stephen White, and Bob Arnot in Cox, *Rethinking the Soviet Collapse.*

34. See James Dale Davidson and Lord William Rees-Mogg, *The Great Reckoning: Protect Yourself in the Coming Depression* (New York: Touchstone Books, 1993).

35. The book in question was Lester Thurow, *Head to Head: The Coming Economic Battle among Japan, Europe, and America* (New York: Morrow, 1992).

36. According to Anthony Giddens, "globalization is almost worth not naming now: it is less a phenomenon, it is simply the way we live. . . . You can forget the word globalization: it is what we are." Cited in John Lloyd, "Interview: Anthony Giddens," *New Statesman*, January 10, 1997.

37. For a materialist though not necessarily orthodox Marxist account of the long history of capitalist economic interdependence, see Fernand Braudel, *Capitalism and Material Life, 1400–1800* (New York: Harper and Row, 1973); *Civilization and Capitalism, 15th–18th Century*, vol. 2, *The Wheels of Commerce* (New York: Harper and Row, 1982); and *Civilization and Capitalism, 15th–18th Century*, vol. 3, *The Perspective of the World* (London: Collins/Fontana, 1984). On Braudel, see Randall Germain, "The Worlds of Finance: A Braudelian Perspective on IPE," *European Journal of International Relations* 2, no. 2 (1996): 201–30.

38. The two radical classics on dependency and development are Paul Baran, *The Political Economy of Growth* (New York: Monthly Review Press, 1957), who later influenced André Gunder Frank, *Capitalism and Underdevelopment in Latin America* (New York: Monthly Review Press, 1969).

39. See Peter Burnham, "Globalisation: States, Markets, and Class Relations," *Historical Materialism* 1, no. 1 (1997): 1–16.

40. See Paul Hirst and Graham Thompson, *Globalization in Question* (Cambridge: Polity, 1996). In her radical critique of the view that states are now powerless to make policy because of globalization, Linda Weiss even talks about "the enhanced importance of state power in the new international environment." See her "Globalization and the

Myth of the Powerless State," *New Left Review* 225 (September–October 1997): 3–27. The Canadian Marxist Leo Panitch is another radical who disputes the notion that globalization has rendered national politics meaningless. See his "Globalization and the State," in *Socialist Register, 1994,* ed. Ralph Miliband and Leo Panitch (London: Merlin, 1994), 60–93.

41. According to the blurb on the back of one noted study on the new "borderless world," "nation states are dinosaurs waiting to die. . . . [they] have lost their ability to control exchange rates and protect their currencies. . . . they no longer generate real economic activity. . . . the fate of nation states is increasingly determined by choices made elsewhere." See Kenichi Ohmae, *The End of the Nation State: The Rise of Regional Economics* (New York: Harper Collins, 1996).

42. See Elmar Altvater and Birgit Mahnkopf, "The World Market Unbound," *Review of International Political Economy* 4 (autumn 1997): 448–71. For useful discussions of the relationship between globalization and inequality, see Andrew Hurrell and Ngaire Woods, "Globalisation and Inequality," *Millennium* 24, no. 3 (1995): 447–70; and Julian Saurin, "Globalisation, Poverty, and the Promises of Modernity," *Millennium* 25, no. 3 (1996): 657–80.

43. Ronen Palan, *Underconsumptionism and Widening Income Inequalities: The Dynamics of Globalization,* Newcastle Discussion Papers in Politics, no. 4 (Newcastle, England: University of Newcastle, 1993), 45.

44. Andrew Sayer and Richard Walker, *The New Social Economy: Reworking the Division of Labour* (Oxford: Oxford University Press, 1992).

45. See James Petras and Morris Morley, "U.S.-French Relations in the New World Order" (July 1997, unpublished), 39.

46. In an attack on what he identified as a "Marxist vision" of a world economic crash, the American economist Lester Thurow argued that elected governments could and would in the end act to prevent the destruction of "both the economic system and democracy itself." See his "The Revolution Is upon Us," *Atlantic Monthly* 279 (March 1997): 97–100.

47. See "Will the World Slump?" *The Economist,* November 15, 1997, 17–18.

48. William Greider, *One World, Ready or Not: The Manic Logic of Global Capitalism* (New York: Penguin, 1997).

49. One well-established Marxist has argued that the era of "financial expansion represents the 'autumn' of a prevailing capitalist order as it slowly gives way to a new order." See Giovanni Arrighi, *The Long Twentieth Century: Money, Power, and the Origins of Our Time* (London: Verso, 1994). See also the article by the German Marxist Elmar Altvater, "Financial Crises on the Threshold of the 21st Century," in *Socialist Register, 1997,* ed. Leo Panitch and Colin Leys (London: Merlin, 1997), 48–74.

50. See Ann Markusen and Joel Yudken, *Dismantling the Cold War Economy* (New York: Basic Books, 1992).

51. Thomas J. McCormick, *America's Half-Century: United States Foreign Policy in the Cold War and After* (Baltimore: Johns Hopkins University Press, 1995).

52. See Michael Cox, *U.S. Foreign Policy after the Cold War: Superpower without a Mission?* (London: Royal Institute of International Affairs, 1995).

53. Goran Therborn, "Dialectics of Modernity: On Critical Theory and the Legacy of Twentieth-Century Marxism," *New Left Review* 215 (January–February 1996): 59–81.

54. For the radical case against U.S. intervention in Bosnia see James Petras and Steve Vieux, "Bosnia and the Revival of U.S. Hegemony," *New Left Review* 218 (July–August 1996): 3–25.

55. Chomsky's discussion of democracy and America's role in supporting it in the postwar period is somewhat more nuanced than the actual title of his book—*Deterring Democracy*—would suggest. See, in particular, "The Decline of the Democratic Ideal," ibid., 331–50.

56. Frank Furedi, *The New Ideology of Imperialism* (London: Pluto, 1994).

57. See Barry Gills, Joel Rocamora, and Richard Wilson, eds., *Low Intensity Democracy: Political Power in the New World Order* (London: Pluto, 1993); and William I. Robinson, *Promoting Polyarchy: Globalization, U.S. Intervention, and Hegemony* (Cambridge: Cambridge University Press, 1996).

58. Michael A. Bernstein and David E. Adler, eds., *Understanding American Economic Decline* (New York: Cambridge University Press, 1995).

59. See Stephen Gill, "American Hegemony: Its Limits and Prospects in the Reagan Era," *Millennium* 15, no. 3 (1986): 311–39; and *American Hegemony and the Trilateral Commission* (Cambridge: Cambridge University Press, 1990). For a critique of hegemonic stability theory from a Marxist perspective see Peter Burnham, *The Political Economy of Postwar Reconstruction* (London: Macmillan, 1990).

60. Alfredo Valladao, *The Twenty-first Century Will Be American* (London: Verso, 1996).

61. See David Held, *Democracy and the Global Order: From the Modern State to Cosmopolitan Governance* (Cambridge: Cambridge University Press, 1997).

62. Robert W. Cox, "The Global Political Economy and Social Choice," in Cox with Sinclair, *Approaches to World Order*, 191–208.

63. See "Global Economy, Local Mayhem," *The Economist*, January 18, 1997, 15–16.

64. Cox, "The Global Political Economy and Social Choice," 192.

65. Eric Hobsbawm, *The Age of Extremes: A History of the World, 1914–1991* (London: Pantheon, 1994), 459.

HOW WE LEARNED TO ESCAPE PHYSICS ENVY AND TO LOVE PLURALISM AND COMPLEXITY

Ernst B. Haas and Peter M. Haas

Introduction

Is cumulative knowledge and progress possible in international relations (IR)? While this essay focuses on international institutions, it may be taken as a mere illustration of much wider issues in the field of IR and social science more generally.

Students of IR remain divided on the implications of international institutions for the understanding of contemporary international relations. This is largely due, we believe, to the incommensurate epistemological and ontological positions within the discipline of IR that characterize most studies and interpretations of international institutions. In this essay we try to frame a pragmatic-constructivist approach for the study of international institutions, and of IR more generally. "Pragmatic" derives from the philosophy of science tradition of "pragmatism."[1]

Because our objective is to sidestep the philosophical chasms now dividing the discipline we also seek to avoid some of the dichotomies that now bedevil us. One such opposes ideographic to nomothetic studies—unnecessarily. Another claims that there is a deep fissure between explanation and understanding—an overstated caricature

This paper was originally prepared for the millennial reflections panel on institutions held at the annual meeting of the International Studies Association, March 16, 2000. We are immensely indebted for critical comments to Anne Clunan, Peter Katzenstein, Craig Murphy, and M. J. Peterson.

of systematic research. Still another opposes positivism to reflectivism. Our method of sidestepping these procrustean constraints on inquiry features a consensus theory of truth: we argue that it is possible for followers of any and all of these approaches to knowledge to agree with one another in solving a problem if and when they can also agree that they accept a given solution to be "true," if only temporarily and for a restricted purpose. We also argue that the means for ascertaining such a "truth"—truth tests—can also become consensual by means of sustained dialogue among theorists and practitioners. Ontologically and epistemologically the truth ascertained by these operations is neither as absolute as positivists and scientific realists demand nor as biased, subject to someone's domination, or hegemonic as relativists proclaim.[2]

Ontology

"Institutions" remains an essentially contested concept. This is irksome since "any discussion of causation must presuppose an ontological framework of entities among which causal relations are to hold, and also an accompanying logical and semantical framework in which these entities can be talked about."[3] Scholars disagree about the meaning and consequences of international institutions. Most neoliberal institutionalists study the consequences of variations in formal arrangements of organizational properties in light of an, often unacknowledged, rational choice approach to an understanding of actors' preferences and motivations. On the other hand, those informed by a more sociological bent tend to focus more intensively on informal institutions. They regard formal institutions as reflecting common goals (and values) at the founding; that is, institutions are artifices that need not be simply efficiency-enhancing, or transaction cost–reducing, contrivances. Moreover, sociologically informed institutionalists consider the effect of transforming the understandings, interests, and preferences of actors in ways that were not anticipated by them at the institution's founding.[4] The dividing line between the kinds of institutionalists is between those who believe in structural determinism as opposed to those who favor actor-initiated change.

Our early modern mentors in international relations theory did not differ over values: both sides preferred peace to war, life to death, wealth to poverty. They differed over the question of freedom of the will, or the agency-structure problem, as we call it today. The proponents of anarchy held (and hold) that structure triumphs, that humankind chooses under frighteningly tight constraints. The defenders of cooperation argued (and argue) that opportunities exist for the exercise of innovative choices, albeit constrained by factors outside human control. This basic difference in the assumptions, propositions, and research associated with each side has not been bridged to this day. There are few signs of either side winning a decisive victory.

It is difficult to formulate a singular theoretical way to study institutions. Our conceptions go back to the very origin of the modern state system and to our theories about it. With a little legerdemain it could even be argued that the fissure was already present in ancient Greek thought, pitting the realism of Thucydides against the idealism of the Stoics. That fissure divides theories of anarchy from notions of contract; doctrines of competition and war from dogma about cooperation and possible peace; Machiavelli, Hobbes, and Rousseau from Grotius, Locke, and Kant. The arguments have become more nuanced, the data much richer, and the methods now include statistics, gaming, and modeling, but the fissure remains as deep as ever. Not only do the ontologies of students of institutions differ, but the epistemological battles among constructivists, neorealists, neoliberal institutionalists, radical political-economy perspectives, and postmodernists continue to rage unabated.

Positivism versus the Tyranny of Competing Epistemologies

Scholars in the natural sciences do not face the problem of reconciling competing protean principles. Their units of analysis lack free will; at least, none has been empirically demonstrated in atoms, molecules, and cells. Therefore, the positivist epistemology that has proved so successful in physics is unlikely to prove equally powerful in the social sciences because the entities studied "talk back" to the scholar. It is relatively simple to agree on what constitutes intellectual progress when there is consensus about methods, about how we establish truth. The schools of international relations scholars to be reviewed here disagree over the espousal of positivism as the sole legitimator of truth; but they agree on rejecting the relativism of postmodernists and some feminist theorists. Hence what may be considered as intellectual progress remains in the realm of contestation.

Neorealists and neoliberals do profess to be positivists. Their tolerance for other approaches is always conditioned by their insistence that the arguments of other schools must meet positivist truth tests. Peace theorists in the Kantian tradition disagree, though those who come from social psychology do not. Many world systems theorists eschew positivism, but they may subscribe to scientific realism or pragmatism. Some constructivists also claim to be scientific realists; others follow the pragmatist tradition. Scientific realism, to our minds, collapses to positivism by default or exhaustion. No constructivist accepts positivism as the sole and authoritative guide to sound knowledge.[5] We consider ourselves evolutionary "epistemologists" who also embrace rigor; rigor is possible without falling prey to the temptation of positivism.

While positivism's achievements in the natural sciences are very impressive, its utility does not carry over unproblematically to the social sciences where social scientists cannot be sure that the "reality" being studied is not a product of the concepts chosen to study it. Even physicists have not uncritically accepted positivist claims. Early physicists Max Planck and Ernst Mach debated the extent to which physics is grounded in actual reality or in intellectual constructs.[6] Such debates require social scientists to carefully assess a positivism based on a glorification of physics as an approach for understanding the social sciences.

Positivism, and to a lesser extent its cousin scientific realism, relies on a correspondence theory of truth and knowledge. The reality to be comprehended is "real," whether we perceive it correctly or not. Not so when it comes to the study of international institutions, where discussion mostly depends on a *social* construction of reality over which various schools of scholarship obviously and painfully disagree.

That being so, many truth tests valid in the natural sciences cannot be made to work in the study of international institutions. While modeling and quantification may well add value to less formal modes of discourse, their weight in validating an explanatory argument is weaker in the social than in the natural sciences, and even feebler when it comes to prediction. That, of course, does not mean that positivist procedures are not entirely appropriate in the social sciences when and where their epistemological requirements do not clash with the social construction of reality, which stresses human intention and perception rather than reliance on fixed conditions expressible as crisp variables.

More often though, and certainly for matters that are important and interesting, social science inquiry is outside the positivist domain. A generative mechanism for behavior eludes this approach to knowledge for fundamental reasons. It is difficult to formulate universal claims over time and across cultures because of the mutable nature of institutions and the potential role of free will (that is, of actors' ability to change their minds and pursue new goals).[7] Researchers may interfere with the subject of study or find themselves subject to the same set of potentially biasing social influences that shape their very object of study. Mathematics may not be the natural language of human interaction, or at least not a sophisticated mathematics that is incapable of autopoetic and recursive calculations.

No wonder Imre Lakatos warned against applying his theory of scientific progress to the social sciences. He did not envision a discipline marked by competition among a number of partly incommensurable intellectual traditions, all enjoying high legitimacy in the eyes of their adherents. He thought of a single established theory undergoing degenerative or progressive evolution, a theory whose adherents shared basic ontological and epistemological commitments. International relations hardly fits this view.

Neorealists accord importance to international institutions—defined as organizations and law—only to the extent that they serve to secure the hegemon's interests. World systems theorists regard institutions as stages in, and beyond, the historical evolution of capitalism or as tools of capitalist exploitation. Neoliberals think of institutions—as behavior patterns or as organizations—as devices for coping with uncertainty and limiting transaction costs. Peace theorists and classical liberals equate institutions with arrangements for improving international cooperation, especially if they have their roots in social psychology or in law.

Constructivists, though they agree that actors construct their own reality and that ideas are important causes of behavior, exhibit at least three different stances with respect to international institutions. Constructivists who stress state identity subordinate interest in institutions as such to the roles assumed by state actors; constructivists who privilege norms as shapers of behavior see the world much as peace theorists do when it comes to international cooperation: they see institutions as agents of change. Finally, constructivists who embrace an evolutionary epistemology regard institutions partly as arenas for designing change and also as arrangements that bring about change as they alter to the perceptions of their members.

Thus, evolutionary constructivists can contribute to a dialogue between observer-scholars and actor-politicians.

These diverse positions are troublesome for intellectual progress for two reasons: the different meanings of core terms inhibit discourse in general, and these differences infuse and confuse the discussion of causality in particular. Realists and neoliberals subscribe to a naturalistic conception of reality, in line with their positivist proclivities. Pragmatist-constructivists disagree with their scientific realist cousins about the extent of social construction.

Can the Study of Institutions Be Rescued?

The difficulty of attaining a consensual theory of international institutions is overwhelming. Differing notions about institutions are usually pitched at different levels of analysis. Bridging levels in a single theory or approach is possible, but experience has shown that one scholar's claim of successful bridging is often not accepted as persuasive by the entire community of scholars. No Lakatosian cumulation occurs because different approaches are embedded in different scholarly traditions whose competing ontological claims continue to burden our intellects. World systems theory is embedded in historical materialism, neorealism and neoliberalism in microeconomics and utilitarianism. Peace theory has its roots in the social psychology of human imperfection; increasingly it is also inspired by general systems thinking of a very abstract kind, by notions of self-organizing systems of ever greater complexity. Constructivists, by and large, see themselves as the heirs of the sociology of collective behavior. Yet they too remain divided over whether to favor structural predominance, "structuration," or the evolutionary logic of change that combines intentional causality with natural selection.

As scholars we are often asked to specify the "research frontier" in our field. Those who call for that specification seem to think that once that elusive frontier is crossed, "progress" has occurred or will be made. In the natural sciences that idea is not problematic. Discoveries about nature shape our ideas of "reality out there." More recent discoveries may demonstrate an imperfect understanding or subsume earlier notions of reality. Yet there is a consensus that incremental increases of understanding of how nature works constitute scientific progress.

In the social sciences nothing is "discovered." Our understanding of social reality is subject to the reflexivity of our minds. Scholars analyze and reanalyze, interpret and reinterpret, conceptualize and reconceptualize the same core questions time after time. Social scientists do not make discoveries in the sense of the natural sciences. Many contemporary discussions of international institutions would be quite accessible to Machiavelli, Grotius, Hobbes, Locke, Rousseau, and certainly to Kant, Bentham, and J. S. Mill. But these foundational scholars would certainly be astonished to learn about new issues on the political agenda that have their origins in global trends and conditions specific to our times. They would be surprised by the advent of a truly global society. The proliferation of new actors would astound them. So would the concerns triggered by humankind's intensified interaction with the material environment.

But would all these novelties amount to new constitutive principles of global order unsuspected by our forerunners? The appreciation of the importance of the value of healthy ecosystems to human survival, and the willingness to sacrifice gains in wealth and power to achieve ecological improvement, may well be the only important change in actors' understanding of their role in the world that cannot be explained through traditional IR theoretical accounts of actors' motivations, understandings, and patterns of behavior.

Even in the natural sciences consensus on basic theory is never permanent, always subject to challenge and to reconceptualization. The grand theories of today—quantum mechanics, the evolutionary synthesis, and the big bang origin of the universe—may not survive unscathed. Why then burden the social sciences to ever emulate the natural sciences in elaborating grand theories of this type, and expect the entire scholarly community to accept them as true?

But the inability of international relations scholars to grasp the positivist grail of discovery is not a sufficient reason for seeking rigor and relevance. We should continually reexamine our theories about institutions and revise them. We ought to continue to debate the significance of international institutions. We as scholars of international relations ought to know more about what these institutions can, or cannot, contribute to peace, wealth creation and distribution, human rights, and sustainable development. We ought to persist in inquiring how institutions fit into larger events and trends, such as growing (or declining) global income inequalities, stronger (or weaker) nation-states. We ought to do this even if basic differences among approaches cannot be synthesized or transcended, if consensual grand theories continue to elude us. We ought to be able to do this without worshipping physics as an exemplar and without embracing positivism as the only valid method.

Pragmatism and Pluralism

When Nobel laureate Robert Solow was asked whether economics had made any progress he replied, "My message is that economics makes progress the way any other discipline makes progress; by thinking carefully and respecting evidence."[8] Since we all think carefully and certainly respect evidence, yet need a meeting of the International Studies Association to discuss whether progress has been made, this advice seems to beg the very question. IR specialists have sought to make progress for more than fifty years; yet they continue to disagree over whether they have produced any. Is there something wrong with the very notion of progress as applied to international studies?

Yes and no. If intellectual work is judged by the Lakatosian measure, progress is not occurring because the deep chasm between believers in free will and adherents of structural determinism is not being bridged. Moreover, this deep chasm entails continuing differences over types of causality.

But students of international institutions are not compelled to judge themselves by these extremely demanding standards. A theoretical contribution may be considered progressive if it changes the way most scholars think about the problem or puzzle that they consider as calling for an explanation *and* if it offers the possibility of bridging existing theories at a level *below that of grand theory.* Under those conditions rival notions of causality can be sidestepped rather than reconciled. Progress occurs, for instance, when two theories, one positivist and tied to a causality of statistical covariation and the other constructivist and based on intentional causality, nevertheless illuminate the same puzzle, or explain away the same problem, or provide synergistic explanatory accounts.[9] In that case fundamentals are not reconciled, but interesting phenomena are confirmed intersubjectively. IR trends may be fruitfully explored, and the causal understanding of the interplay between forces typically analyzed by discrete schools is advanced.

Pragmatists, including ourselves, while remaining within the family of scholars who believe in the possibility of establishing the

truth of propositions about the world, nevertheless differ from positivists because we eschew any crisp notion of causality.

Pragmatism rests on the following foundations, and thus is particularly attractive to constructivists.[10] The world is not immediately accessible to actors. Actors behave willfully, but not all share
common perspectives or understandings. Willful actors, through intersubjective activities, construct the world. Institutions are thus
causes and effects of this process. Different propositions need to be
developed to deal with each step. Understanding can only be made
intelligible via a consensus theory of truth, since our concepts and
understandings about the world do not necessarily correspond to the
world as such. Consensus works by shared epistemological commitments by a community of scholars embedded in a receptive and supportive milieu. Knowledge cumulation is a social activity conducted
by communities of scholars rather than by individuals working in
isolation. Conclusions reached through a consensual process are
more likely than individual efforts based on a correspondence theory
of truth, and a positivist approach to understanding, to yield policy-
relevant solutions that work. Because the determinations are more
likely to be true in a limited sense, having been derived through a
collective debate, and because the conclusions themselves are politically attractive, they are seen in democratic societies to be impartial
and uncompromised by political bias. Finally, pragmatists retain the
Enlightenment faith in reason that political emancipation may be
achieved through publicizing warranted social findings through the
double hermeneutic or reflexive social science. Unlike positivism,
such results are collective and warranted by group appraisal. Truth—
an emancipatory political project—is most likely to arise in a democratic culture of tolerance for public discourse and intellectual cu-
riosity and with some independence from funding sources. Unlike
radical interpretivism, truth claims are warranted by the process by
which they are generated rather than their resonance with actors'
norms.

Pragmatists hold that truth is provisional. They prefer to think in
terms of complex relations among variables, not simply "A is explained by B" because the two are logically associated with each
other. Unfortunately, some positivists mistake statistical association for causation, and also for a direct correspondence with the "natural world." They also make their peace with the short half-life of
most theories, and thus few aim at finding general covering laws.
Some constructivists, however, shade into a commitment to scien-

tific realist epistemology because they wish to demonstrate the reality of phenomena not amenable to direct observation, an ability most other constructivists do not claim to possess.

Progress can be had if we lower our ambitions. There will be no consensual grand theory for us. Neither synthesis nor cumulation seems within our grasp. What to do? We might focus our explorations on substantive areas of general concern. Instead of asking, "How do we explain the origin of institutions?" we should ask "Which institutions are most likely to bring about a peaceful (or egalitarian, or wealthy) world?" Or we might profitably ask, "Why have international institutions failed to deliver significant economic development?" or, "Under what circumstances may institutions with particular designs affect behavior in a desirable way?" It makes sense to speak of a problem-focused synthesis rather than continuing to pitch progress at the macrotheoretical level because different approaches may well illuminate different aspects of the puzzle and still allow a comprehensive response to the question.[11] If the strictures of positivism or realism can be satisfied in the conduct of this research, so much the better. If not, all ought to be able to make their peace with the looser notion of causality urged by pragmatists.

It bears repeating that the evolutionary epistemologist stance, a variant of pragmatist-constructivism, is by no means consistently hostile to all aspects of positivism, though it is less positivistic than are constructivists who focus on state identity. Positivism supposedly undergirds "rational" ways of studying international institutions; constructivism is alleged to rely on *Verstehen*, on "reflection," on "interpretive sociology." It is simply incorrect to argue, as some do, that all branches of constructivism ought to be sharply juxtaposed to the epistemologies of "hard science."

Max Weber, the inventor of interpretive sociology, was more judicious in his formulation. He distinguished between "observational" and "explanatory" understanding. The former involves directly watching and then interpreting the significance of some item of actor conduct, such as joy or anger. The latter calls for the determination of the actor's reason for acting in the observed manner, the study of motivation. Weber is careful to specify that the mode of explanatory understanding is "rational understanding of motivation, which consists in placing the act in an intelligible and more inclusive context of meaning."[12] Actors are assumed to be acting in accordance with what they see as the best way to attain their objectives; motives are "rational" in that sense, even if not in the perspective of microeconomics or game theory. Therefore they can be studied with systematic methods and subjected to rigorous hypotheses that may even be falsifiable. Interpretation does not have to be the equivalent of mushiness. Hence patterns of behavior ascertained by such methods can be fully consistent with the assumptions of evolutionary epistemology. Nevertheless, the progressive cumulation of knowledge of the Lakatosian positivist universe is not likely in the more contingent style of inquiry of this branch of constructivism.

Moreover, policy relevance remains possible if concerns are kept modest. Even though IR scholars cannot claim to have made important discoveries at more modest levels of discourse, something like progress occurs. All schools of thought in international relations (except for the realists) now agree that the shape of things has fundamentally changed because of these developments in the real world of the last fifty years: sovereignty has become a contested concept, global civil society is emerging, domestic civil society has blown up the unitary state, equality among states is becoming more than a legal conceit, the redistribution of wealth is accepted as given by most actors, sustainable development is a goal for all. Theory has always followed diplomatic and military practice. The arrival of these notions makes it evident that theory and practice continue to reinfect each other in the face of macrotheoretical commitments that ignore more modest insights.

Methodological Injunctions

If knowledge is socially constructed, how can one, within a social setting, analyze social processes? We suggest that unpackaging types of social construction can accomplish this. Fundamentally, there are three different types of knowledge, as defined by philosophers of science. "Brute facts" are those that are subject to intersubjective observation and verification by analysts.[13] This is the traditional area of natural science where, ultimately, nature can bite back. Second, there are "hybrid facts," where analysts apply frames in excess of their principal understanding of the phenomena. These domains are much more common in the study of international institutions, including environmental and economic regimes. Last is the domain of "social facts," which exist ultimately by definition and have no meaning independent of the social world in which they exist, such as international law, human rights, and even military deterrence. Being self-conscious about each of these types of "fact" is essential for making a methodologically sound constructivist argument. Jumping from one to the other, such as mistaking a hybrid fact for a social fact and back again, discredits the reliability of constructivism.

Cumulative progress in creating consensual knowledge about institutions rests on a number of individual steps: making individual claims in single works done in the constructivist style; reconciling individual claims within constructivism (intraparadigm progress); and conducting interparadigm midlevel discussions that try to resolve different interpretations of similar phenomena and conceptual applications that may lead, ultimately, to some degree of provisional closure and dispute resolution between paradigms.

First is the development of good work by individuals, an exercise that is closest to positivism in the need for rigor and self-conscious assumptions, or of the propositions that guide the research. Individual claims should rest on the logical consistency behind the analysis, possible falsification of the underlying claims, and some degree of empirical testing. By way of methods, constructivist work that heeds seriously the epistemological injunctions about theorizing about ineffable actor beliefs is probably best performed with qualitative methods, rather than the statistical and behavioral ones typically associated with positivism, because of the difficulty of developing reliable indicators of such variables. Thus, focused comparative studies, process tracing, and even counterfactuals are able to focus attention on the vital variables that constructivists believe to drive institutional politics.[14] Reconciling individual contributions within a common theoretical tradition should be possible through the same techniques of careful testing of propositions and findings in compatible domains.

Cumulation and progress may occur when lessons are drawn from such individual contributions. How do they fit with views from other approaches, are they complementary in terms of assumptions, and do they qualify or challenge key beliefs? Ideally progress should occur between paradigms via a Lakatosian process of hypothesis testing and Popperian falsification, with an eye toward the value of contributions to developing new insights rather than marginal improvements on a given tradition. However, we have difficulty recalling the last time we saw scholars admit to error or publicly change their minds on the basis of these procedures.

In practice cumulation probably occurs over a span of generations through a sociological process of cohorts of trained graduate students replacing a previous generation of scholars. In the shorter term debates are often characterized by rhetorical and polemical interparadigm debates that convince no one. Still, there are pragmatic institutional design lessons about how to promote consensus through cumulative exercises that inhibit egregious bias. Conscientious debates among well-intentioned scholars should be encouraged in peer-reviewed journals, including multiauthored works and edited volumes organized around common themes.

Conclusion

Our notion of progress implies the legitimacy of a plurality of approaches. It suggests tolerance for competing ontologies and epistemologies. However, we are not being tolerant for the sake of being tolerant, of being nice to our intellectual antagonists. Tolerance is an inevitable by-product of the double hermeneutic in which we, as pragmatist-constructivists, are stuck. Intellectual pluralism is inescapable because of the commitment to pragmatism. We concede that our social construction of reality cannot be proved superior to anyone else's. In analyzing the social construction of actors we remain embedded in our own, which will differ from those of other scholars. The achievement of modest progress depends on continuing the conversation among all of us.

Nobody finally wins or loses in this perspective. The grand theoretical stakes are low because any cumulating that may be achieved is temporally and spatially limited and unlikely to challenge any deep commitments. But a few puzzles get solved along the way.

Notes

1. A good collection of the seminal articles is presented in Louis Menand, ed., *Pragmatism* (New York: Vintage Books, 1997).
2. The philosophy of science against which these categories are constructed is elaborated in Michael Martin and Lee C. McIntyre, eds., *Readings in the Philosophy of Social Science* (Cambridge: MIT Press, 1994); Richard J. Bernstein, *Beyond Objectivism and Relativism* (Philadelphia: University of Pennsylvania Press, 1983); Ernest Sosa and Michael Tooley, eds., *Causation* (Oxford: Oxford University Press, 1993); David Braybrooke, *Philosophy of Social Science* (Englewood Cliffs, N.J.: Prentice Hall, 1987); John Searle, *The Construction of Social Reality* (New York: Free Press, 1995); Anthony Giddens, *The Constitution of*

Society (Berkeley: University of California Press, 1984); Martin Hollis and Steve Smith, *Explaining and Understanding International Relations* (Oxford: Oxford University Press, 1990).

3. Jaegwon Kim, *Philosophy of Mind* (Boulder, Colo.: Westview, 1996), 5.

4. Peter M. Haas and Ernst B. Haas, "Learning to Learn," *Global Governance* 1 (September–December 1995): 255–84; Ernst B. Haas, *When Knowledge Is Power* (Berkeley: University of California Press, 1990).

5. We use these philosophy of science categories as explained in Larry Laudan, *Science and Relativism* (Chicago: University of Chicago Press, 1990). See also his *Beyond Positivism and Relativism* (Boulder, Colo.: Westview, 1996) for the notion of pragmatism as we use it. Evolutionary epistemology is defined and explicated by Donald T. Campbell in "Evolutionary Epistemology," in *The Philosophy of Karl Popper*, P. A. Schilpp (La Salle, Ill.: Open Court Publishing, 1974), 413–63; and Kai Hallweg and C. A. Hooker, eds., *Issues in Evolutionary Epistemology* (Albany: State University of New York Press, 1989). For more on the application of evolutionary epistemology and consensus theories of truth see Donald T. Campbell, *Methodology and Epistemology for Social Sciences* (Chicago: University of Chicago Press, 1988); and Steven Toulmin, *Human Understanding* (Princeton, N.J.: Princeton University Press, 1972), app. 1.

6. Stephen Toulmin, ed., *Physical Reality* (New York: Harper Torchbooks, 1970).

7. R. Harre and P. F. Secord, *The Explanation of Social Behavior* (Oxford, England: Basil Blackwell, 1972), 9–12ff.

8. *Bulletin of the American Academy of Arts and Sciences*, December 1982, 30.

9. Syncretic individual volumes include Glenn H. Snyder and Paul Diesing, *Conflict among Nations* (Princeton, N.J.: Princeton University Press, 1977); Janice Gross Stein and Raymond Tanter, *Rational Decision-Making* (Columbus: Ohio State University Press, 1980); Graham Allison, *The Essence of Decision* (Boston: Little, Brown, 1971); Peter M. Haas, *Saving the Mediterranean* (New York: Columbia University Press, 1990); Daniel Deudney and G. John Ikenberry, "Soviet Reform and the End of the Cold War," *Review of International Studies* 17 (July 1991); Daniel Deudney and G. John Ikenberry, "Who Won the Cold War?" *Foreign Policy* 87 (summer 1992); Richard Ned Lebow and Thomas Risse-Kappen, eds., *International Relations Theory and the End of the Cold War* (New York: Columbia University Press, 1995). For complementary works that include different approaches and yet address a similar question, see the following. On the Cuban missile crisis see James Bright, *Cuba on the Brink* (New York: Parthenon, 1993); and James Bright and David Welch, *On the Brink* (New York: Hill and Wang, 1989). For environmental studies from multiple perspectives see Richard Benedick, *Ozone Diplomacy* (Cambridge: Harvard University Press, 1998); Karen Litfin, *Ozone Discourses* (New York: Columbia University Press, 1994); Peter M. Haas, "Banning Chlorofluorocarbons," in *Knowledge, Power, and International Policy Coordination*, ed. Peter M. Haas (Columbia: University of South Carolina Press, 1997); and Edward Parson, "Pro-

tecting the Ozone Layer," in *Institutions for the Earth*, ed. Peter M. Haas, Marc A. Levy, and Robert O. Keohane (Cambridge: MIT Press, 1993).

10. Prominent pragmatists who are clustered together for the purpose of this summary include Charles Peirce, William James, John Dewey, Jurgen Habermas, Paul Ricoeur, Charles Taylor, Hilary Putnam, and Richard Rorty. See Menand, *Pragmatism*, for a useful summary.

11. We are comforted by this dictum of Max Weber's: "Meaningfulness naturally does not coincide with laws as such, and the more general the law the less the coincidence. For the specific meaning which a phenomenon has for us is naturally *not* to be found in those relationships which it shares with other phenomena. . . . In the cultural sciences the knowledge of the universal or the general is never valuable in itself." Quoted by David Dessler in "Constructivism within Positivist Social Science," *Review of International Studies* 25 (1999): 136. Emphasis in original. Taken from Max Weber, "'Objectivity' in Social Science and Social Policy," in *Methodology of the Social Sciences*, ed. E. Shils and H. Finch (Glencoe, Ill.: Free Press, 1949), 76.

12. Max Weber, "The Interpretive Understanding of Social Action," in *Readings in the Philosophy of the Social Sciences*, ed. May Brodbeck (New York: Macmillan, 1968), 25–26. For an extended argument that this mode of inquiry is consistent with positivism, albeit not with its most demanding form that insists on strict correspondence between nature and the concepts used in discovery, see Gil Friedman and Harvey Starr, *Agency, Structure, and International Politics* (New York: Routledge, 1997), ch. 4.

13. G. E. M. Anscombe, "On Brute Facts," *Analysis*, no. 184 (March 1958): 69–73.

14. Alexander L. George and Timothy J. McKeown, "Case Studies and Theories of Organizational Decision-Making," *Advances in Information Process in Organizations* 2 (1985): 21–58; David Collier, "The Comparative Method," in *Political Science: The State of the Discipline*, ed. Ada W. Finifter (Washington, D.C.: American Political Science Association, 1993); Andrew Bennett and Alexander George, eds., *Case Studies and Theory Development* (Cambridge: MIT Press, forthcoming).

EN ROUTE TO KNOWLEDGE

Is There a "Third Path" (in the Third Debate)?

Yosef Lapid

A third path leads beyond modern and postmodern methodological debates in the social sciences, history, and the humanities. It turns out that choices between the routes of science and interpretation, history and theory, objectivism and relativism are more illusionary than real.[1]

Notwithstanding the general understanding that the end of the millennium may well represent an arbitrary or insignificant temporal marker, few scholarly disciplines (international relations [IR] included) have been able to resist the temptation of using this festive occasion as a pretext for another round of extensive and vigorous stock taking. Michael Burawoy, a Berkeley sociologist, perceptively notes that at stake in such evaluative exercises is not so much "what we don't know, but how to interpret what we do know"[2] in our respective disciplinary domains. Our presentation guidelines suggest that such was also the intent behind the ten "millennial panels" that occasioned this theoretical collection. Participants were invited to address six carefully formulated and closely related tasks. Of these, however, only the last one (dealing with future themes and research agendas) addressed specifically the issue of what we "don't know" (or what we need to know) in international relations. The other five engaged in different ways the far more difficult task of interpreting or assessing what we (think) "we do know" about our notoriously elusive subject matter.

In the following, I focus my comments on the first and most general task, namely a "self-critical state-of-the-art reflection on accomplishments and failures." In accord with my panel assignment, "alternative and critical perspectives" will be the referent object of my comments. However, insofar as the meaning of being "critical" (or alternative) is anything but self-evident, some preliminary clarifications are in order. In the aftermath of more than a decade of "third debating," it should be evident that there is no unitary "alternative" position, nor a simple or single way of demarcating the "critical" from the "noncritical." In international relations as in other scholarly fields critical voices are informed by vastly different (neo-Marxist, poststructuralist, feminist, postpositivist, and so on) ontological and epistemological premises. Reproducing multiple lines of division evident more generally in recent social theory, IR's alternative and critical perspectives thus constitute a fragmented and slippery domain that firmly resists undifferentiated assessments.

Since a suitably nuanced mapping of this vigorously contested domain is precluded by the limited scope of this essay, I will engage the issue of IR criticality through the related concepts of *pluralism, dialogue, and reflexivity*. To be sure, such a demarcation of criticality will be deemed excessively narrow and anemic, especially by those who insist on infusing critique with a massive dosage of political engagement. As it happens, I tend to agree that a high level of social concern on the part of the scientist is indeed a defining attribute of any scholarly enterprise that claims a "critical" mantle. However, consistent with the main argument developed in this paper, with respect to the question of how "emancipatory" can a critical inquiry become without compromising its scholarly value, I wish to highlight, in particular, the wisdom of exploring more fully the promise of possible, but currently still submerged, "third way/middle ground" positions.[3]

At least two justifications can be invoked at this point in support of the following attempt to assess accomplishments and failures of critical and alternative IR approaches with a triple optic of pluralism, dialogue, and reflexivity. First, pluralism, dialogue, and reflexivity are widely recognized across the humanities and the social sciences to be both closely associated with, and supportive of, critical and alternative agendas. Second, and perhaps more important, pluralism, dialogue, and reflexivity have been widely recognized as potential moments of special productivity in IR's disciplinary transition known as the "third debate." Initiated by a loose coalition of postpositivist/postmodernist/poststructuralist/constructivist/feminist/normative and other "critical" and/or "dissident" challengers, the third debate registered extensive demands for radical change. These included calls for a reflexive reexamination of ontological, epistemological, and axiological premises and a serious reassessment of disciplinary options and practices in a rapidly changing intellectual and political landscape. Some envisioned an epistemologically more pluralistic and creative discipline, willing to experiment with new ways of doing science. Others sought an intellectually less parochial, less insular, and more interdisciplinary knowledge-producing enterprise. Still others hoped to institute "interpretation" or "emancipation" (as opposed to "explanation") as the defining telos of a more vibrant science of international relations. Most, however, looked forward to a more open, inclusive, and dialogically engaged scholarly community capable of communicating effectively (if not consensually) across separate categories of all sorts (levels of analysis, paradigms, disciplines, genders, continents, and so on). In this sense, pluralism, dialogue, and reflexivity are properly understood as common denominators of sorts in the change-oriented disciplinary transition known as the third debate.

To the detriment of the entire third-debate project, most of these initial demands were put on the table by some of the most vocal and polemical proponents of radical change. As a result, it was initially rather difficult to discern that this "opening-up" momentum was tacitly sustained also by a more general sentiment (spreading deep into "mainstream" positions) that things have become excessively stale in the study of international relations. My main argument in this paper is based on the premise (and hope) that this polarized situation may now be finally changing. In recent years, we have witnessed multiple (but only partially convergent) attempts to nudge the center of gravity in the third debate away from polarized (either/ or) confrontations in the direction of more moderate via media (both/ and) type postures. This median space is still consolidating and will likely face mounting opposition from both mainstream and critical theoretical quarters. Should it prevail, however, disciplinary ramifications for pluralism, dialogue, and reflexivity can be far reaching and largely positive.[4]

With this general argument in mind, and with the benefit of more than a decade's hindsight, I now revisit the merits of contending disciplinary responses triggered by the third-debate transition. I do so in two stages. First, I offer a brief impressionistic reading of the current status of the three disciplinary responses (i.e., despair, celebration, and reconstruction) mentioned originally in my third-debate article published in 1989.[5] Building on this reading, I then engage in a more detailed discussion of how the IR discipline may better situate itself to become a main beneficiary of the current interest in via media solutions to seemingly insoluble knowledge problems. Throughout this discussion, the main questions remain the same: What is the relationship between the third debate and theoretical progress in international relations? Was the third debate able to, at least partly, honor its promise of a vastly improved scholarly enterprise? Are we still in the third debate or have we moved, as Ole Waever and others argue, to a "fourth" or perhaps "fifth" debate?[6] And, finally, are there any reasons to be guardedly optimistic regarding the "next stage" in IR's continuing disciplinary transition?

A Decade Later: Despair, Celebration, or Reconstruction?

In view of the fact that knockout-type eliminations are as rare in international relations as in other social sciences, it is hardly surprising that all three responses (despair, celebration, and reconstruction) that were embryonically present back in 1989 are still visible today. This is, however, different from affirming a static or stagnant picture. For subtle changes in both the constitution and relative standing of these three responses are clearly evident. Starting with the despairing response, my sense is that it has largely maintained its relative vigor and standing in the IR domain. One detects, however, a noteworthy change in the constitution of this response. Back in 1989, the despairing camp drew most of its support from manifestly alarmed mainstream quarters. At the time, mainstream opponents seemed intent on stemming the tide of what they perceived to be cleverly camouflaged "knowledge viruses," ingeniously designed by sinister third-debate programmers to infect, erase, and/or otherwise "deconstruct" the meager fund of "positive" knowledge that had been slowly accumulating in the IR field. Switching metaphors, in the late 1980s and early 1990s, mainstream opponents operated with a crude "roach motel" image of the third debate: IR theories checked in, but they did not check out. Needless to add, such a negative posture left little room for optimism regarding the third debate.

As evidenced, however, by the recent spectacular rise of constructivism in international relations, mainstream circles are nowadays far less suspicious or paranoid about third debate–minted ideas. This more relaxed attitude may have been there already in 1989, but it was fully eclipsed by the fiercely polarizing logic of the opening salvos in the third debate. For our present purposes, suffice it to say that the despairing camp has not been seriously weakened by recent mainstream defections because of parallel new defections of deeply disillusioned scholars from the reconstructive and/or celebratory camps. Many applicable examples come to mind. Barry Buzan and Ole Waever—whose work on identity and security, for instance, is exemplary in the theoretical "reconstruction" mode—have come up recently with separate and rather strong indictments of the IR theoretical enterprise.[7] Similarly, Ann Tickner—whose initial response to the third debate was rather celebratory—has grown, over time, increasingly pessimistic over the prospects of ever reaching a meaningful conversational encounter between IR feminists and the IR mainstream.[8] And, finally, Steve Smith's contribution to this millennial panel offers yet another compelling example of a despairing retreat into pessimism on account of a putatively decisive victory by the U.S./IR academic mainstream in its battle with critical and alternative approaches over the authorization of knowledge in international relations.

As in 1989, I remain fairly skeptical of such despairing disciplinary stories. I continue to believe that it is simply wrong and counterproductive to invoke the imagery of a scholarly expedition aboard a *Titanic,* tragically headed toward some epistemological, ontological, or axiological "iceberg." Ten years into the third debate, IR's journey to the land of better knowledge continues. Having taken, or at least scouted, the interpretive, the linguistic, the constructivist, the rhetorical, the normative, the critical, the spatial, and many other real or imaginary "turns," the IR scholarly expedition has not stumbled into any unscientific black hole. To the contrary, as noted recently by Samuel Makinda, "A distinctive feature of recent IR debates is that most theorists tend to address more critically such themes as science and interpretation; objectivity and subjectivity; norms and practices; and materialism and idealism."[9] To that extent, the journey has become more pluralistic, more lively, and also more promising.

Which takes me directly to the celebratory response. Back in 1989, I paid almost exclusive attention to this optimistic reaction because, at the time, it seemed to be ascendant in the IR field. The situation is quite different today. In recent years the celebratory camp has been constantly losing altitude, as serious pessimism started to set in regarding the actual limits of the revitalizing theoretical energy released by the third debate. To better understand the reason why this growing pessimism has managed to gain such momentum, it is helpful to distinguish between two items on the celebratory agenda that happened to be destined to very different fates in the actual unfolding of the third debate.

The first agenda item can be provisionally characterized as an "opening-up/pluralism" project. It sought a more open, diverse, and interdisciplinary theoretical enterprise. It tried to drive home the message that having a productive discipline in no way requires that diversity and interdisciplinarity be suppressed. This agenda item registered in my view significant and, most likely, irreversible achievements. To be sure, additional work remains to be done, for instance, on the "IR-as-an-American-discipline" front. There is also considerable substance to the lingering suspicion that much of this "opening" may have been more cosmetic and cynical than real.[10] But things cannot be so terribly wrong if even as disgruntled a participant as David Campbell can now concede that "where once we were all caught in the headlights of the large North American car of international relations theory, now the continental sportster of critical theories has long since left behind the border guards and toll collectors of the mainstream—who can be observed in the rearview mirror waving their arms wildly still demanding papers and the price of admission—as the occupants go on their way in search of another political problem to explore."[11] Arguably, what holds true for "the continental sportster of critical theories" is equally true for many other approaches whatever their destination, preferred mode of transportation, and location vis-à-vis "the large North American car of international relations theory." Further testimony that such is the case can be adduced, for instance, from James Der Derian (the actual originator of the catchy "large North American car" metaphor) who in a recent publication simply refuses to offer any apologies for his "eclectic group of travel companions" and flatly asserts instead that "whichever theorist helps me best understand the subject of my inquiry gets to the head of the class."[12]

There was, however, a second, and far less successful, item on the third-debate agenda. This second agenda item expressed the hope for a more dialogically oriented and communicatively engaged scholarly enterprise. To the extent that scholarly disciplines are well described as conversational communities with a tradition of argumentation, it is clear that the third debate has energized "argumentation" at the expense of "conversation." Under the third debate, IR theoretical discourses have proliferated, and some have become considerably more vibrant but also correspondingly less "engaged." The growing disarray of concepts, theories, and approaches has, in fact, become so overwhelming as to prompt descriptions of the IR field as a "paradigmatic dysfunctional family."[13] Occasional attempts to engage in sustained dialogues have been regularly undermined by oppositional rhetoric that quickly turned them into bitterly contested battlegrounds. Lost in such escalations was the realization that a discipline's (communicative) ability to impart or share information is not necessarily less important than its (epistemological) ability to produce and certify "true" knowledge, and the two are, of course, intimately related.

The problem is now well understood in our discipline, and the urgent desire to find new workable solutions seems nearly universal. This became evident, for instance, in a Visions of International Relations series held recently under the auspices of the Walker Institute at the University of South Carolina. In his introduction to a forthcoming volume based on this project, Donald Puchala forcefully captures this sentiment. "Pluralism," he says,

> with positive affect attached, turns up in text after text, and a definite point of convergence among the contributors is their common concern about the fragmentation of scholarship in International Relations—the "insularity of scholarship," the "incommensurability of discourses," the "mutual inattentiveness" of specialists, the growing intolerance of intellectual diversity, and even the degeneration of civility in the academy are all bemoaned. The call of almost all in this volume is for "bridge building" across the paradigmatic divides, "dialogue" and "interaction" among contending schools and different specializations, avoiding extremes, seeking the *via media* while generally attending to the task of trying to better understand the real world despite the distractions of academia.[14]

The same sentiment was voiced in the annual addresses of two past ISA presidents.[15] Finally, a similar concern was echoed also by Thomas Biersteker in his opening editorial article for a newly (re)launched IR journal, where he suggests that we must "give primacy to approaches that can accommodate incompatible or incommensurable differences, rather than to try to choose a single 'winner' out of competing claims."[16]

It is against this general background that the question posed in the title of this essay can be best understood. If our main disciplinary problem today is the eruption of "flabby"—as opposed to "engaged"—pluralism,[17] is taking the third way in the third debate a possible solution? Is there, in other words, an intellectually viable middle ground that carries the promise of dialogue and deliberation (but not necessarily consensus or agreement) across deeply divisive ontological, epistemological, and axiological lines? In the next section, I cautiously answer this question in the affirmative. Caution is needed because there is nothing automatically or necessarily redeeming in the median space. To the contrary, the idea lends itself to serious misunderstanding and misappropriation. Indeed, there are already some reasons to suspect that the recent popularization of the via media idea through IR constructivism (Emanuel Adler and Alex Wendt, in particular) may turn out to be detrimental to a broader and more rewarding disciplinary engagement with the median space.

The Third Way: From "Flabby" to "Engaged" Pluralism in International Relations

An interesting set of developments, both internal and external to the IR discipline, has combined to elevate the appeal of third way–type reasoning. Whatever its intellectual or political merits, third way thinking seems now increasingly in tune with the emerging spirit of our times.[18] Such is particularly the case in the academic world, where one detects a growing fascination with, and broadening support for, via media positions. In a recently published book Francois Dosse vividly captures the rising centrality of this intellectual median space, which, in his view, opens up exciting possibilities for new alliances between the exact sciences, the social sciences, and the humanities.[19] Interestingly enough, a parallel reorientation toward the middle ground is now tentatively evident also in international relations.[20] This is, I submit, a promising but far from risk-free development. If properly managed, it may eventually blossom into a productive disciplinary discussion regarding the "next stage" of the third debate.

To facilitate such an outcome, in the following, I sketch a more analytical understanding of the median space (i.e., the third way, via media, middle ground) idea and spell out some of its ramifications for reconfiguring pluralism, dialogue, and reflexivity in the IR domain. The main objective throughout will be to explore the possibility of transcending sterile paradigmatic fragmentation with a more carefully fine-tuned third way heuristic. Erik Doxtader's insightful elucidation of the "communicative qualities" of the "middle" in public life will start us in this general direction.[21] Doxtader argues "that a manifold exploration of the middle of public life may help to unravel the puzzle of how public transgression and opposition facilitates dialogue and mutual agreement."[22] His rich and philosophically informed discussion presents the middle as a "space of deliberation that contains both opposition and agreement"; as a "movement between transgressive and intersubjective modes of communication"; and as a "norm that moderates but does not mediate the dynamic elements of public deliberation."[23] Following Hegel, Doxtader portrays the middle as a productive space that is both "found" and "created"; it is also a reflective space "which is simultaneously interior and exterior to the self."[24] To reiterate, however, Doxtader's main interest in the middle is as a "heuristic" that explains "how the negativity of opposition can create the ground of mutual dialogue."[25]

At the end of his article, Doxtader extends an open invitation to all scholars to "find other middles and investigate their communicative qualities."[26] I suggest that the IR scholarly community would be well advised to accept this invitation and proceed with a serious and reflective investigation of the "middle" of the third debate. Unfortunately, with few exceptions, this is not the direction in which the rising IR interest in the median space is currently evolving.[27] International relations' via media may be "under construction," but there is little evidence of a plausible and imaginative architectural design to guide a productive implementation of such a critical disciplinary project.[28] Missing, in particular, is any sustained reflection on whether and how this third way can facilitate new types of pluralism, dialogue, and reflexivity in international relations. And yet, in lieu of such reflection, there is ironically a serious risk that the via media project may itself become an additional bone of contention in an already overly fragmented and polarized discipline.

Spirited, if often confused, responses elicited by high-powered constructivist claims to exclusive ownership of the median space in the current disciplinary debate vividly attest to the gravity of the aforementioned risk.[29] While clearly justifiable, the decision of some English School proponents to present a historical counterclaim to the

very same space may be equally misguided.[30] Indeed, facile presenta-
tions of such claims and counterclaims can only invite further third
way maneuvers (from international law, for instance) "that would
make even Prime Minister Tony Blair proud."[31] Whether such maneuvers can also make the IR discipline proud is, of course, another
matter.

Now, to the extent that with respect to the middle ground, the
point is "not to argue in favour of any specific approach,"[32] what else
can IR scholars do with it in the context of the third debate? My
answer returns to the themes of pluralism, dialogue, and reflexivity.
To further explicate the promise of rethinking these three themes in
the context of a via media approach, I refer briefly to the work of
Eviatar Zerubavel (a Rutgers sociologist), who profiles three intellectual "mind-sets" (the rigid, the fuzzy, and the flexible) that correspond
to three modes of "sculpting" academic identities.[33] The rigid mind-
set feels most comfortable in a context of clear-cut distinctions and
sharp demarcations. It promotes a world made up of discrete, insular
entities. It discourages contacts and bridge building between such entities, and it leads a sustained campaign against the vague, the in-
between, and the nested. In the academic context, the result is a
highly compartmentalized, that is, fortresslike, pluralism. The fuzzy
mind-set is the diametrical opposite (the Other) of the rigid mind-set.
It is suspicious of all borders and resentful of all efforts to curb curi-
osity and focus intellectual attention. When applied to an academic
context, the fuzzy mind-set results in nondisciplinary, or even con-
tradisciplinary, sculpting practices, as it refuses to partake in the constitution and sedimentation of separate academic identities. The result is "flabby" (i.e., "anything goes") pluralism. Zerubavel prefers,
however, the flexible mind-set, which offers an attractive via media
between absolute rigid-mindedness and virtual fuzzy-mindedness. In
his own words, the flexible mind-set "fosters an intellectual environment that would allow for both order and creativity, structure and
open-mindedness, focus and change."[34]

Against this background, it is reassuring to note that the emergence of a flexible mind-set/middle ground orientation as a guiding
vision for would-be disciplinary "sculptors" may be sufficiently important to justify speculations on a new stage in IR's evolving disciplinary debate.[35] Relevant in this context is the fact that academic
identities sculpted under the influence of the flexible mind-set can
mature into a type of pluralism approvingly described by Richard
Bernstein as "engaged pluralism." Bernstein believes that this type

of pluralism "has been characteristic of what is best in our own American philosophic tradition. . . . One accepts the multiplicity of perspectives and interpretations. One rejects the quest for certainty, the craving for absolutes, and the idea of a totality in which all differences are finally reconciled. But such a pluralism demands an openness to what is different and other, a willingness to risk one's prejudgements, seeking for common ground without any guarantees that it will be found."[36] To that extent, via media–type pluralism can teach us how "to think and act in the 'in-between' interstices of forced reconciliation and radical dispersion."[37]

A better understanding of the manner in which via media approaches may facilitate new and more productive understandings of pluralism in the social sciences (IR included) also brings to the fore the realization that some lingering scholarly disagreements may be rooted in "differing ideas about the nature of dialogue, or about how social scientists participate in dialogue."[38] Indeed, a better understanding of the communicative qualities of different types of dialogical encounters can be a prime benefit of a more energetic engagement with the middle of the third debate along the lines advocated in this essay. As aptly pointed out by Nicholas Burbules, "Dialogue represents, to one view or another, a way of reconciling differences; a means of promoting empathy and understanding for others; a mode of collaborative inquiry; a method of critically comparing and testing alternative hypotheses; a form of constructivist teaching and learning; a forum for deliberation and negotiation about public policy differences; a therapeutic engagement of self-and Other-exploration; and a basis for shaping uncoerced social and political consensus."[39] Furthermore, dialogues can yield a wide range of possible outcomes including agreement, consensus, understanding, tolerance, and even communicative failure or "incommensurability." For as pointed out by Burbules, "There are instances in which the very encounter with a radically different, unreconciled, and unreconcilable point of view, value, voice, or belief can serve important educational purposes; to cause us to question the horizons of our own assumptions, to explore within ourselves (and not only within the other) the cause of why dialogue 'fails' and to consider the possibility of a radically different way of approaching the world. Dialogue in the mode of resolving or dissolving differences provides no tools for coping with such encounters or deriving meaning from them; it regards them as failures or breakdowns, and not as limitations within the model of dialogue itself."[40]

It is at this point that the themes of dialogue and pluralism tie into the broader theme of reflexivity. As noted by many observers reflexivity can be, and has been, practiced dogmatically in the IR domain even by "critical," "dissident," or "alternative" scholars.[41] An additional promise of the median space is to facilitate more genuinely reflexive practices in the IR domain. That such a promise is entailed in a third way reorientation is suggested by Zerubavel's notion of a "flexible mind-set," by Doxtader's depiction of the middle as a "reflexive space," and by Bernstein's ideal of "engaged pluralism." To date, the IR scholarly community seems only dimly aware of the many intellectual and communicative opportunities that can be seized by a serious engagement with the middle of the third debate. It is, however, to the credit of this "discipline-defining" debate that the possibility that we may actually seize upon these opportunities cannot be entirely precluded.

Concluding Remarks: Bringing Goldilocks Back into IR Theory?

Evaluative appraisals of the kind undertaken in this essay are frequently referred to nowadays as disciplinary "stories" or "fairy tales." If so, this was neither a "Sleeping Beauty and the prince" nor a "*Titanic* and the iceberg" story. Rather, it was a "bringing Goldilocks back into IR theory" story. Scientists refer to the idea that a planet needs to be "just right" (i.e., neither "too hard" nor "too soft") to support life as the "Goldilocks principle." I submit that a Goldilocks principle of sorts is at work also in the constitution and operation of vibrant scholarly communities. My argument in this paper suggests that the "next stage" in the third debate may depend to a great extent on our understanding of where the IR discipline is situated today vis-à-vis this principle.

To be sure, there is nothing original or new in such third way contentions. Inside and outside the academic world, they have been known to please some people and to infuriate others. I can readily anticipate similar reactions to this presentation. Indeed, as with any other trail, good things and bad things may, and do, happen on the third path depending on human choices and actions. As noted by Tim Dunne (with respect to the English School), theories located in the middle ground can be prone to misidentification and "open to predatory strategies of assimilation or rejection."[42] Similarly, critical and postmodernist scholars have good reasons to be nervous about rampant bridge building because, as Cynthia Weber justly notes, "often the bridge becomes the alien other's back."[43] Besides, difficult analytical choices will always await IR scholars of different theoretical persuasions willing to venture into the middle ground. For, as aptly put by John Ruggie, "even coalitions of the willing may find the going tough as they discover analytical limits beyond which their respective approaches cannot be pushed."[44] And those who naively, or strategically, decide to nonetheless push against such "limits" may end up producing meaningless or monstrous togetherness in which "several incompatible things are . . . being bolted together."[45]

Be that as it may, I still believe that the facilitation of new and intellectually better-equipped "coalitions of the willing" should be prioritized at this stage of the disciplinary debate. Despite its numerous imperfections, the third path seems highly promising in this respect. Triumphant, unreflective, and/or hegemonic "middle-groundism"—under which all IR scholars would mindlessly line up and embrace each other on the third path—is undesirable and, of course, also impossible. As a pluralist, I would be first to concede that the third way is itself but one trail in the forest (albeit an important and, until recently, also a rarely traveled one). All considered, however, a reflective cost-benefit analysis still leaves us, I think, deep inside positive terrain. "Would it not be refreshing," asks Donald Puchala, "if such continuing conversation, and not periodic great debates, becomes the intellectual mode of International Relations?"[46] The third way in the third debate may help turn this vision into a reachable goal.

Notes

1. John R. Hall, *Cultures of Inquiry* (Cambridge: Cambridge University Press, 1999), 1.
2. Michael Burawoy, "A Sociology for the Second Great Transformation?" *Annual Review of Sociology* 26 (2000): 693.
3. Noretta Koertge, "Science, Values, and the Value of Science," *Philosophy of Science* 67, no. 3 (2000): S45–S57; for an early articulation of a similar position in IR, see Yosef Lapid, "*Quo Vadis* International Relations? Further Reflections on the 'Next Stage' of International Theory," *Millennium: Journal of International Studies* 18, no. 1 (1989): 84–85.
4. Yosef Lapid, "Sculpting the Academic Identity: Disciplinary Reflections at the Dawn of a New Millennium," in *Visions of International Relations: Assessing an Academic Field*, ed. Donald Puchala (forthcoming).
5. Yosef Lapid, "The Third Debate," *International Studies Quarterly* 33 (1989): 235–54.

6. Ole Waever, "Figures of International Thought: Introducing Persons instead of Paradigms," in *The Future of International Relations*, ed. Iver B. Neumann and Ole Waever (New York: Routledge, 1997), 1–37.
7. Barry Buzan and Richard Little, "Why International Relations Has Failed as an Intellectual Project and What to Do about It?" (paper presented at the annual convention of the International Studies Association, Los Angeles, Calif., March 14–18, 2000); Ole Waever, "The Sociology of a Not So International Discipline," *International Organization* 52, no. 4 (1998): 687–727.
8. Ann Tickner, "You Just Don't Understand: Troubled Engagements between Feminists and IR Theorists," *International Studies Quarterly* 41, no. 4 (1997): 611–32.
9. Samuel Makinda, "Reading and Writing International Relations," *Australian Journal of International Affairs* 54, no. 3 (2000): 389.
10. Cynthia Weber, "IR: The Resurrection or New Frontiers of Incorporation," *European Journal of International Relations* 5, no. 4 (1999): 435–50.
11. David Campbell, *Writing Security*, 2d ed. (Minneapolis: University of Minnesota Press, 1999), 215.
12. James Der Derian, "Virtuous War/Virtual Theory," *International Affairs* 76, no. 4 (2000): 778.
13. David Bederman, "Constructivism, Positivism, and Empiricism in International Law," *Georgetown Law Journal* 89, no. 2 (2001): 469.
14. Donald Puchala, "Visions of International Relations: Continuing the Dialogue among Scholars," in Puchala, *Visions of International Relations*, 7.
15. Margaret Hermann, "One Field, Many Perspectives: Building the Foundation for Dialogue," *International Studies Quarterly* 42 (1998): 605–24; Michael Brecher, "International Studies in the Twentieth Century and Beyond: Flawed Dichotomies, Synthesis, Cumulation," *International Studies Quarterly* 43 (1999): 213–64.
16. Thomas Biersteker, "Eroding Boundaries, Contested Terrain," *International Studies Review* 1, no. 1 (1999): 8.
17. Richard Bernstein, *The New Constellation* (Cambridge: MIT Press, 1992).
18. For a different opinion see Stephen Walt, "Fads, Fevers, and Firestorms," *Foreign Policy*, no. 121 (November–December 2000): 37.
19. Francois Dosse, *Empire of Meaning: The Humanization of the Social Sciences* (Minneapolis: University of Minnesota Press, 1999), xix.
20. See Alexander Wendt, "On the Via Media: A Response to the Critics," *Review of International Studies* 26 (2000): 165–80; Gillian Wylie, "International Relations' *Via Media*: Still under Construction," *International Studies Review* 2, no. 3 (2001): 123–26; Georg Sorensen, "IR Theory after the Cold War," *Review of International Studies* 24 (1998): 83–100; Marc Doucet, "Standing Nowhere: Navigating the Third Route on the Question of Foundation in International Theory," *Millennium: Journal of International Studies* 28, no. 2 (1999): 289–310; Emanuel Adler, "Seizing the Middle Ground: Constructivism in World Politics," *European Journal of International Relations* 3, no. 3 (1997): 319–63; Nich-

olas Onuf, "Constructivism: A User's Manual," in *International Relations in a Constructed World*, ed. Vendulka Kubalkova, Nicholas Onuf, and Paul Kowert (London: Sharpe, 1998).

21. Erik Doxtader, "Characters in the Middle of Public Life: Consensus, Dissent, and Ethos," *Philosophy and Rhetoric* 33, no. 4 (2000): 336–69.
22. Ibid., 338.
23. Ibid., 339.
24. Ibid., 346–47.
25. Ibid., 351.
26. Ibid., 362.
27. See in particular Sorensen, "IR Theory after the Cold War," 85–92.
28. Wylie, "International Relations' *Via Media*," 123–26. Exemplifying this problem, Wylie locates the main weakness of Wendt's otherwise impressive new book in "Wendt's determination to forge a *via media* through the 'Third Debate,'" 124.
29. Wendt, "On the Via Media: A Response to the Critics," 165–80.
30. Richard Little, "The English School's Contribution to the Study of International Relations," *European Journal of International Relations* 6, no. 3 (2000): 395–422.
31. Bederman, "Constructivism, Positivism, and Empiricism in International Law," 469.
32. Sorensen, "IR Theory after the Cold War," 91.
33. Eviatar Zerubavel, "The Rigid, the Fuzzy, and the Flexible: Notes on the Mental Sculpting of Academic Identity," *Social Research* 64, no. 4 (1995): 1093–98.
34. Ibid., 1097.
35. Waever, "Figures of International Thought," in Neumann and Waever, *The Future of International Relations*, 25.
36. Richard Bernstein, "Metaphysics, Critique and Utopia," *Review of Metaphysics* 42 (1988): 257.
37. Richard Bernstein, *The New Constellation* (Cambridge: MIT Press, 1992), 9.
38. James Bohman, "Pluralism, Indeterminacy, and the Social Sciences: Reply to Ingram and Meehan," *Human Studies* 20, no. 4 (1997): 452.
39. Nicholas Burbules, "The Limits of Dialogue as a Critical Pedagogy," in *Revolutionary Pedagogies: Cultural Politics, Instituting Education, and the Discourse of Theory*, ed. Peter Trifonas (New York: Routledge, 2000), 252.
40. Ibid., 260.
41. Mark Neufeld, "Reflexivity and International Relations Theory," *Millennium* 22, no. 1 (1993): 53–76.
42. Tim Dunne, "Constructivism and the Altered Landscape of IR Theory" (paper presented at the annual meeting of the International Studies Association, Washington, D.C., February 1999), 10.
43. Cynthia Weber, "IR: The Resurrection or New Frontiers of Incorporation," 446.
44. John Ruggie, "What Makes the World Hang Together? Neo-Utilitarianism and the Social Constructivist Challenge," *International Organization* 52, no. 4 (1998): 883.

45. Friedrich Kratochwil, "Constructing a New Orthodoxy? Wendt's 'Social Theory of International Politics' and the Constructivist Challenge," *Millennium* 29, no. 1 (2000): 73–101.
46. Donald Puchala, "Marking a Weberian Moment: Our Discipline Looks Ahead," *International Studies Perspectives* 1, no. 2 (2000): 142.

ALTERNATIVE, CRITICAL, POLITICAL

R. B. J. Walker

This paper offers a necessarily highly condensed argument about what it might mean to make judgments about the state of international relations or international studies as a scholarly discipline from some kind of alternative or critical perspective. I begin by sketching some tentative grounds on which I would presume to make judgments about judgments in this context. I then identify what I take to be four among many possible areas of convergence among the heterogeneous literatures that are currently identified, and disciplined, as alternative and critical. I then conclude by emphasizing my overall concern with practices of authorization, both in a specific discipline and in the practices that discipline seeks to examine, and try to end on an upbeat.

I apologize in advance for the density and unqualified character of some of the formulations. I hope it will be clear that the whole business of offering judgments about judgments is a complex matter, one fraught with contradictions that are constitutive of what it is we think we are referring to when speaking of international relations/studies. I also hope it will be clear that the issues I try to emphasize here are important less in relation to the relatively trivial debates that occur in a specific academic site than to questions of authority that arise in relation to substantive claims provoked by analyses of the rapidly changing character of contemporary political life.

My primary argument in brief, though I make no pretense to work through its underlying logic in any detail, is that the literatures that can be loosely even if controversially classified as alternative and critical are interesting primarily as attempts to politicize practices that have been profoundly depoliticized. This, I might add, is hardly a novel preoccupation. My secondary argument is that, read in this way, these literatures lead to engagements with the constitutive practices of a specifically modern politics, especially with the practices of sovereign authorization—again a familiar and longstanding concern. Linking these arguments is a claim that even though these literatures might be framed in relation to some kind of "outside," whether as phenomena that are somehow (temporally) post- or as phenomena that are somehow (spatially) beyond (while also being constitutive of) the state, they express a renewed skepticism about a modern politics of autonomous subjectivities "inside."

What impresses me about much of the theoretical literature that has been portrayed in recent popular culture as radically different is less the claim that something has been left behind (modernity, structuralism, and so on) than the rather single-minded and often extremely rigorous engagement with what it could possibly mean to be radically different. In a formulation I have used too many times already, though one that I think remains especially important for thinking about the explicitly spatial preoccupations of international relations theory, one way of understanding many of the problems of contemporary politics is to think of the difficulties of imagining an outside to a politics that is already constituted as a structure of insides and outsides.[1] This formulation can also be framed as the difficulty of imagining an alternative to a politics that already expresses a structure of the norm and the alternative (or the exception, or the state of nature, or the international anarchy, or the barbarian, or the oriental, or the romantic, or the utopian, to name only some of the best-known variations on this theme). It can also be framed, in a way that I currently find more interesting, as the difficulty of imagining forms of critique other than those depicted in the standard modern (Kantian) opposition between dogmatism and critique.[2]

Some might argue that there is no need to pose such problems. Many eminent people would agree with them. I wish them well. I also wish they would stop justifying themselves by making highly contentious claims about the real, the rational, the unchanging necessities of modern political life, or the natural goodness of modern liberalism: claims that often amount to much the same thing. I take it as fairly obvious that contemporary political life is changing more rapidly than our capacity to comprehend such change. This is especially so given that modern politics rests upon a specific understanding of the relationship between stasis (as norm) and change (as exception), or, more portentously/pretentiously, between space and time. The extraordinary explosion of diverse meanings awkwardly subsumed by the term *globalization,* or the barely articulated forms of dissent to currently hegemonic governmentalities expressed since the Seattle trade talks, offers some indication of the limits of the modern political imagination in this respect.

What we see in so many disciplinary and disciplining responses to the attempt to articulate alternative and critical approaches can be understood very largely as a repetition of familiar dogmatic assertions of the natural necessity of the categories of modern liberalism. These are categories that I, along with many of the canonical liberal texts, would insist are a site of very difficult problems rather than of principles that must be upheld so as to save us from anarchy and damnation, or worse, relativism. Many of these canonical texts have long insisted that liberalism *must* turn dogmatic at the limit. This, one might say, is the whole point of all those "political realisms" that now seem so embarrassing (and why they nevertheless remain much more interesting than their more stridently utilitarian successors). It is also why so many theorists of international relations constantly bowdlerize Hobbes and Kant (or refuse to look Max Weber or Carl Schmitt in the face, or look no further than John Rawls and the local economics department to construct their account of what liberalism involves) in order to sustain a systematic refusal to engage with the conditions under which the categories of modern liberalism could be naturalized.

In this context, it is hardly surprising that attempts to repose questions about politics are so often met with reenactments of Hobbes's arbitrary assertion of the sovereign authority that guarantees legitimate knowledge. Still, there is considerable irony (and some crucial political practices to be analyzed) in the deployment of metaphors of a state of nature (accusations of relativism, immorality, absent foundations, and absent knowledge) in a discipline that has so often (and so unwisely) invoked this metaphor to describe its most essential problematic.

More positively, what I find interesting about contemporary international relations/studies is that it is becoming a key site at which the necessity to reengage with questions about authority and the authorization of authority is becoming most obvious. I would readily admit that some people may not find this interesting at all. Such questions can be a little disruptive to scholars who are more or less content to accept prevailing ontological and ideological assumptions and just want to get on with the specific research that interests them. Nevertheless, the most important contestations in any discipline of knowledge concern the questions that are authorized to be interesting or even askable/answerable. This is why, I will suggest, it is so much easier to invoke the name of Hobbes (to take only the most obvious example) as a guide to the alternative and the critical than as an expression of conventions and necessities that must be obeyed.

It is also important to insist at the outset that there is no field, subfield, or scholarly community that can be identified easily or un-contentiously as *alternative* or *critical* in relation to a practice called international studies/relations. In the first place, to identify an *alternative* is to assume a norm against which exceptions are to be identified. Here one might point, to take only three obvious lines of analysis, to (1) a hegemonic system of institutional practices (to be examined in terms of, say, the sociology of a profession, its recruitment practices, and so on); (2) a hegemonic discourse identifying the intellectual traditions through which scholarship should be constituted and judged (to be examined in terms of any of the now vast family of analyses that were once so easily referred to as ideology-critique); (3) a hegemonic account of the core problem or problems that enable prevailing intellectual traditions and institutional practices (to be examined especially in relation to claims about the canonical inheritance and central debates).

For my present purposes, I assume that these three possibilities are identified in increasing order of importance. I recognize that what count as alternative or as critical approaches have been driven in very large part by the quite extraordinarily controlled, elitist, and nationalist character of the way in which "international relations" has been shaped as a subfield in the specific American discipline of "political science," as well as by the more ideologically driven and shoddy formulation of many of the intellectual traditions that have become conventionalized in this context. Nevertheless, the appropriate tools for analyzing institutional and discursive hegemonies are fairly readily to hand even in the traditional crafts of the history of ideas and the sociology of knowledge. Consequently, I take it that it is in relation to the formulation and legitimation of core questions and debates that what have been framed as alternative approaches have been most sustained and serious. Insofar as one can judge the achievements and limits of these approaches, it is primarily in terms of their effect on what counts as an interesting and important scholarly agenda, and thus on the authorization of what counts as a legitimate repertoire of scholarly questions.

This is a theme that concerns not only this specific discipline. It is also central to the more general problems faced by attempts to develop forms of political pluralism that are sensitive to claims to "difference." It is in this context especially that I would identify many of the key disagreements among those who think of themselves as somehow alternative in the specific context of international relations/studies. The key and in many ways quite obvious difficulty here is not the need to increase sensitivities to differences and pluralisms. It is the need to come to terms with the historically specific framing of the relationship between identity and difference, or universal and plural, that has set up modern political practice as a series of impossible but necessary antinomies, not least between the necessary and the possible, the norm and the exception, the natural and the critical.

In the second place, to identify something as *critical* is to encounter a complex field of both popular and technical usages of this hopelessly overburdened term. In some of its popular senses, and in some of the literatures about international relations/studies, critique might encompass distaste, whining, and doctrinal disagreement. In most of its technical and scholarly senses it refers to some (of the many) versions of the Kantian distinction between the critical and the dogmatic. Complexities then arise not least because there are so many ways of insisting on the need to insist on a proper (critical) awareness of the conditions under which claims to knowledge are made (an insistence that applies to all forms of scholarly knowledge, whether empirical or hermeneutic as well as the supposedly alternative) and because of the ease with which claims to critical knowledge turn into forms of dogmatism (again whether empirical, hermeneutic, alternative, or critical).

The Kantian distinction between the critical and the dogmatic remains an unavoidable point of orientation (even if one that is very difficult to sustain in recognizably Kantian terms). I would also claim that what is most interesting in those intellectual traditions that have been framed as radically different, especially as Foucauldian, Deleuzean, Derridian, and so on, remains tied to the possibility of sustaining and extending this distinction, though it does so by recognizing that the grounds for critique must be immanent rather than transcendent. Moreover, I hope that notice of this assumption is sufficient to ward off the abusive identification of the alternative and the critical with rabble-rousing accounts of some postmodernity, and to insist that indictments of some kind of relativism, nihilism, or Thrasymachian antiethics from some presumed position of rationality or modernity are merely expressions of problems that need to be addressed with great seriousness rather than a tactic about which anyone can be proud.

To be clear here: my comments rest on the assumption that the distinction between the critical and the dogmatic remains crucial, even if difficult. It applies across all fields of knowledge. From this ground, most of the other distinctions and categories through which the possibility of critique has been raised in international relations/studies—the pretense to distinctions between first, second, third, and nth debates, between realists and liberals, between modernists and postmodernists, and between either rationalists or empiricists and either reflectivists or constructivists are perhaps the most perplexing, but there are many others—are almost entirely irrelevant. Most of these disciplinary artifacts constitute a philosophical swamp, a sign that a little knowledge is indeed a dangerous thing, especially in the hands of those who would be disciplinary king. They are a massive hindrance to constructive discussion. Quite apart from all the wasted energy required to negotiate this swamp, however, the pursuit of critical knowledge has always been a very tricky affair, and it has certainly not become any less tricky over the past few decades.

Insofar as one can judge the achievements and limits of approaches that aspire to be critical in the specific context of a professional discipline, it is perhaps primarily in terms of their capacity to successfully insist on the very necessity of critique in the face of entrenched institutionalized conventions. But the challenge of critique in international studies is especially interesting because this possibility is necessarily raised in and through the various contemporary challenges to the subject of modernity—the (free, equal, autonomous, and so on) individual subject constituted as citizen in and by the (sovereign, national) state—that has for so long been both the ground and aspiration of the possibility of critique. The institutionalized practices of a discipline may be annoying, not to say career destroying, but as a site for engaging with the crucial questions of contemporary politics, "the international" poses enormous intellectual challenges for which even our most sophisticated traditions are clearly wearing very thin. (This, I might add, is why forms of critical possibility associated with Habermas, cosmopolitanism, Critical Theory, and related attempts to privilege a Subject of History, seem to me to be expressions of rather than positive responses to the problem at hand.)

To put this in a slightly different language, if international studies/relations is somehow concerned with "the state," then it also has to be concerned with the question of authority—that is, not only with the effects of the state as the most effective site of modern authority but with the practices of authorization that have enabled the state. Hobbes may be the patron saint of international relations, but only to the extent that, like Machiavelli, Kant, and all the other poor abused caricatures of the prevailing canon, he is understood to have been concerned precisely with the practices of authorization.

Hobbes is especially important as a paradigmatic account of the practices of discrimination and authorization necessary for reading texts and making claims to scholarly knowledge quite as much as for the practices of states, legal regimes, and declarations of war. Hobbes's questions, I would say, like the questions of a Machiavelli, a Rousseau, a Kant, and many others, are much closer to the questions posed by various alternative and critical theorists than to most of what is claimed in their name in the standard disciplinary texts. This is not surprising in that they were asking about the very possibility of a modern politics. Their answers, of course, or the procedures through which they tried to work out their answers, are a different matter.

Again, one might want to claim that their questions are uninteresting, or merely historical, or merely theoretical, or culturally parochial, or even that their answers are perfectly adequate. Such claims might be debated. But they can be debated usefully only while recognizing that it is difficult to find much of a theory of international relations in *any* of these canonical sources—accounts of the practices of authorization certainly, accounts of a (always highly problematic) relationship between a political community and an absence of political community also, but clear accounts of what international relations is really like, very rarely. That enterprise starts much later and has a very interesting history, a history that makes it into the standard texts in the most extraordinarily simple-minded form we all know and loathe. Every introductory student learns it. The categories are hammered into memory, then it's social science all the way. Good-bye questions about authorization, about the very possibility of a modern politics, let alone a politics that is not monopolized by the modern state. Hello the desperate need for critique.

The key achievement of supposedly alternative and critical literatures over the past two decades has been to open up at least some possibility of asking questions about the location and character of the political. Or rather, this is the context in which I would try to make judgments about the contributions of alternative and critical literatures. Moreover, I would want to insist that areas of scholarship that are not formally identified as alternative and critical also have much to say. I would say this especially of some feminist political theory, some postcolonial theory, some political economy, some literary theory, some cultural theory, some legal theory, some ecological theory, some empirical theory, some rationalist theory, some institutional theory, and so on. In all cases, the emphasis is on the some: not all claims to critique are critical; not all claims to be alternative are alternative; not all claims made under the signs of empiricism, rationalism, and the rest are conventional or dogmatic. Difficult questions of judgment here are all too often erased by caricatured identities and a mania for easy classifications. Moreover, it is not as though alternative and critical theories of international relations/studies can be considered as closed communities, no matter how much people identified with these categories might hang around together in the annual meetings of the professional associations. I doubt very much that publications about either alternative/critical international relations/studies or publications about the professional discipline of international relations/studies in general account for more than a very small proportion of what any of us read in order to make sense of what is going on, or to keep up with the concepts and techniques necessary for either research or teaching. Indeed, I would consider it to be a sign of professional incompetence if this were the case.

What I think ultimately links many of those who are located as alternative and critical in relation to international studies/relations, then, is a deep skepticism about the received account of where and what the political must be. This is an account that is notoriously expressed as a simple fact of life by those who claim to speak of a political realism in international relations and naturalized even by many if not most attempts to challenge the presumptions of political realism. This skepticism, this concern with the contemporary fate of modern practices of authorization, provokes different scholars to move in many theoretical directions. The differences among these directions is perhaps much more interesting than what unites them as somehow alternative or critical, but for purposes of this discussion I will focus on some commonalities.

There seems, to me at least, to be a shared concern with four core themes. First, the tendency to interrogate the received assumptions about what the world is taken to be—that is, to privilege the critical analysis of categories that express (and help constitute) assumptions about the ontology of politics. Second, the tendency to engage with sovereignty as an enormously complicated site of political practice, one that most accounts of modern politics pass over in silence. Third, the tendency to get very annoyed when told that difficult questions about ontology and sovereignty ought to be adjudicated on the ground of epistemology and method. And fourth, the insistence that there are interesting parallels (not to say ironies) between the constitution of international relations as a discipline concerned with the study of crisis and the constitution of accounts of what it means to have alternative or critical perspectives on that discipline.

Of course it would come as no surprise to me to learn that others who have come to represent the alternative and the critical find that this way of framing a specific site of scholarly engagement completely misses the point of what they are up to. Moreover, each of these four themes can be made to seem highly arcane, trivial, philosophical, and so on; the rhetorical procedures are familiar. Nevertheless, these four themes seem to get at political practices that are of considerable practical importance. My own experience has been that it's much easier to talk about them with policymakers and activists than with theorists of international relations. Whether one takes this claim to practical relevance seriously or not, however, I would want to insist that it has to be couched not in terms of the familiar and profoundly ideological distinction between theory and practice, but of questions about the conditions under which claims about the arcane, the trivial, the theoretical, and the practical get to be authorized as authoritative.

First, then, perhaps the most crucial constitutive move of modern Anglo-American social science has been to insist that all theoretical disputes be resolved on the ground of epistemology, a ground that is then usually narrowed either to the possibilities of empiricism, the techniques of method, or both. Not everyone, not even most (or perhaps even many) Anglo-American social scientists have been fooled by this move, but it has been especially influential in the political science subfield of international relations.

There are two obvious countermoves to this insistence on the priority of epistemology and method. One is to note that the very possibility of modern epistemology has depended on a specifically modern ontology, classically a dualism of spatially differentiated subjects and objects. This is an observation that might at least serve to emphasize the highly contested character of contemporary accounts of legitimate knowledge rather than to legitimize claims about a store of scientific techniques. The problem of knowledge, one might say, is precisely a problem, and a very interesting and important one at that. The other countermove is to note that all the noise about epistemology and method has largely served to mask a sustained silence about the ontological categories and assumptions that are thereby reified.

It is in both contexts that we can understand much of the insistence in various critical and alternative literatures on and importance of examining, and largely rejecting, assumptions that are taken for granted in many claims about the priority of epistemological adjudication. Sometimes this rejection is made on grounds of philosophical incoherence and sometimes on grounds that these assumptions are politically interested/suspect; the possibilities are obviously extensive. Thus, if there were an opportunity to survey these literatures in detail, I would especially stress the implications of the following:

- Critiques of various practices of reification (in the senses identified by both Georg Lukacs[3]—as commodification—and Alfred North Whitehead[4]—as the fallacy of misplaced concreteness), especially in relation to claims about state, nation, history, structure, cultural identity, gender, power, rationality, and the necessary virtue of the standard liberal antinomies (as assumed not least in the familiar "levels of analysis" schema). Hence the "post-" in poststructuralism, the methods of genealogy, the injunctions to privilege verbs and actions rather than nouns and things, and so on.
- Refusals of Cartesian and Lockean accounts of the relation between language and world (and thus a concern with the politics of representation and questions of authorization rather than with, say, the "influence" of "ideas" or "culture").

- Explorations of multiple subjectivities in relation to claims about cultures, genders, political communities, citizenships, rights, ecologies, and so on.
- Explorations of spatiotemporal configurations other than those identified as national histories contained in horizontal territories (and thus of "speed," flows, lines of flight, rhizomatics, networks, horizons, global/locals, and so on).

To privilege questions about ontology is, of course, to question the most basic constitutive categories of the discipline. On the one hand it is hard to see how this is anything to which anyone could object, given the degree to which these categories have been challenged by just about everyone else. On the other, it is easy to see how these questions are unlikely to find favor in disciplines that depend on these categories for their very legitimation.

Second, to focus on questions of ontology is especially to focus attention on the principle that is claimed to define the phenomena that is international studies/relations studies and yet that is simply taken for granted by those studies. This is the principle (and practice, and institution, and problem) of sovereignty, a principle that, not least, offers our paradigmatic account of how questions about ontology and questions about epistemology should be related.

International relations theory typically takes sovereignty to be an expression of (the already achieved condition of) a plurality of communities, communities that are always potentially in conflict because of the absence of any common community. It is only rarely taken to be a practice through which the relation between plurality and commonality is produced and reproduced. (This, I have argued elsewhere is the crucial cause and effect of the discourses through which "international relations" has been distinguished from "political theory.")[5] Sovereignty then ceases to be a site of contradictions and paradoxes—of, to invoke the terms of a variety of analytical traditions, the paradox of founding, of the groundless authorization of a ground of authority, of the ontotheological production of ontology, and of a decision to include/exclude that defines what can then be included/excluded. It is no longer understood to be the site of a politics that constitutes a politics (Hobbes, standing on the shoulders of Plato and Aristotle) or a site at which exceptions are made to the norm (Schmitt, the distiller of epigrams from logics worked out by Hobbes, Kant, and Weber), or a site at which the sign of rationality asserts itself on a ground of charade, rhetoric, irrationality, and the yawning gap between word and thing (the standard puzzle of nominalism bereft of transcendental guarantees). Sovereignty becomes merely an achieved condition, though we might have some interesting and important debates about exactly when it was achieved, if ever. Indeed, one might, and I would, want to insist that sovereignty can never be an achieved condition, in principle; careful readings of Hobbes are especially helpful in this context.

There is, though, a paradox in the way the discipline of international relations has so easily assumed sovereignty as a foundation (been mesmerized by the top turtle, perhaps) and then constituted itself as the study of a world of multiple sovereignties. The rise of various alternative and critical modes of analysis can be explained in large part as a consequence of conditions under which it is no longer sensible to allow this paradox to work as if it is the most natural thing in the world.

Hobbes, of course, hoped that his account of the necessity of sovereign necessity would seem to be the most natural thing in the world, indeed insisted that it must be so if we moderns are to forestall the necessary consequence of liberal individualism: relativism. Kant is not so very different in this respect. If Hobbes and Kant are still to be used as canonical figures in thinking about international relations/studies, then at least they ought to be read seriously as sites in which the problem of sovereignty is explored rather than as the dim-witted utilitarians and protodemocrats that pop up in so many texts in this field. It may be the case that much of the alternative and the critical is articulated with the help of writers who seem excessively post- or excessively Parisian, or excessively literary, or excessively philosophical. Still, it can hardly be said that the ways in which they engage precisely with the sovereign practice of authorization has only marginal relevance to international relations/studies. In any case, excessive reification is arguably a far, far worse problem, one that is far more common, and, of course, one that is subject to a multitude of rhetorical tactics intended to make it seem utterly benign.

Third, questions about how we know what we claim to know are dependent on what we assume we are trying to know. If one starts from an Augustinian distinction between necessity and free will, for example, one will end up doing the familiar dance of structure and action. One might prefer the tango—or at least try to come to terms with how modern accounts of sovereign authority constitute a modern account of freedom as necessity, whether under the law of the state or the law of universal morality. We are free to act, as we have been told time and time again, as long as we do what we have to do. This is a contradiction that plays rather a large role in the constitution of most of our modern political categories, not least those that are used in claims about rational action. It is not one that is likely to be resolved by epistemology, though it is one that we might begin to see as very poorly framed in the first place. Epistemologies have their place, but they are the product of ontological contestation, not referees; they are authorized grounds for contestation in which referees can be deployed, not authorizations of those authorized grounds.

Epistemology remains crucially important. Many of the characteristic concerns of alternative and critical theories are not directed against the importance of epistemological matters, indeed quite the contrary, but against the prevalence of caricatured accounts of what it means to make knowledge claims about the world. These caricatures, moreover, have now become almost inseparable from a utilitarian or instrumental account of rational action that serves as an obvious ideology of more or less identifiable political interests. Furthermore, much of what actually goes on under the rubric of epistemology turns out to be a more or less elaborate production of classifications, of inclusions and exclusions, about which a great deal might and should be said from a critical perspective.

In any case, demands that critical and alternative scholarship submit to the arbitrary and long-contested accounts of what a proper social science should look like are unpersuasive, to say the least. However, demands that all claims to knowledge be susceptible to critical analyses of their conditions of possibility remain crucial. Critique trumps social science, not the other way around. Or rather, there is no social or any other kind of science without critique. Contestations arise in this context because there are so many claimants to the status of critique—and hence many opportunities for epistemological debate—but also so many attempts to claim this status by fiat, and hence so many tactics for the practice of discipline building.

Fourth, there are grounds to be skeptical about many scholarly claims produced by the discipline of international relations. These grounds are not sufficient to undermine its importance as a characteristic discourse of the modern state, whether as, for example, an expression of its constitutive outside, as the negation of the modern claim to political identity and community that serves to affirm the

claims to identity and community that is being negated, as a legitimation of specifically modern practices of nationalism, as a sequence
of claims about where and what modern politics must be, or as a set
of profoundly normative codes framed as the most realistic of natural
necessities. At least, these are the characteristics of a contemporary
site of political practice that have interested me.

The practices of authorization in this discipline reproduce practices
of authorization in the phenomena it seeks to study. Forms of critique
and claims about alternatives in the discipline express wider doubts
about modern authorizations of authority. This is why I think there
is something quite interesting about the ways in which a discipline
that has been framed more than any other as being about crisis—
about war and necessary violence at the point at which authority
disappears—should be said to be somehow in crisis.

It is perhaps telling that we are now so willing to speak about
policy, about governance, about governmentalities, about regimes,
about global *civil* societies, about global *social* movements, about
nongovernmental organizations and international nongovernmental
organizations, and perhaps now especially about ethics, yet we remain so reluctant to speak about politics. It is also perhaps telling
that so many of the practices of the discipline still largely depend on
the framing of the key debates on precisely the dyadic possibilities
that both enabled and reproduced modern accounts of sovereign ne-
cessity/freedom. This is apparent not least in the recent constitution
of various strands of social constructivism, a term that makes little
sense to me unless taken as some vintage opposition to a claim to
nature, to essence, or a methodological injunction to reify; in this
context, surely the key issue is not *whether* constructivism (see, for
start, Hobbes, Locke, Rousseau, Smith, Marx, Mill, Weber, and the
rest) but what kind, and especially what ontologies are being described as an act of construction and why we should refer to this act
as *social* rather than *political*.

Modern politics, of course, hinges on a capacity to draw the line—
between humans and citizens, legal and illegal, norm and exception,
public and private, political and nonpolitical, political and economic, political and ethical, political and cultural, and not least, the
domestic and the international. It is thus of considerable interest to
see how this discipline, which has been framed especially as a concern with life on the edge, with the state of emergency, with the
inscription and transgression of boundaries, continues to enact lines
of sovereign jurisdiction and legitimate authority.

My own view is that the extensive metaphorical/discursive field through which lines drawn in (Euclidean) space have come to be read as lines between the legitimate and the illegitimate, or the included and the excluded, offers an increasingly (but always) difficult ground on which to understand contemporary accounts of both subjectivity and authority. It is not a ground on which I would try to fix an analysis of contemporary political life. The modern art of discrimination, in both the positive and negative sense of this term, is in trouble.

At this historical juncture, it may make very little sense to speak of critical and alternative perspectives in international studies/relations except as the familiar Other that serves to legitimize some prevailing norm. The tight corsets of the cold war years have clearly come unstuck, but hardly as a result of a handful of scholars who had read some political, social, and literary theory. Intellectual horizons may have been reshaped and broadened, some possibilities explored, many new connections made across disciplines and institutions, but these depended on broader historical changes that made the existing order unsustainable in any case. In some ways, the relatively open and cosmopolitan character of contemporary international studies is quite remarkable, especially given the state of the discipline thirty years ago. This openness may still have fairly obvious limits, which become even more obvious as one moves toward the key institutions of intellectual hegemony. Still, it does seem to me that questions about authorization, about the political practices through which authorities are constituted and reconstituted, can now be asked in more and more interesting ways. Such questioning is, of course, the very opposite of the claim to political realism as we have come to know it in this context, although it is far from unknown in some of the key sources of this claim, among which I would especially single out Max Weber. It is also precisely what would interest a Machiavelli, a Hobbes, or a Kant, as well as the Foucauldians, Derridians, and Deleuzeans, even if the contemporary plague of Benthamites might wish us to believe—and I insist on the word believe—otherwise.

But let me try to be clear here also: to insist on the necessity of critique, something that seems to me to be rather conventional (which is why I read Foucault, Derrida, Deleuze, and the rest as people engaged with rather conventional questions and problems, even if in provocative and I think quite productive ways), is also to insist that the very meaning of critique, and of what it might mean to engage with alternatives, is highly contentious. The standard Hobbesian, Kantian, and Schmittean authorizations of authority are increasingly difficult to sustain, as are all the other less stringent liberal attempts to draw the line that ultimately rests upon these more dramatic theorists of the limit condition. The meaning of critique is contentious because modern forms of authorization are in widespread dispute. The authorizations of this specific discipline are interesting because the realm of international relations/studies is one in which difficulties of authorization are so obviously acute. Hence, presumably, all those synonyms that try to elude references to politics. Hence also the difficulty of coming to terms with contemporary authorizations enacted in the World Trade Organization, the European Union, the United Nations, the conventions on this and that, and so on. And hence, consequently, the good old-fashioned wisdom of looking for politics in places where it is not supposed to be.

In the end, then, it is this fourth set of convergences that seems to me to be the most significant. The great paradox of modern international relations/studies is that its disciplinary conventions have for so long discouraged any concern with the practices of authorization, and yet the problem of authorization (the Hobbesian *problem* of sovereignty rather than the supposedly bare Bodinian or Westphalian fact of sovereignty if one prefers, and thus all those myriad practices through which sovereign authorizations are authorized and reauthorized) is perhaps nowhere as interesting as in the phenomena these conventions seek to examine. In the end, the key feature of international relations theory, as of its enabling twin, modern political theory, has been an almost complete refusal to take the problem of sovereignty seriously (and I might add that modern political theorists have generally been even more irresponsible than modern theorists of international relations in this respect). I at least take it as a sign of some progress that this refusal, while still popular, is increasingly treated as a sign of sloppy scholarship, as indeed I would insist it is, and on the most conventional of grounds.

Contrary to various attempts to link critique, alternatives, emancipations, and so on to the discovery of firm foundations in ethics, economics-in-the-last-instance, or some such extrapolitical realm, it is important to stress that these grounds are anything but certain. These are, after all, the grounds on which modern politics, and thereby modern international relations, was initially constituted against theocracy and empire, even if this was on terms always susceptible to a reversion to theological models of authorization in the horizontal spaces of modern states rather than the vertical space of empire. But then, perhaps we really are now being asked to conform to the necessities of empire. Perhaps questions about authorization have become redundant. Perhaps a further deification of the market and its rational actors is all we can look forward to. If not, there is certainly a lot of work to be done.

Notes

1. This is the puzzle I seek to examine in my *International Relations as Political Theory* (Cambridge: Cambridge University Press, 1993).
2. For an attempt to explore what this might involve, see my *After the Globe/Before the World* (Cambridge: Cambridge University Press, forthcoming).
3. Georg Lukacs, *History and Class Consciousness* (1923; London: Merlin, 1971).
4. Alfred North Whitehead, *Science and the Modern World* (New York: Macmillan, 1925).
5. R. B. J. Walker, *Inside/Outside: International Relations as Political Theory* (Cambridge: Cambridge University Press, 1993).

THE GLOBALIZATION OF GLOBALIZATION

James N. Rosenau

As one whose professional life exceeds that of the International Studies Association, I have mixed feelings about the invitation to reflect critically on the accomplishments, failures, debates, standards, approaches, and future agendas of international relations (IR) and its subfields. On the one hand, I have no doubt that our shared past is marked by enormous growth and progress. The conceptual and methodological equipment with which IR is probed today is far more elaborate, incisive, and diverse than was the case at the outset—back in the 1950s when a few isolated, non–Ivy League scholars first came together around common interests to form a professional association, replete with a journal (called *Background* before being changed to the *International Studies Quarterly*) and with a membership so small that it convened annually on campuses because it was unable to reach the minimum registration required for reduced rates at hotels. On the other hand, for all the progress that has marked IR's evolution, I am plagued with doubts about the field's capacity for adapting to the transformations at work in the world today. And my doubts extend to questioning the wisdom of engaging in introspective assessments of inter- and intraparadigmatic debates—perhaps out of fatigue generated by a history of vigorous involvement in such debates and perhaps because I have progressively

This paper was prepared for presentation at a millennial reflections panel at the annual meeting of the International Studies Association, Los Angeles, Calif., March 16, 2000.

moved away from the IR mainstream, but more likely out of a conviction that change has left us so far in arrears that we need to focus our energies on assessing substantive dynamics rather than evaluating our colleagues, their theories, and their standards. Several years ago I gave up wondering, worrying, and writing about the fit between my thinking and that of realists and liberals. To articulate such concerns struck me as needless ritual that diverted valuable time and space from focusing on what was transpiring outside academe in what students call "the real world." The problem was me and my understanding, which required an agenda framed by my own reasoning and not one devised by others. Put differently, exercises like the present one can be a substitute for thinking about the nature of the world and how it should be studied, and I think that too often we resort to this substitute when the course of events seems too complex and obscure to comprehend.

So the ensuing paragraphs stray beyond the assigned topics. They are rooted in a sense of déjà vu all over again, to quote an insightful philosopher. In 1968 I wrote that all the signs were pointing in the same direction, that a spate of articles, textbooks, conferences, and curricula signified the emergence of a subfield (comparative foreign policy),[1] and now an even greater variety and number of indicators are heralding the arrival of another new preoccupation, one that is so pervasive that it has not only spread quickly through our ivory towers, but it has also galvanized action in the world's streets, markets, foreign offices, boardrooms, legislative chambers, city halls, cyberspaces, and every other site where people converge. And its pervasiveness in academe is such that it may emerge as our field and not just as a subfield. On Tuesday, January 19, 2000, while preparing a syllabus for a new course on globalization, three insightful newspaper stories, two soon-to-be-published manuscripts, a large book of readings, invitations to two conferences (one in Washington and one in Israel), and the lead article in the December issue of *Foreign Affairs* came my way—all of them concentrating on one or another aspect of globalization. That was just one day's take. Previously the flow of such indicators was no less continuous or voluminous, with word of new courses, conferences, dissertations, books, and papers on the subject amounting to a flow of tidal proportions. In effect, the preoccupation with the dynamics of globalization, both good and bad, has undergone globalization.

But there is a difference between the 1968 article and the recent déjà vu experience. The former involved a flow located entirely in the IR academic community, whereas the second is predominantly inundating other communities both outside and within the academy. The outside flow is evident in the huge extent to which globalization encompasses a cluster of issues at the top of the agenda of communities at every level of aggregation. The inside preoccupation with such issues is sustained by scholars in anthropology, sociology, economics, geography, and social psychology, with political science and IR trailing way behind. More accurately, within the American IR community, globalization is not a primary focus of most inquiries. The articles, books, and conference proposals I received January 19 were the work either of colleagues abroad or of journalists, defense officials, and economists. It is almost as if our political science and IR communities are shying away from the forces of globalization because their complexity does not fit readily within the extant frameworks. These forces are so pervaded by nonlinear feedback mechanisms, by confounding nuances, that confronting them runs the risk of finding that one's hard-won intellectual perspectives are inadequate to the explanatory tasks and may have to be abandoned, or at least greatly modified.

If that seems like sour grapes and a violation of my commitment not to worry or write about the approach of others, let me articulate my out-of-the-mainstream perspectives not in terms of others having gone astray but in terms of four major dimensions of globalization that strike me as urgently needing to be addressed. There are, of course, a number of other dimensions that should command focused attention, but these four can be seen as prerequisites to focusing on the others.

Change

If one assumes, as I do, that the world, its societies and its people, is undergoing transformations so profound as not to be fully appreciated, then a major conceptual challenge needs to be faced: how do we know change when we see it? How do we differentiate between evolutionary and breakpoint change? At what levels of aggregation are deep and enduring changes most likely? Do changes at, say, micro levels necessitate comparable changes at macro levels, and vice versa? Are some forms of change illusory, amounting to no more than brief disruptions of underlying patterns? With few exceptions, such questions have not been the focus of conceptual inquiries by IR scholars.[2] Most of us tend to take for granted that salient changes in the actors and structures of world affairs will be manifest as they unfold. Sure, when a regime collapses or an alliance breaks up, when terrorists demolish skyscrapers, when markets decline precipitously, or when situations deteriorate abruptly, we have little difficulty discerning the end of one historical sequence and the onset of another. Ascribing change to such developments is easy, but assessing the durability of the changes, or discerning the early indicators of regime, alliance, terrorist-induced, situational, or market collapses, is where our conceptual equipment is rudimentary, if not altogether lacking. This is why all too often we are surprised by the turn of events.

There are, of course, no magic formulas for understanding and anticipating different forms of change. Still, there are ways of maximizing our ability to assess when transformations may ensue. One is to assume that systems are always on the edge of collapse, an assumption that compels us to be sensitive to, even in awe of, the capacity of systems to get from one moment, week, year, or decade in time to the next. To proceed from the opposite assumption—that systems are likely to persist—is to limit our readiness to recognize the formation and early stages of change dynamics. Another way of coping with the challenge of change is to allow our variables to vary—that is, to mentally imagine a wide range of possible shifts in the values of all the variables relevant to our concerns. Most of us, for example, did not allow for the possibility that the cold war and the Soviet Union would come to abrupt ends. In retrospect, such failures border on the inexcusable. Or at least if we had been more sensitive to the susceptibility of systemic collapse and thus been alert to variations in the two structures expressive of such tendencies, it may have been less surprising.

Fragmegration

Of the numerous change dynamics presently shaping world affairs, two clusters stand out as paramount—those that foster globalization, centralization, and integration on the one hand and those that promote localization, decentralization, and fragmentation on the other. While these polarities move the course of events in opposite directions, they are continuously, simultaneously, and often causally interactive, giving rise to the prime tensions with which individuals and their collectivities must contend. To capture the inextricable and pervasive character of these interactions, I use the concept of "fragmegration," which is admittedly awkward and grating but at the same time reminds us that the processes of fragmentation and integration are interactive and, often, causally linked.[3] Indeed, it can readily be argued that the emergent epoch is one of fragmegration and not simply one of globalization. The so-called battle of Seattle in late November 1999 offers a quintessential illustration of fragmegrative dynamics: as the representatives of states gathered for the integrative purpose of negotiating new trade agreements, so did various nongovernmental organizations (NGOs) and individuals take to the streets to demonstrate their opposition and to highlight the fragmenting nature of such agreements. And the terrorist actions against the United States might well be described as the "mother" of all fragmegrative situations: they pulled the country together even as they destroyed one of its major landmarks.

While anthropologists, sociologists, journalists, and business executives have recognized the importance of fragmegrative processes[4] and even coined their own labels for them,[5] these crucial dynamics have not been accorded centrality by the IR community. To the extent that globalizing or localizing forces are examined, they tend to be explored and traced separately, with only passing attention being paid to the ways in which each set of forces affects the other. One reason for this conceptual gap probably concerns the simultaneity of fragmegrative dynamics. The processes whereby the several polarities are linked to each other are comprised largely of feedback mechanisms, of nonlinear sequences that present enormous methodological dilemmas (see last section of essay). Most of us are accustomed to linear analysis, to discerning how dependent variables vary in response to the operation of various independent variables. The idea that each dependent variable becomes instantaneously an independent variable tends to be too mind-boggling to acknowledge, much less serve as the basis for inquiry. So fragmegrative studies languish for want of an effective methodology.

Equally important, the conceptual gap is bypassed because of the number and variety of sources that contribute to and sustain the processes of fragmegration. One of these sources consists of what I have elsewhere labeled "the skill revolution" wherein people everywhere are increasingly able to construct scenarios that trace the course of distant events back into their homes and pocketbooks.[6] A second source involves the large degree to which collectivities around the world are undergoing authority crises, by which is meant the paralysis and stalemates that prevent them from framing and moving toward their goals. A third focuses on the bifurcation of global structures whereby the long-standing statecentric world now has a rival in an emergent multicentric world of diverse actors such as ethnic minorities, NGOs, professional societies, transnational corporations, and the many other types of private collectivities that now crowd the global stage. A fourth is what I call the "organizational explosion" that has witnessed a huge proliferation of associations and networks at every level of community. A fifth I call the "mobility upheaval," by which is meant the vast and ever-growing movement of people around the world, a movement that includes everyone from the tourist to the terrorist and from the jet-setter to the immigrant. A sixth consists of the many microelectronic and transportational technologies that have collapsed time and space. A seventh involves the complex processes through which territoriality, states, and sovereignty have weakened to the point where it can be reasonably asserted that landscapes have been supplemented—and in some cases replaced—by mediascapes, financescapes, technoscapes, ethnoscapes, and ideoscapes.[7] An eighth concerns the large degree to which national economies have been globalized. How these eight major sources (and doubtless others could be identified) interactively generate and sustain the dynamics of fragmegration is an enormous analytic challenge, but even prior to assessing their interaction is the need to probe each of them for their fragmegrative content and consequences.[8]

Micro-Macro Links

Still another critical aspect of fragmegrative dynamics involves the links between individuals at the micro level and collectivities at the macro level. Like change and fragmegration, these links have not been the focus of extensive conceptualization and investigation. While few analysts would deny that the flow between the two levels is central to how collectivities come into being and sustain themselves through time, how their macro-macro relationships are configured, and how people are shaped by the collectivities to which they belong, the interaction across these levels has been largely taken for granted or, in one well-known case, assessed to be beyond systematic comprehension.[9] We simply do not have any viable theory that anticipates how individuals will vary in response to varying macroinputs or how the structures and policies of macrocollectivities might be undermined, redirected, sustained, or otherwise af-

fected by new patterns at the micro level. Again, this is a preoccupation in some of the social sciences,[10] but IR scholars have
essentially ignored the puzzles posed by the links among the levels
of aggregation. Indeed, a major paradigm in the field, realism, pro-
ceeds from the premise that the only relevant action is that of states
at the macro level, that individuals at the micro level can be assumed
to follow the lead of their states.

The reasons for this seeming obliviousness to micro-macro links
are not difficult to identify. Tracing such links is extremely difficult
theoretically and thus even more challenging empirically. Those of
us who do not subscribe to realist formulations intuitively know
that the links are endlessly operative, that what collectivities and
individuals do on the global stage is in part reactions to each other,
but faced with the task of tracing their interactions, we tend to find
it easier to take them for granted than to wrestle with the puzzles
they pose. I do not claim to have made any progress in solving the
puzzles, but I do contend that comprehension of world affairs increasingly requires us to address the challenge and frame models that
offer a chance to fit some of the pieces of the puzzles together.[11] As
the skill revolution, authority crises, structural bifurcation, the organization explosion, the mobility upheaval, microelectronic technologies, the weakening of territoriality, states, and sovereignty, and
the globalization of national economies accelerate and extend their
impact on fragmegrative dynamics, so does it become all the more
urgent that we collectively work to confront the causal interactions
thereby established. Table 1 is an effort to highlight the vast domain
across which such theorizing must roam. The entries in its cells are
no more than impressionistic hypotheses about how the sources of
fragmegration may play out at the micro, macro, macro-macro, and
micro-macro levels, but hopefully they are suggestive of some of the
paths inquiry into such relationships should follow.

Methodology

The conceptual challenges posed by the dynamics of change, fragmegration, and micro-macro interactions share a methodological dilemma. Each is pervaded with feedback processes, and thus they pose
the difficult question of how to explore them systematically. In other
words, each is rooted in events that unfold virtually simultaneously,
making it fruitless to cast analyses in terms of the interaction of
independent and dependent variables. More accurately, analyses cast

in a conventional linear framework seem bound to fall short in terms of capturing the interactive, high-speed nature of the phenomena of interest. How, then, to proceed? What methodologies might be available for probing nonlinear sequences of interaction? Are we bound to rely exclusively on case studies that, hopefully, somehow reveal the underlying tendencies that drive the transformative impacts of fragmegration and micro-macro links? Can nonlinear methodologies drawn from mathematics and statistics be adapted to the needs of the IR student? If we are not ourselves adept at such methods, how do we make an effective case for students employing them?

Never having been very sophisticated as a methodologist, I do not have very precise answers to these questions. I know they are important, and I presume there are colleagues who can answer them with some authority. Still, ignorance is no excuse. If the mysteries of a fragmegrative world are to be fathomed, we cannot shy away from the methodological questions on the grounds of inexperience. Herewith, then, a partial, somewhat informed response to the methodological challenge: while case studies can surely be of value, there are also nonlinear procedures that have become more feasible as a result of advances in computer technologies. As I understand it, there is now the prospect of computer chips that will be ten billion (yes, ten billion) times faster than those in use today.[12] This heightens the potential of using computer simulations based on complexity theory, of building nonlinear feedback mechanisms into models that simulate the dynamics of change, fragmegration, and micro-macro interactions. To recur to points made earlier, conceptualizations of these three sets of dynamics are in short supply and obviously need to be refined before computer models can be applied. If it is assumed that such refinements will eventually be developed, however, then computer simulations may prove to be a useful methodology in unraveling the mysteries of a fragmegrative world.

As for the problem of motivating and equipping students to take advantage of the technological advances that lie ahead, let me report on a teaching aid that I have found highly effective semester after semester for the last several years. It is a book entitled *Complexity: The Emerging Science at the Edge of Order and Chaos,* by M. Mitchell Waldrop.[13] In fifty-one years of teaching I have never given an assignment that has had such pervasive consequences. Each semester the first week's assignment is to read the entire book and write a five-page evaluation of it. The reactions are consistently impressive. Even though the book refers only occasionally and peripherally

Table 1. Some Possible Sources of Fragmegration at Four Levels of Aggregation

Sources of Fragmegration	Levels of Aggregation			
	Micro	*Macro*	*Macro–Macro*	*Micro–Macro*
Skill revolution	Expands people's horizons on a global scale; sensitizes them to the relevance of distant events; facilitates a reversion to local concerns	Enlarges the capacity of government agencies to think "out of the box," seize opportunities, and analyze challenges	Multiplies quantity and enhances quality of links among states; solidifies their alliances and enmities	Constrains policy-making through increased capacity of individuals to know when, where, and how to engage in collective action
Authority crises	Redirect loyalties; encourage individuals to replace traditional criteria of legitimacy with performance criteria	Weaken ability of both governments and other organizations to frame and implement policies	Enlarge the competence of some IGOs and NGOs; encourage diplomatic wariness in negotiations	Facilitate the capacity of publics to press and/or paralyze their governments, the WTO, and other organizations
Bifurcation of global structures	Adds to role conflicts, divides loyalties, and foments tensions among individuals; orients people toward local spheres of authority	Facilitates formation of new spheres of authority and consolidation of existing spheres in the multicentric world	Generates institutional arrangements for cooperation on major global issues such as trade, human rights, the environment, etc.	Empowers transnational advocacy groups and special interests to pursue influence through diverse channels
Organizational explosion	Facilitates multiple identities, subgroupism, and affiliation with transnational networks	Increases capacity of opposition groups to form and press for altered policies; divides publics from their elites	Renders the global stage ever more transnational and dense with nongovernmental actors	Contributes to the pluralism and dispersion of authority; heightens the probability of authority crises

Mobility upheaval	Stimulates imaginations and provides more extensive contacts with foreign cultures; heightens salience of the outsider	Enlarges the size and relevance of subcultures, diasporas, and ethnic conflicts as people seek new opportunities abroad	Heightens need for international cooperation to control the flow of drugs, money, immigrants, and terrorists	Increases movement across borders that lessens capacity of governments to control national boundaries
Microelectronic technologies	Enable like-minded people to be in touch with each other anywhere in the world	Empower governments to mobilize support; renders their secrets vulnerable to spying	Accelerate diplomatic processes; facilitate electronic surveillance and intelligence work	Constrain governments by enabling opposition groups to mobilize more effectively
Weakening of territoriality, states, and sovereignty	Undermines national loyalties and increases distrust of governments and other institutions	Adds to the porosity of national boundaries and the difficulty of framing national policies	Increases need for interstate cooperation on global issues; lessens control over cascading events	Lessens confidence in governments; renders nationwide consensus difficult to achieve and maintain
Globalization of national economies	Swells ranks of consumers; promotes uniform tastes; heightens concerns for jobs	Complicates tasks of state governments vis-à-vis markets; promotes business alliances	Intensifies trade and investment conflicts; generates incentives for building global financial institutions	Increases efforts to protect local cultures and industries; facilitates vigor of protest movements

to the relevance of complexity theory for world affairs, and even though much of the book is about matters far removed from the concerns of social science—it is the story of the Santa Fe Institute in New Mexico—the students find the outlines of complexity theory eye-opening and virtually every week of the semester one or another student mentions the book and voices an idea he or she picked up from it. No book I have ever assigned lingers so persistently in the memory banks of students. In the last few years several students have rethought their study plans in the direction of tooling up in computer science.

In sum, I find myself persuaded that the future of our field, its capacity to confront the huge conceptual and methodological challenges that have eluded our generation, lies in the training of those who will enter the field in the future. We need to acknowledge our own limitations and alert those we train to the necessity of their breaking with past paradigmatic assumptions and finding new ways of understanding and probing the enormous challenges posed by the dynamics of change, fragmegration, and micro-macro interactions. If we can orient our students along these lines, the globalization of globalization will have moved on to a higher and more secure analytic plane.

Notes

1. James N. Rosenau, "Comparative Foreign Policy: Fad, Fantasy, or Field?" *International Studies Quarterly* 12 (September 1968): 296–329.
2. Among the exceptions are Barry Buzan and R. J. Barry Jones, eds., *Change and the Study of International Relations: The Evaded Dimension* (London: Pinter, 1981); K. R. Dark, *The Waves of Time: Long-Term Change and International Relations* (London: Pinter, 1998); Joshua Goldstein, *Long Cycles: Prosperity and War in the Modern Age* (New Haven, Conn.: Yale University Press, 1988); K. J. Holsti, *Change in the International System: Essays on the Theory and Practice of International Relations* (Brookfield, Vt.: Elgar, 1991); and George Modelski, *Long Cycles in World Politics* (New York: Macmillan, 1987).
3. The fragmegration concept was first developed in James N. Rosenau, "'Fragmegrative' Challenges to National Security," in *Understanding U.S. Strategy: A Reader*, ed. Terry Heyns (Washington, D.C.: National Defense University, 1983), 65–82. For a subsequent and more elaborate formulation, see James N. Rosenau, *Along the Domestic-Foreign Frontier: Exploring Governance in a Turbulent World* (Cambridge: Cambridge University Press, 1997), chap. 6.
4. See, for example, Stuart Hall, "Old and New Identities, Old and New Ethnicities," in *Culture, Globalization, and the World-System: Contemporary Conditions for the Representation of Identity*, ed. Anthony

D. King (Minneapolis: University of Minnesota Press, 1997); Ulf Han-
nerz, *Transnational Connections: Culture, People, Places* (London:
Routledge, 1996); Arjun Appadurai, *Modernity at Large: Cultural Dimensions of Globalization* (Minneapolis: University of Minnesota Press,
1996); and Kevin R. Cox, ed., *Spaces of Globalization: Reasserting the
Power of the Local* (New York: Guilford Press, 1997). For fragmegrative
analyses by business executives and journalists, see Dee Hock, *Birth of
the Chaordic Age* (San Francisco: Berrett-Koehler, 1999); and Thomas L.
Friedman, *The Lexus and the Olive Tree* (New York: Farrar, Straus and
Giroux, 1999).

5. Among the single-word labels designed to suggest the contradictory tensions that pull systems toward both coherence and collapse are
   "chaord," a label that juxtaposes the dynamics of chaos and order; "glocalization," which points to the simultaneity of globalizing and localizing dynamics; and "regcal," a term designed to focus attention on the
   links between regional and local phenomena. The chaord designation is
   proposed in Hock, *Birth of the Chaordic Age*; the glocalization concept
   is elaborately developed in Roland Robertson, "Glocalization: Time-
   Space and Homogeneity-Heterogeneity," in *Global Modernities*, ed.
   Mike Featherstone, Scott Lash, and Roland Robertson (Thousand Oaks,
   Calif.: Sage, 1995), 25–44; and the regcal formulation can be found in
   Susan H. C. Tai and Y. H. Wong, "Advertising Decision Making in Asia:
   'Glocal' versus 'Regcal' Approach," *Journal of Managerial Issues* 10 (fall
   1998): 318–39. I prefer the term "fragmegration" because it does not
   imply a territorial scale and broadens the focus to include tensions at
   work in organizations as well as those that pervade communities.

6. For a full discussion of the skill revolution as a microdynamic, see James
   N. Rosenau, *Turbulence in World Politics: A Theory of Change and
   Continuity* (Princeton, N.J.: Princeton University Press, 1990), passim.
   For a test of the skill revolution as an empirical hypothesis, see James
   N. Rosenau and W. Michael Fagen, "Increasingly Skillful Citizens: A
   New Dynamism in World Politics?" *International Studies Quarterly* 41
   (December 1997): 655–86.

7. These "scapes" are discussed in Arjun Appadurai, *Modernity at Large:
   Cultural Dimensions of Globalization* (Minneapolis: University of Minnesota Press, 1996), 33–36.

8. For a brief discussion of the eight sources of fragmegration, see James
   N. Rosenau, "Emergent Spaces, New Places, and Old Faces: Proliferating
   Identities in a Globalizing World," in *Worlds on the Move: Globalization, Migration, and Cultural Scarcity*, ed. Jonathan Friedman and Shal-
   ini Randeria (London: I. B. Tauris, forthcoming).

9. J. David Singer, "The Levels-of-Analysis Problem in International Relations," *World Politics* 14 (October 1961): 77–92.

10. See, for example, J. C. Alexander et al., eds., *The Micro-Macro Link*
    (Berkeley: University of California Press, 1987); and K. D. Knorr-Cetina
    and A. V. Cicourel, eds., *Advances in Social Theory and Methodology:
    Toward an Integration of Micro- and Macro-Sociologies* (Boston: Rout-
    ledge and Kegan Paul, 1981).

11. Recently I have undertaken to address the challenge in James N. Rosenau, *Distant Proximities: Dynamics beyond Globalization* (Princeton, N.J.: Princeton University Press, forthcoming).
12. John Markoff, "Tiniest Circuits Hold Prospect of Explosive Computer Speeds," *New York Times*, July 16, 1999, A1.
13. Torchbooks (Simon and Schuster), New York 1992.

FEMINIST THEORY
AND GENDER PERSPECTIVES

THE FISH AND THE TURTLE

Multiple Worlds as Method

L. H. M. Ling

Once upon a time, there lived a colorful and proud little fish. He had lots of friends and loved the water surrounding him. He swam swiftly, quickly, and gracefully—and was very agile at getting his food. One day he met a turtle, an old friend whom he had not seen in a long time.

The fish greeted the turtle. "Hello, Sister Turtle, how are you? I have not seen you in a long time. Where have you been?"

The turtle replied, "I am fine, thank you, Fish. I was away on earth for an errand."

"Oh, really? What is earth? Is there something beyond this lovely water?"

"Very much so."

"What does it look like?"

The turtle paused. It was difficult to find the right words to describe something that the fish had neither experienced nor seen. But the impatient fish interrupted the turtle's thoughts.

"Is earth like water?" "Uh, no. . . ."

"Can you swim in it?" "No."

"Do you feel the same pressure as you go deeper?" "No, it's not like that at all. . . ."

"Does it dance with sparkling lights when the sun shines on it?" "No, not really. . . ."

Impatient, the fish got mad. "I have asked you many questions about earth, and all you can answer is no. As far as I am concerned, that earth of

Many thanks to Anna M. Agathangelou, Celine M. Larkin, Thanh-Dam Truong, and Augusta del Zotto for their comments on this paper. The paper was prepared for a millennial reflections panel on feminist theory and gender studies held at the annual meeting of the International Studies Association, Los Angeles, Calif., March 15–20, 2000.

yours does not exist." And with a disdainful flash of his colorful tail, he swam proudly away.

The turtle sighed, "How can one know something *new* when one's questions are based on the prejudices of the *old*?"[1]

This Vietnamese folktale illustrates for me the central *problematique* facing our discipline of international relations (IR) today: multiple worlds and how to know them. In the case of IR, the fish is more like a whale. The latter not only rules the seas; it can experience another life above the sea—when it surfaces to spout, for example—but chooses not to recognize it as so.

For too long, the whale of IR—realism[2]—has subjected our discipline to an illusory universalism propagated through notions of power and the state. Though many states now populate our "international system" and each exercises power within its limits, these facts alone do not verify the claim that, therefore, every state is the same and acts on power in the same way. Doing so would require two, related corollaries: (1) state making and power construction are identical processes across time and space *because* (2) the Westphalian interstate system has succeeded in eradicating all previous "imagined communities" of clan, tribe, nation, language, religion, and/or civilization. Precisely because this is not so (September 11 is the latest example), realists vow to renew the fight against "instability," "pariahs," and "the clash of civilizations."

Feminists and other critical theorists have led the charge against such realist one-worldism.[3] First, they have identified this perspective as precisely that. Neither an objective law of nature nor an intrinsic element of the human condition, realist one-worldism is but one *representation* of the world. Its longevity relies on a deceptively simple self-justification: that is, because realists believe that the world is nasty, brutish, lonely, poor, and short, they behave accordingly, thereby ensuring that the world is indeed so, which in turn affirms their belief that the world is nasty, brutish, lonely, poor, and short. Meanwhile, realists proclaim loudly their goal of averting a global holocaust by entrenching us further into this one-world logic—of which the latest manifestation is rational choice theory.

More than other critical theorists, feminists have exposed the inherently *gendered* nature of such world making. Not only is realist one-worldism a social construction, but it reflects the experiences, practices, norms, and institutions of a particularly small segment of the world's population: propertied, white males. What traditional IR has passed off as "universal" or "human," feminists have pointed out, should be described more accurately as "particular" and "androcentric." For this reason, IR as a field of study and practice implicitly discriminates against anyone who does not or cannot abide by realism's version of hegemonic masculinity—even those bodies that may be white, male, propertied, and even heterosexual but who may subscribe to an alternative logic of understanding or constructing the world.

In this sense, feminists have highlighted at least two worlds operating in IR: one of men, masculinity, and patriarchy and a second, *hidden* one of women, femininity, and matriarchy. Cutting-edge theorists like Cynthia Weber have deconstructed this binary further to include a "queer," third world of blurred pairings between men/women, masculinity/femininity, patriarchy/matriarchy.[4] In her analysis of U.S. foreign policy toward five Caribbean neighbors (Cuba, Dominican Republic, Grenada, Panama, Haiti), Weber has found a consistent resort to hypermasculine tactics (invasion, bombing, kidnapping, embargo) on the part of the U.S. government to cover for a sense of national emasculation that burns from unrequited desire. Similarly, in my own work,[5] I have shown how the West's historical conviction that Asia must be a woman who should be conquered (with Puccini's *Madame Butterfly* as cultural exemplar) actually reveals a quaking, lovesick, inverted Western Butterfly who wants nothing more than to be *loved* by the Oriental Other (with David Henry Hwang's *M. Butterfly* as counterexemplar).

Herein lies the challenge for feminist and critical theorizing in IR. While feminist theorizing has helped us realize the world's gendered split and multiple personalities, we need further explorations into *other worlds and their ways of world making*. Postcolonial feminists, for instance, have surfaced a deep-sea "whale" within liberal (white, Western) feminism.[6] It proclaims "global sisterhood" for all but denies equal standing for nonliberal (nonwhite, non-Western) feminisms and feminists.[7] Liberal feminism presumes that gender supersedes race, class, and culture, thereby allocating one categorical patriarchy to rule over all. Doing so effectively upholds a de facto hegemonic identity that is white, heterosexual, and North American/western European.[8] In silencing unequal power relations *among* women, liberal feminism reframes "difference" into the familiar model of "pluralism." That is, while difference acknowledges deeply embedded, multiple "lifeworlds" in constituting who and what we are, pluralism cares not for the content of such lifeworlds but merely recognizes their form. Indeed, according to Anthony Arblaster, "inclusion" in liberal theory historically means tolerance of, not acceptance of or, more important, engagement with difference.[9]

This pluralist logic invariably objectifies women, despite feminist avowals to the contrary. Celebratory of a linear, progressive logic of capitalist development, it returns Third World women (including those in the First World) to a center/periphery dichotomy. White women always sit comfortably in the center while Others either "crouch" (to use Frantz Fanon's famous characterization of the colonized) covetously on the periphery or straddle precipitously on the "borderlands" of multiple worlds.[10] Such hegemonic self-involvement loses out on potential alliances that could be forged *among* feminists who, despite their differences, still share a common purpose in social emancipation. Equally important, such hegemonic self-involvement prohibits learning about who and what *we* are.

Accordingly, the question remains: *how* to know multiple worlds, let alone communicate across them? Various strategies have been suggested: "strong objectivity,"[11] cultural "conversations,"[12] "empathetic cooperation,"[13] "mobile subjectivities,"[14] cultural "traveling."[15] These efforts are reinforced by a greater recognition of "contact zones"[16] between cultures—specifically those of colonizer and colonized—that allow their common progeny to "autoethnographize" their own subjectivities.

Even so, the concept of subjectivity remains unitary. Despite all this "traveling," "conversing," "cooperating," "mobilizing," or "autoethnographizing," an implicit assumption still holds: that is, subjectivity as an analytical unit may be multiplied—even "deconstructed"—to reflect greater complexity in real-life experience, but it remains intact as a core or essential source of difference. Harding's notion of "strong objectivity" serves as an apt example. She calls for an additive approach to multicultural knowledge: that is, by hearing from more voices, especially those that have been silenced or marginalized, we may "know" more. But the very condition of communicating across multiple worlds induces an intimate *mixing* of subjectivities, where the Self's boundaries begin to blur with those of the Other. Distinct labels like "southern," "minority," or "Other" do not simply *add* to more familiar ones like "northern," "majority," or "Self." Instead, the interaction between these two identities triggers the eventual rise of a third, hybrid subjectivity. It compels a recognition that the southern, minority, Other exists in part *within* the northern, majority, Self, and vice versa.

Put in terms of the folktale that opened this essay, we need the fish and the turtle, first and foremost, to continue their mutual inquiry.[17] But the turtle needs to speak up. It cannot just react to the impatient fish/whale's questions that, essentially, reconstruct the unfamiliar in terms of the familiar, thereby never getting access to the unfamiliar.[18] The turtle needs to show the fish/whale how to "see" the other, unfamiliar world through its *relationship* to the familiar one. (Alas, epistemological richness is both a privilege and a burden!) The turtle can best accomplish this task by discarding the temptation to objectify either Self or Other as distinct identities. Instead, we must recognize history as it *is* and *always has been*:[19] a constant process of hybrid world making to ensure survival.[20] For her part, the turtle needs to search within her own subjectivity for that commonality that binds all turtles, fishes, and whales. The fish/whale, in turn, should *listen*, patiently and openly, while developing a method or hermeneutic of *asking questions*.[21] These must pertain to the turtle's knowledge, rather than reaffirm what the fish/whale already knows. For such knowledge is not just an interesting aside that adds spice to life, nor does it simply cumulate information for predictive purposes, nor is it the "right" or "fair" thing to do. Rather, the turtle's wisdom helps the fish/whale *survive better* in a universe of multiple worlds, each fraught with hazardous rocks, coasts, currents, and beaches. For this reason alone, the fish/whale has a vested interest in forgoing age-old hierarchies of anarchy/order, center/periphery, Self/Other, or masculinity/femininity. The whale of IR must learn, finally, that these offer the mere illusion, rather than actuality, of power and control.

Notes

1. Many thanks to Thanh-Dam Truong for recounting this folktale to me.
2. By realism, I refer to the classical tradition of Hans Morgenthau and Henry Kissinger but also include its latest variant: neoliberal institutionalism.
3. Ann Tickner has characterized this condition of nonunderstanding between conventional and critical/feminist IR theorists as one of talking across whole worlds. Robert Keohane has taken this gap to mean the difference between problem-solving theory (which accepts the world as is) and critical theory (which seeks to change the world). As a counter to Tickner, he cited Hans Morgenthau as one realist who problem solved in order to change the world. But Tickner's point, reinforced here, was that Morgenthau and other like-minded realists still believed in *one* world. Hence, whether he sought to change the world or not was irrel-

evant. Ultimately, Morgenthau subscribed to an authoritarian assumption *about* the world. J. A. Tickner, "You Just Don't Understand: Troubled Engagements between Feminists and IR Theorists," *International Studies Quarterly* 41 (1997): 611–32; R. O. Keohane, "Beyond Dichotomy: Conversations between International Relations and Feminist Theory," *International Studies Quarterly* 42 (1998): 193–98.

4. C. Weber, *Faking It: U.S. Hegemony in a "Post-Phallic" Era* (Minneapolis: University of Minnesota Press, 2000).

5. L. H. M. Ling, *Postcolonial International Relations: Conquest and Desire between Asia and the West* (London: Palgrave, 2001).

6. This critique could be applied to Marxian feminism as well. But liberal feminism takes the brunt of this charge given its spread through neoliberal globalization in the world today.

7. Well-known feminists like Susan Moller Okin and Martha Nussbaum, for example, have argued that only Western liberalism can "save" Third World women from their Third World traditions. Neither recognizes that there are elements of Third World traditions that may be as emancipatory as their own liberal one, nor that Western liberalism may be as incarcerating as some Third World traditions. S. M. Okin, "Is Multiculturalism Bad for Women?" in *Is Multiculturalism Bad for Women? Susan Moller Okin with Respondents*, ed. J. Cohen, M. Howard, and M. C. Nussbaum (Princeton, N.J.: Princeton University Press, 1999), 7–26; M. Nussbaum, introduction and "Emotions and Women's Capabilities," in *Women, Culture, and Development*, ed. M. Nussbaum and J. Glover (Oxford, England: Clarendon, 1995), 1–15, 360–95.

8. This hegemonic subjectivity excludes even those descendants of white, heterosexual, North American/western Europeans in former colonial locations like Australia, New Zealand, and Latin America. Similarly, it exiles those from transitional societies in Russia and eastern Europe who may be categorized as racially "white" but considered "Third World" politically, economically, and culturally.

9. A. Arblaster, *The Rise and Decline of Western Liberalism* (London: Basil Blackwell, 1984).

10. While we should not ignore the pain, confusion, and sheer tediousness of those caught "in between" or belonging to "neither-nor" worlds (see C. Moraga and G. Anzaldua, eds., *This Bridge Called My Back* [New York: Kitchen Table, Women of Color Press, 1983]), neither should we project a glorious "centeredness" for those who are not considered "ethnics," "minorities," or "Third World." Such a presumption is not only self-defeating ("we are never centered") but also inaccurate. R. W. Connell has shown in his work on masculinities that even those who are supposedly the most centered in today's world—heterosexual, white men—face similar dilemmas of dealing with a societally imposed identity that may conflict with or undermine their personal subjectivity. R. W. Connell, *Masculinities* (Berkeley: University of California Press, 1996).

11. S. Harding, *Is Science Multicultural?* (Bloomington: Indiana University Press, 1998).

12. D. L. Blaney and I. Inayatullah, "Prelude to a Conversation of Cultures in International Society? Todorov and Nandy on the Possibility of Dialogue," *Alternatives* 19 (1994): 23–51.

13. C. Sylvester, *Feminist Theory and International Relations in a Postmodern Era* (Cambridge: Cambridge University Press, 1994).

14. K. Ferguson, *The Man Question* (Berkeley: University of California Press, 1993).

15. Moraga and Anzaldua, *This Bridge Called My Back.*

16. M. L. Pratt, *Imperial Eyes* (London: Routledge, 1992).

17. In this sense, the dialogue between Keohane ("Beyond Dichotomy: Conversations between International Relations and Feminist Theory") and Tickner is a good beginning. Tickner, "You Just Don't Understand," 611–32.

18. Keohane's continued attempt to reframe feminist IR into conventional positivist categories of hypothesis testing and question formation, despite avowals to the contrary, is but one example of this. Keohane, "Beyond Dichotomy."

19. As Stuart Hall noted: "In this 'post-colonial' moment, these transverse, transnational, transcultural movements, which were always inscribed in the history of 'colonisation,' but carefully overwritten by more binary forms of narrativisation, have, of course, emerged in new forms to disrupt the settled relations of domination and resistance inscribed in other ways of living and telling these stories." S. Hall, "When was 'the Post-Colonial'? Thinking at the Limit," in *The Post-Colonial Question: Common Skies, Divided Horizons*, ed. Iain Chambers and Lidia Curti (London: Routledge, 1996), 251.

20. For example, Robert Wright has posited that evolution favors systems that figure out ways of coexistence, rather than the old Darwinian model of survival of the fittest. R. Wright, *The Moral Animal: Evolutionary Psychology and Everyday Life* (New York: Vintage Books, 1995).

21. Trinh T. Minh-ha has described this as an attitude of learning through indirection: "One can only approach things indirectly. Because, in doing so, one not only goes toward the subject of one's focus without killing it, but one also allows oneself to get acquainted with the envelope, that is, all the elements which surround, situate or simply relate to it." Trinh T. Minh-ha (in conversation with Annamaria Morelli), "The Undone Interval," in Chambers and Curti, *The Post-Colonial Question*, 4. Gayatri Chakravorty Spivak has offered another suggestion. It would apply to all "Selves" coping with their "Others": "Rather than imagining that women automatically have something identifiable in common, why not say, humbly and practically, my first obligation in understanding solidarity is to learn her mother-tongue. You will see immediately what the differences are. You will also feel the solidarity every day as you make the attempt to learn the language in which the other woman learnt to recognize reality at her mother's knee. This is preparation for the intimacy of cultural translation." Quoted in C. Bulbeck, *Re-Orienting Western Feminisms: Women's Diversity in a Postcolonial World* (Cambridge: Cambridge University Press, 1998), vi.

ON THE CUT(TING) EDGE

V. Spike Peterson

I would first like to thank the editors for inviting me to contribute to the Millennial Reflections Project. In preparing my remarks I have had the benefit of reading the essays presented at the "Feminist Theory and Gender Studies" and "Alternative and Critical Perspectives" panels. Indeed, my remarks often build on points elaborated by my colleagues and are especially indebted to Marysia Zalewski's essay. The latter inspired the themes and the title of my own contribution. Rather than repeat arguments already articulated, my essay focuses on identifying the strengths of feminist international relations (IR)—what renders it "cutting edge"—and considering how these strengths are related to the successes of feminisms and feminist IR. I will also consider how these very strengths of feminisms are related to the "failures" of feminist IR—what renders it "cut"—in relation to mainstream IR. In other words, I wish to explore more fully Zalewski's key insight: that feminisms' strengths explain both why and how feminist IR is cutting edge and why and how it also gets cut by the mainstream. Finally, I will consider these strengths in relation to the current state of IR and cutting-edge horizons.

Feminisms and Feminist IR

Before proceeding, I feel obliged to clarify in my own words how feminisms constitute a wide spectrum of analytical and political positions. A variety of overlapping feminist projects constitute a continuum that spans positivist and "alternative" (postpositivist, poststructuralist) orientations. Typically, feminist interventions in any discipline begin by exposing the omission of actual women and their activities, while also documenting how "woman" is represented as deviant from or deficient in respect to male-as-norm criteria. For example, the model of human nature (as atomistic, self-interested, acquisitive, and competitive) that underpins the dominant discourse in IR is in fact based upon interpretations by and of a particular subset of humans (elite males) in a particular context (modern Europe). Hence, these are suspicious as universalizing claims about *all* humans—or even all males—at all times.

Probably the most familiar feminist work involves the subsequent project that "corrects" androcentric bias by asking "where are women and gender?" in the context of conventional topics.[1] "Adding women" exposes the androcentric assumptions of conventional accounts, inserts actual (embodied) women in our picture of "reality," and reveals women as agents and activists, as well as victims of violence and the poorest of the poor. But it also, and significantly, forces a rethinking of foundational categories by revealing the extent to which excluding women/femininity is a fundamental structuring principle of conventional thought. Indeed, women cannot simply be "added" to concepts and categories that are constitutively masculine: the public sphere, the military, rationality, political identity, objectivity. Either women as feminine cannot be added (that is, women must become like men) or the constructions themselves are transformed (that is, adding women as feminine alters masculine premises and conceptual boundaries).

For many feminists, these studies reveal gender as not simply a trait of embodied individuals but a historically institutionalized, *structural* feature of social life: it is a socially imposed and internalized "lens" through which individuals perceive themselves and the world, *and* the pervasiveness of gendered meanings shapes concepts, practices, identities, and institutions in patterned ways. In short, gender is not simply an empirical category referring to substantive men and women but an *analytical* category, pervasively shaping how we conceptualize, think, and "know." How we think, of course, both shapes and is shaped by who we (think we) are, how we relate and act, and what we do. Understanding gender as an analytical category enables feminists to criticize not only the exclusion and/or denigration of females (as a sex category) but also the masculinist constructs that underpin philosophy (reason, abstraction), political theory (atomistic individualism, sovereignty), economic models (waged labor, rational choice), and science (objectivity, dichotomies). It thus links "women" and gender in the more complex project of reconstructing theory.

As we move along the continuum, feminisms focus less on sex as an empirical variable and more on exploring the interdependence of masculine-feminine, the centrality of gendered identities, and the significance of gender in how we conceptualize and theorize. Conventional categories and dichotomies are not taken for granted but problematized, and there is more attention to symbols, discourse, foundational claims, epistemologies, and theoretical debates. The point here is to reiterate that feminisms are not only about "adding women"—as an empirical category—to existing frameworks and the IR mainstream. These are crucial projects, but understanding gender *only* as an empirical category misses too much of what makes feminisms intellectually exciting and politically transformative. Perhaps we could even say that it is gender as an *analytical* category that makes feminisms truly cutting edge.

Feminist IR as Analytically and Politically Cutting Edge

Zalewski identifies feminisms as cutting edge because they so thoroughly destabilize "what we think we already know and how we know it."[2] In this sense, feminisms force us to reexamine presumed givens and stretch us to address the resulting "shake up" of "conventional ideas about subjectivity, epistemology, ontology, agency and political action in IR." What I want to explore in more detail is how feminisms and more specifically, feminist IR, are cutting edge both analytically *and* politically.[3] I will subsequently consider how this positions feminist IR positively and negatively in relation to mainstream IR.

Analytically

There are numerous interweaving threads in the claim that feminisms are cutting edge and also destabilizing.[4] First, given that gendered identities, bodies, concepts, and practices *permeate* social relations and empirical conditions, the study of gender requires and produces transdisciplinary orientations. We can observe that institutionally (if not intellectually or ideologically), conventional disciplines tend toward conceptual and methodological reification. This suits certain purposes (e.g., cumulative knowledge claims, or

Cox's "problem-solving" theory) and inhibits others (e.g., diachronic reflection, or Cox's "critical theory"). An extensive literature argues the advantages and disadvantages of each. Not surprisingly, cutting-edge work is favored by (but not exclusive to) transdisciplinary orientations insofar as these by definition stretch or transgress familiar and often constraining boundaries. Similarly, transdisciplinary scholars are more likely to be exposed to, and therefore be aware of and engaged with, a plurality of methods and interdisciplinary debates, and these conditions favor (without ensuring!) an epistemological sophistication that is less required or cultivated by monodisciplinary orientations. As one consequence, from transdisciplinary starting points feminists generate more wide-ranging and encompassing analyses of social relations. For example, in their study of world politics feminists draw upon and link areas of inquiry (e.g., developmental psychology, family relations, domestic violence, welfare economics, heterosexist religion, ecological issues) neglected in mainstream accounts. Providing a different example, Christine Sylvester notes how Cynthia Enloe "spots the internationally destined woman as body beautiful—Carmen Miranda—*and* links it to international trade in tropical fruits *and* discusses it in the context of America's Good Neighbor Policy of yesteryear *and* also says something about land reform in Latin American development strategies."[5]

As these examples suggest, the ubiquity of gender prompts feminists to transgress not only disciplinary boundaries but the boundaries separating public and private and "levels of analysis"—boundaries that are paradigmatic in political science and IR. For example, feminists examine how individual internalization of gender stereotypes (e.g., masculinity as competitive, unemotional, and "in control") interacts with sociocultural inputs (e.g., patriarchal religious beliefs, pornography, violent entertainment) and with gendered divisions of labor (e.g., politics and the military as "men's work") to fuel international relations that are competitive and conflictual (e.g., dominated by competitive men seeking autonomy and control through direct and indirect violence). This linking of the personal (and psychological) to the cultural, political, and international is especially well developed in feminist studies of nationalism, which exemplify feminisms' cutting-edge status in relation to analyses of identity.[6]

As Jindy Pettman notes in her essay, "feminists have particular interests and investments in the politics of identification, with gender and sexuality crucial components in themselves, as well as constituting and marking other boundaries and power relations."⁷ Whereas feminists have an enduring interest in the politics of identity, scholars in political science and IR have conventionally neglected these areas of inquiry. Until recently, the latter disciplines tended to take for granted both a Eurocentric model of the modern subject (identified as unitary, autonomous, interest maximizing, and rational) and a (Eurocentric) spatial model of public sphere agency and territorial states. In these accounts, the dichotomy of public-private locates political action and identity in one but not the other sphere; the dichotomy of internal-external distinguishes the identity of citizens and order within from "Others" and anarchy without; and the dichotomy of culture-nature (civilized-primitive, advanced-backward, developed-undeveloped) "naturalizes" First and Third World identities coded by uneven geopolitical power.

Empirical and epistemological transformations challenge the adequacy of these conventional accounts. In terms of the former, state-centric political identity increasingly shares the stage with nonterritorial claimants. Subnational and transnational social movements transgress territorial boundaries in favor of identities "grounded" on ecological, antinuclear, ethnic, feminist, religious, and other non-state-based commitments. Uneven flows of information, culture, people, technology, and capital involve human migrations and diasporic identities that complicate territorial frames of reference. The globalization of production and finance undercuts national economic planning, eroding state sovereignty and the political identities it presupposes, even as supranational forces alter state power and subnational conflicts expose the illusion of homogeneity promoted in nationalist narratives. In short, identities conventionally "grounded" in state territoriality are losing ground to a politics of new or even "non" space(s). In terms of epistemological transformations, critiques of positivist empiricism have altered our understanding of agents, identity, and subjectivity. In contrast to the modernist conception of a unitary rational actor, contemporary social theory illuminates the multiplicity of subject locations (implying multiple identifications) and their dynamic interaction "within" the self *and* in relation to the self's environment. In short, identities are socially constructed as ongoing processes: they are embedded in and interact with historically specific social contexts composed of intersubjective meaning systems, practices, institutional structures, and material conditions. Hence, the study of identities must be historical, contextual, and dynamic: asking not only how identities are located in time and space but also how they are (re)produced, resisted, and reconfigured. These remarks suggest that any cutting-edge scholarship must engage the theory and practice of identity, identification, and subjectivity, and feminists are at the forefront of such work.

It is not simply that attention to identity raises issues that are typically neglected in mainstream accounts (where positivist-empiricist orientations marginalize them as psychological, private sphere, emotional, and too subjective). It is also that feminists bring identity and subjectivity *into relation* with more familiar features of mainstream study. My own work casts this relational orientation as an alternative analytical framing, or "triad analytics." The latter posits identities, social practices/institutions, and meaning systems as three co-constituting dimensions of social reality. More specifically, it juxtaposes "who we are" (identity, subjectivity, sexuality, allegiance, etc.), "what we do" (actions, practices, social structures, etc.), and "how we think" (concepts, discourse, ideology, etc.). This triadic framing moves away from dichotomized constructions in favor of understanding the material (empirical, structural) and symbolic (analytical, discursive) relationally, that is, as *interdependent* (mutually constituting), and it insists that "what we do" and "how we think" are also inextricable from "who we are." It thus affords an interactive, multilevel, multivariable, and transdisciplinary orientation and can facilitate conversations among diverse theoretical perspectives. On the one hand, the triad makes reference to, or can be linked with, features of social life that are familiar in modernist, positivist, and critical accounts (e.g., agents, ideology, institutions). On the other hand, the triad takes subject formation seriously, privileges relational rather than dichotomized analytics, and "opens new spaces" for theory/practice; these are "moves" more familiar in critical and "alternative" accounts.

To return to an earlier example, consider how gender is a structural feature of nationalist projects in codetermining senses: the identities mobilized in nationalist activities are gender differentiated (resolute leaders, supportive caretakers); the practices of nationalism are gender differentiated (men at the war front, women at the home front), and the symbols and discourse of nationalism are deeply gendered (masculine protectors of the motherland, feminine signifiers of the nation and cultural identity). We see these relationships horrifically at work in the example of rape as a weapon of war. "Men" are expected to defend their motherland and protect "their women."

Rape is not only a metaphor of national humiliation, suggesting the failure of men to defend their territory and the loss of manhood in defeat, but also an embodied practice whereby the Other threatens group reproduction by impregnating the group's women with "alien" seed. Ethnonationalist conflicts in the 1990s have demonstrated all too well how rape is a weapon of war, how performing gender identities involves violence, and how the female body is not only figuratively but literally a battleground. In short, the gendering of nationalisms is not a coincidence but integral to how we identify with, think about, and go about making war.

The point here is that feminisms are cutting edge analytically in part because they are transdisciplinary, translevel, and multidimensional, in part because they pioneered studies of identity, and in part because they address complexity through innovative and relational analytics. The nationalism example begins to suggest the linkages between feminisms as cutting edge not just analytically but politically.

Politically

Feminists acknowledge that their work is informed by normative/political commitments. The specifics of that commitment vary tremendously, but the very acknowledgment of a commitment to "improving the conditions of women" links and strengthens feminists even as it also works against feminist projects by fueling resistance from those who deny the politics of all knowledge claims or denounce gender equality.

By definition and conviction, then, feminists are engaged in critical studies, analyzing and resisting status quo masculinism and gender hierarchy. But self-reflection and critical politics are integral to feminist theory/practice in several additional senses. First, like all marginalized and subordinated groups, feminists must be consciously "political" if they are to survive, much less prosper, in a typically indifferent and frequently hostile environment. For feminist academics, this involves career- and life-defining trade-offs in the pursuit of research, publishing, professional, personal, teaching, mentoring, and activist priorities. An important consideration is how the need to build and sustain an institutional/professional presence for feminist IR diverts precious time from more "serious" (read: research and publishing) activities. Given uninstructed and resistant audiences, feminists must also spend precious time defending their research orientation and repeating basic argumentation, which depletes time available for forging ahead with an expansive research agenda. The lived politics of this struggle are part of what my colleagues mean by debating whether to "ask feminist questions in IR" or "IR questions in feminism."[8]

Second, and very significantly, the diversity among women has forced feminists to reflect critically (and uncomfortably) on the meaning of feminism, definitions of "woman," the politics of representation, and the dangers of universalizing claims. "Sisterhood" aspirations have always been in tension with differences of ethnicity/race, class, age, physical ability, sexuality, and nationality, especially so in the global context that engages feminist IR. As Lily Ling reminds us, postcolonial feminists "have surfaced a deep-sea 'whale' within liberal (white, Western) feminism [that] proclaims 'global sisterhood' for all but denies equal standing for nonliberal (nonwhite, non-Western) feminisms and feminists."[9]

However one assesses the success or failure of feminisms to address the challenges of difference, I believe feminists have taken those challenges more seriously, and moved more responsibly to address them, than most oppositional groups. This is due in part to taking their commitment to social justice seriously (an uneven record) and in part, I believe, to the unique situation of feminists in the academy. Struggling with these complicated and arduous challenges, feminists both drew upon and expanded their transdisciplinary orientations and, especially, their analyses of identity and identification. These were somewhat unique resources, and the resulting scholarship is surely one of feminisms' claims to cutting-edge status. At the same time, addressing these questions involved analytical development in additional respects, for example, in regard to ontological claims, epistemological debates, and theoretical advances. No less significant, addressing these questions involved developments in political practice, for example, in regard to movement priorities, organizational politics, and long-term, "big picture" strategies.

What I want to emphasize is the inextricable link between analytics and politics, which is especially evident in feminist theory/practice in regard to structural hierarchies. On the one hand, feminisms have transdisciplinary and complex analytical resources for investigating and theorizing about identity, difference, and historically specific hierarchies of oppression (heterosexism, racism, classism, etc.). On the other hand, feminist claims to political relevance and critique have "forced" them to address embodied differences of power: compared with other academic units, feminist scholars are expected to "walk" their (egalitarian) "talk." In struggling to do so, feminists draw on and expand their analytical resources, and generate cutting-edge analyses of hierarchical power.

The particular contribution I have in mind demonstrates these points and illustrates the transformative implications of gender as an analytical category. I refer to the feminist analysis of gender hierarchy as fundamental to domination in its *many* guises. Viewed empirically, females suffer disproportionally under systems of domination insofar as females constitute one-half of most subordinated groups and are systematically rendered more vulnerable to sexual and other violence, inadequate health care, political subordination, and economic impoverishment. Viewed analytically, the naturalization of women's oppression—taking gender hierarchy as "given" rather than historically, politically constructed—*serves* as the model for depoliticizing exploitation more generally, whether of groups or of nature. That is, feminists argue that the subordination of women and femininity to men and that which is privileged as masculine is not "natural" or inevitable—as it is typically represented—but socially constructed and historically contingent. Dominant (masculinist) ways of thinking, however, naturalize the marginalization, objectification, and corollary exploitation of all who are denigrated by association with the feminine: not only "women" but also nature, racialized minorities, effeminate men, and colonized Others. The ostensible "naturalness" of sex difference and masculine dominance is thus generalized to other forms of domination, which has the effect of legitimating them as equally "natural" hierarchies. Eliminating the justification of oppression as natural does not eliminate oppression, nor preclude other justifications of it. But the ideology that treats hierarchies as natural serves powerfully to legitimate and reproduce domination: through the internalization of oppression, the silencing of protest, and the depoliticization of exploitative rule and global hierarchies.[10]

In this crucial sense, feminist critiques are not simply about male-female relations but about all social hierarchies that are naturalized (depoliticized, legitimated) by denigration of the feminine. The transformative insight that this affords is that "adding women" (as an empirical category) may be an effective strategy for improving the lives of (some) "women," but it falls far short of taking gender (as an analytical category) seriously. The latter entails deconstructing the naturalization of structural hierarchies in their multiple (and intersecting) forms. Hence, it involves improving the lives of *all*—not just women—whose oppression is naturalized by denigration of the feminine.

The point here is the uniqueness of feminisms in transforming an initial critique of patriarchy into cutting-edge theory/practice that not only takes difference seriously and analyzes the intersection of structural hierarchies but also informs and enacts emancipatory political practice. Perhaps we could even say that this constitutes "progress"?

Feminist IR as the Cut Edge

Zalewski identifies feminisms as "cut" by the IR mainstream because destabilizing "what we think we already know and how we know it" is not attractive to all knowers (or to any knower at all times). Considered through conventional IR lenses, the transgression of disciplinary boundaries, of public-private divides, or of levels of analysis is typically not even considered worthwhile, much less applauded. For those steeped in positivist empiricism, identities and subjectivities are detours at best, derailments at worst, in the pursuit of "objective" social science. Moreover, embracing complexity and framing analyses relationally are unlikely—even counterproductive—paths if one is seeking parsimonious explanation. In short, what renders feminisms analytically cutting edge effectively cuts them out of the picture framed by dominant starting points in IR.

Similarly, acknowledging the politics of making knowledge claims is not a commonplace in IR. There are several overlapping issues here. First, positivist commitments preclude such acknowledgment and prevent discussions of power in epistemological debates. Quite simply, it is deemed epistemologically "incorrect" to associate knowledge with power. Second, positivist disavowal of power cultivates a silence in regard to power at work in the discipline and its disciplining practices. We rarely hear the mainstream engage in critique of gatekeeping practices; old boy networks; U.S. dominance of the discipline; or race, gender, class, and nationality exclusions. Quite simply, privilege seems to be taken for granted and not interrogated, as if differential power were not of interest in the study of world politics (!) or had no effect on the quality of our scholarship and our collective lives. Third, insofar as allegiance to specific political commitments/policies is acknowledged, liberalism (in the broadest sense) would seem to be the norm among the mainstream. Suffice it to say that this is a limited breeding ground for activists seeking structural transformation, and it is little surprise that the mainstream literature is so muted in regard to self-reflection or radical critique. In short, what renders feminisms politically cutting edge is cut down as suspicious and inappropriate by a mainstream that claims its knowledge is apolitical, its privilege is either irrelevant or unproblematic, and its desire for change is limited.

That IR has little time for the cutting edge of feminisms is not to say that it cuts out all feminisms or all contributions of feminist IR. By reference to the continuum identified earlier, IR feminists have been especially productive in regard to research and publications that "add women" to existing frames of reference. Simply making this research available makes a difference in the discipline: for giving feminism and gender questions visibility; for easier access to empirical data and feminist analyses; for encouraging would-be feminist graduate students and scholars; and for adding feminist materials to mainstream courses and expanding resources for specifically feminist courses. Given the distance we have traveled in little more than a decade, and the variety of obstacles we have confronted, I consider these no small successes. We earned them the hard way and are right to be proud of them.

But even work that simply adds women and thus conforms to the discipline's preferred empirical methods has a limited impact on the mainstream insofar as the latter remains focused on traditional topics where women are "apparently" absent: politics, foreign policy, military and security activities. In the absence of more complex understandings of power, the intersection of public and private, the force of identity politics, and so on, adding women does little to affect mainstream analyses. Stated differently, as long as IR understands gender only as an empirical category (e.g., how do women in the military affect the conduct of war?), feminisms appear largely irrelevant to the discipline's primary questions and inquiry.

Understanding gender as an analytical category opens up entirely new areas and reframes old questions (e.g., how does masculinism affect—even entail—warring identities, attitudes, and practices?). But positivist commitments preclude seeing, much less appreciating, this expanded and admittedly less stable terrain. In the absence of a willingness to transgress conventional boundaries and deconstruct foundational dichotomies, gender as an analytical category is "out of sight" for the mainstream of IR. More specifically, the intellectually exciting and politically transformative work in feminist IR *theory* is effectively invisible because it is outside of what the mainstream can *see* through positivist and politically conservative lenses.[11]

Conclusion: Feminisms, Feminist IR, IR, and the Future

With many of my feminist and alternative theory colleagues, I am persuaded that positivist commitments[12] dominating the discipline are a major impediment to more productive conversations between feminists (many of whom subscribe to alternative perspectives), alternative theorists (some of whom are feminists), and the IR mainstream (who differ among themselves, but share key epistemological commitments). In particular, these commitments prevent understanding of gender as an analytical category and foreclose the openings and transformations this insight provides. That I consider this situation a loss for all concerned, and devastating for the quality and relevance of our scholarship, is no surprise. But what is to be done?[13]

Although feminist work has had a limited impact, and abandoning IR terrain in favor of "asking IR questions in feminism" has a certain logic (and emotional appeal!), there are good reasons for continuing to "ask feminist questions in IR." It is important to remember that limited impact is not the same as no impact, and I believe that IR *needs* feminist and other critical interventions. First, continuing to work "within IR" is important for the differences it already makes and will continue to make. Not least among these is the availability of feminist IR (and other critical studies) as an area of inquiry for students and an academic option for graduates. In the absence of more transdisciplinary offerings and job placements, building critical subfields directly benefits participants and indirectly promotes changes in the mainstream.

Second, IR as a discipline needs to enhance its analytical contributions to our understanding of the world(s) we live in, and feminisms have important resources to share in this regard. Given the importance of transnational and global dynamics in our lives today, one might expect that IR would be the prominent discipline offering sophisticated analyses of these dynamics and possible responses to them. That this is not the case is due in part to epistemological starting points and analytical frameworks that preclude socially relevant questions being asked and limit the political relevance of explanations delivered. IR's analytical toolkit is demonstrably inadequate. In spite of the strengths of conventional approaches, their glaring failure to predict the collapse of communism suggests important limitations, even if the scale of local-national-regional-global problems and the accelerating pace of change did not otherwise demand revising and expanding our analytical capacities. The world "needs" more adequate and more relevant analytics in regard to globalization, and IR should be one important source of these. Perhaps we could even say that IR must take the cutting edge more seriously if it is to be relevant as a substantive area of inquiry and as a contributor to contemporary social theory.

Third, and related, IR as practice has important political effects, yet the discipline (in contrast to many feminisms)[14] engages in little self-reflection about its role in reproducing power relations. Consider the lack of attention to structural hierarchies and exclusionary practices within the discipline, as reflected, for example, in the organization and composition of the millennial reflections panels. Let me say first that the inclusion of feminist and alternative panels was no doubt well intended, and panel participants acknowledged this. But they also pointed out that "separate" panels effectively reproduces a division between mainstream panels engaging in "real" research and "Other" panels doing whatever it is that they do. Even more telling is the composition of the panels: of forty-eight participants "only five are from outside North America, and only ten are women."[15] Racial diversity is not quantified here, but it seems reasonable to note that diversity has not traditionally been a prominent feature of International Studies Association meetings, its mainstream panels, or its leadership rosters. This is not to deny that many individuals bemoan these conditions and that small efforts are made to "improve the numbers"—but we can hardly claim that racial diversity is a priority for the association or the discipline more generally.

Of particular concern (and effectively reproducing these conditions), is how racism *as a feature of international relations*—that is, as worthy of study—appears almost nowhere in mainstream scholarship. A growing number of critical, postcolonial, and feminist scholars, myself included, argue that this "omission" is especially indefensible in today's world. When we "leave race aside," we not only produce deficient scholarship but we also are complicit in reproducing structural oppression. And we know that structural oppression—whatever other factors must also be recognized—is key to conflict both within and between nation-states. In short, however great the strengths of conventional approaches, their glaring failure to take racism (and other structural oppressions) seriously has impaired our analyses of power and reproduced conflictual relations. Perhaps we can even say that the objective of a cutting-edge IR would be to understand and transform structural hierarchies and their violence-making effects. Perhaps most of the discipline shares this objective. But I am persuaded we cannot achieve it as long as we cut out critical, alternative, postcolonial, and feminist IR.

Notes

1. Betty Reardon *Sexism and the War System* [New York: Columbia University Teachers College, 1985]), Jean Bethke Elshtain (*Women and War* [New York: Basic Books, 1987]), and Cynthia Enloe (*Bananas, Beaches, and Bases: Making Feminist Sense of International Politics* [Berkeley: University of California Press, 1990]) pioneered this line of inquiry in IR, and feminist IR scholars followed by exploring gender in/and security (J. Ann Tickner, *Gender in International Relations: Feminist Perspectives on Achieving Global Security* [New York: Columbia University Press, 1992]), states (V. Spike Peterson, ed., *Gendered States: (Re)Visions of International Relations Theory* [Boulder, Colo.: Lynne Rienner, 1992]), foreign policy (Nancy E. McGlen and Meredith Reid Sarkees, eds., *Women in Foreign Policy: The Insiders* [New York: Routledge, 1993]; Cynthia Weber, *Faking It: U.S. Hegemony in a "Post-Phallic" Era* [Minneapolis: University of Minnesota Press, 1999]), world politics (V. Spike Peterson and Anne Sisson Runyan, *Global Gender Issues*, 2d ed. [Boulder, Colo.: Westview, 1993/1999]; Peter Beckman and Francine D'Amico, eds., *Women, Gender, and World Politics* [Westport, Conn.: Bergin and Garvey, 1994]; Francine D'Amico and Peter Beckman, eds., *Women in World Politics: An Introduction* [Westport, Conn.: Bergin and Garvey, 1995]; Jan Jindy Pettman, *Worlding Women: A Feminist International Politics* [London: Routledge, 1996]; Jill Steans, *Gender and International Relations* [New Brunswick, N.J.: Rutgers University Press, 1998]), international organizations (Deborah Stienstra, *Women's Movements and International Organization* [New York: St. Martin's Press, 1994]; Sandra Whitworth, *Feminism and International Relations: Towards a Political Economy of Gender in Interstate and Non-Governmental Institutions* [London: Macmillan, 1994]), development (Marianne Marchand and Jane Parpart, *Feminism, Postmodernism, Development* [London: Routledge, 1994]), revolution (Mary Ann Tetreault, ed., *Women and Revolution in Africa, Asia, and the New World* [Columbia: University of South Carolina Press, 1994]), peace studies (Simona Sharoni, *Gender and the Israeli-Palestinian Conflict* [Syracuse: Syracuse University Press, 1995]), international political economy (Eileen Boris and Elisabeth Prügl, eds., *Homeworkers in Global Perspective* [New York: Routledge, 1996]; Christine B. Chin, *In Service and Servitude: Foreign Female Domestic Workers and the Malaysian "Moder-*

nity" Project [New York: Columbia University Press, 1998]; Marianne Marchand and Anne Sisson Runyan, eds., *Gender and Global Restructuring: Sightings, Sites, and Resistance* [London: Routledge, 2000]), and IR theory (Gillian Youngs, *International Relations in a Global Age* [Cambridge, England: Polity, 1999]).

2. Marysia Zalewski, "Feminism and/in International Relations: An Exhausted Conversation?" in this collection.
3. I hasten to add that I understand analytics (theory, knowledge) and politics (practice, power) as inextricable; I separate them here for heuristic and organizational purposes only.
4. Again, not all feminisms or all IR feminists conform to the generalizations presented here.
5. Christine Sylvester, "'Progress' as Feminist International Relations," in this collection.
6. For a discussion of the importance of identities in feminist theory/practice, see V. Spike Peterson, "Sexing Political Identity/Nationalism as Heterosexism," *International Feminist Journal of Politics* 1, no. 1 (1999): 21–52; on gendered identities in IR, see Marysia Zalewski and Cynthia Enloe, "Questions about Identity in International Relations," in *International Relations Theory Today*, ed. Ken Booth and Steve Smith (Oxford, England: Polity, 1995); Marysia Zalewski and Jane Parpart, eds., *The "Man" Question in International Relations* (Boulder, Colo.: Westview, 1998).
7. Jan Jindy Pettman, "Critical Paradigms in International Studies: Bringing It All Back Home?" in this collection.
8. Zalewski, "Feminism and/in International Relations: An Exhausted Conversation?" and Sylvester, "'Progress' as Feminist International Relations," in this collection.
9. Lily Ling, "The Fish and the Turtle: Multiple Worlds as Method," in this collection.
10. Consider how the reigning ideology of neoliberalism both naturalizes "obscene global inequalities" and demonizes any attempt to criticize these practices and effects as "unnatural." Zillah Eisenstein, *Global Obscenities: Patriarchy, Capitalism, and the Lure of Cyberfantasy* (New York: New York University Press, 1998).
11. Although divided by the panel organizers, alternative scholars share with feminists this critique of the mainstream's resistance to recognizing a plurality of methods and epistemologies, which effectively delegitimizes alternative and feminist theorizing.
12. See, for example, J. Ann Tickner ("Feminist Theory and Gender Studies: Reflections for the Millennium" in this collection) on positivist methodologies as inadequate for analyzing gender, hierarchical social relations, or the mutual constitution of theory and practice; and Steve Smith ("Alternative and Critical Perspectives" in this collection) on the dominance of U.S.-style positivism as delegitimizing alternative perspectives as "outside the standards of social science."
13. Ultimately, of course, what to do is a personal decision, and my own perspective is simply that. My comments here follow the discussion I have elaborated.

14. The point here is less that feminists have "the answers" or offer a definitive model than that their efforts, while continually warranting critical reflection and improvement, produce more diversity and inclusion than manifested in conventional ISA panels and activities.
15. Steve Smith, "Alternative and Critical Perspectives," in this collection.

CRITICAL PARADIGMS IN INTERNATIONAL STUDIES

Bringing It All Back Home?

Jan Jindy Pettman

It is a daunting task to respond to the challenge to assess the state of the art of international studies (IS), or more particularly, feminist IS: to reflect on where we've come from and where we are now (and indeed who "we" are); and to ask, What's at stake here?

For me, writing as a feminist in IS, there is always a double edge, asking both what happens to the international when we take feminism seriously in IS and what happens to women, sex, gender, and feminism when we take the international seriously. I argue that IS needs feminism, to give better and more inclusive accounts of the world; and that feminism needs an international perspective, especially in these days of intensifying globalization. This double move is typical of feminist IS, working both in and beyond—or even against—the discipline.

I begin with several claims regarding feminism and IS, before elaborating on the difference I think feminism has made to our understanding of "the international." This elaboration provides an opportunity to assess "progress"[1] and to address the questions that guide this collection. I will conclude with two illustrations of feminist approaches, regarding war and the Asian crisis.

Making Claims

1. Feminism came late to IS. The first thirty years of the International Studies Association (ISA) were largely feminist free. Femi-

nism began its formalized presence in the ISA with the establish-
ment of the Feminist Theory and Gender Studies section (FTGS) in
1990, much later than equivalent sections and caucuses in other
disciplinary fields. Does this late coming say something about the
ways IS is constituted as a field, and its particular masculinisms?
Or does it say something about feminism, as less useful for or amenable to IS?

2. Feminism appears to have had comparatively little effect on IS
judging by most course offerings, articles or chapters, or references
in many IS texts. But while the center holds, feminism does have a
remarkably robust, diverse, and productive presence in and around
IS—as a glance at the FTGS-sponsored panels in recent ISA conventions and the contents pages of the recently launched *International
Feminist Journal of Politics* (*IFjP*)[2] demonstrates.

3. Disciplinary recognition of and concern about women and gender lag behind the increasing (though still marginal) visibility of
women and feminist-informed critique in the "real world" in terms
of international agenda items, media reporting, international nongovernmental organization and UN forums, and some state rhetoric
(though not necessarily state practice). Even the World Bank now
declares an interest in women, and in gender-sensitive data. This lag
is worth reflecting on. One way to apply "standards" or judgments
to assess theoretical insights of both mainstream IS and its various
subfields is to ask how good at or close to reflecting or making sense
of the "real world" each is. However, this is tricky—for the world
is experienced rather differently by different people, whose identity,
location, political interests, and power (or lack thereof) translate into
different investments in and understandings of world politics.

Nowadays, Euro-North American media frequently notice
women.[3] There are for example exceptional women in world politics—Madeleine Albright, one of the most powerful people in the
world under the U.S. Clinton administration; or Aung San Suu Kyi,
whose influence rests on democratic support and peaceful challenge to militarized violence in Burma. Often, though, women appear as victims or as symbols of the costs of world politics—of war,
civil strife, environmental disaster. Women figure as problems for
the international community or organization, through representations as the majority of refugees, or amongst the poorest of the poor.
Women are now a category with special needs or a separate section
in UN and agency reports. (Note that this category is often actually
one of "womenandchildren." This effectively invisibilizes the ef-

fects both of/on youth and young children and fails to "gender" the account by discriminating between boy and girl children's experiences of war, violence, work, sex tourism, and so on.) Such representations do make women visible, but usually in ways that perpetuate the men/doer–women/done dichotomy, presenting men as the agents and women as the victims of world politics, whatever individual men or women are doing.

At times, women do appear in more positive guises, as survivors or witnesses, as for example in the recent international war tribunal held in Tokyo against Japanese military sexual slavery in World War II. Some women do figure as actors, advocates, or claimants in international politics. Women function as a (difficult) identity or constituency. Women have long organized across state boundaries, especially in the cause of peace or women's rights. International conferences have proved to be rich sites for such organizing. Women's caucuses and networks flourished through the 1990s, around the 1992 Rio Environment and Development Conference, the 1993 Vienna Human Rights Conference, the 1994 Cairo Population and Development Conference, and the 1995 Women's International Conference in Beijing. As well, many women network and politic transnationally, in alliances built around shared experiences or advocacy, against sex tourism or military base sex, for example. They have succeeded in introducing "new" issues to the international agenda. Those now visible in the media and international forums include war rape, international trafficking of women and children, international service industries, labor migration, child soldiers, restructuring, and international health issues. This coverage is often a long way short of analyses that reveal how gender functions to constitute other identities and power relations, but it does provide clues and signs that still often get missed in IS.

Recognizing that women are in international politics and attending to women as international actors opens up new spaces for feminist work; though how "feminism" figures here is another puzzle. There is no simple or single feminist position on/in IS (and it continues to surprise me how often I'm asked to give the lecture or write *the* chapter on feminism and . . .). Different kinds of feminism have been mapped for/in IS too,[4] including schema naming feminist divides along liberal/empiricist, standpoint, socialist/materialist, postmodern, and more recently postcolonial lines. Some have commented on the difficult relations or lack of conversation between feminists in IS, too.[5] Critical approaches with an explicit emphasis on theoretical issues predominate in feminist IS, though these do not necessarily exclude more empirical work. But while feminist IS as a collective is more likely associated with other critical approaches in IS, its relations with nonfeminist critical IS scholars, too, can be difficult or occasional.

Feminism Comes to IS

Feminism in IS is one of many manifestations of second-wave feminism, driven by a fascinating and at times awkward combination of women's advocacy and academic critique. (The relationship between the category *women,* women's movements, and feminisms in the academy remains problematic in the international context, too.) Coming to the discipline comparatively late has consequences for feminism in IS, for there were already many feminisms, including nuanced and sophisticated offerings in relevant areas. Notable amongst these relate to development, peace and war, nationalism, and citizenship. As well, there are years of fierce feminist controversy around identity and difference between women to draw on. These differences often reflect the social impact of international processes and relations, including colonization, migration, race, and ethnicity. These relations have also attracted very little attention amongst most IS scholars and remain marginal.[6]

Until the last decade, and still in many places and texts, women, gender, and feminist scholarship were effectively excluded from IS. The assumption appeared to be either that IS was gender neutral, affecting women and men in similar ways, or that IS was indeed men's business, as its practitioners in the discipline and the management of world politics seemed to confirm. Some saw these positions as stemming in part from IS's failure to notice people, preferring a focus on states, markets, and other apparently impersonal forces. First-generation feminists in IS sought to deconstruct IS, to refute these assumptions and challenge routine, taken-for-granted exclusions. These works made space for "women," and in the process posed questions about the discipline more broadly, including about who owns IS and what its territory, subjects, concepts, and questions should be. Issues of identity, including but not only gender, were often central.

Unsurprisingly, feminists have particular interests and investments in the politics of identification, with gender and sexuality crucial components in themselves, as well as constituting and marking other boundaries and power relations.[7] As well, serious political or intellectual interest in "women" needs notice that women are many things, and what these things are can never be taken for granted. This relates to but is a different problem from that of tracking gender through all social relations including international politics and IS . . . a point I will return to.

The Difference Feminism Makes?

An evaluation of feminism's impact, or lack of impact, on IS might make for discouraging reading. Rather, I wish to consider the contribution of feminist IS, the ways feminists have contributed, on its own terms[8] (the question of the relations between the discipline and "its" feminists is taken up by the other feminist contributors to this collection).

Feminists working in IS

1. radically expand the kinds of topics, issues, and content in IS, as a glance through the ISA program reveals. For example, the ISA 2001 program includes feminist panels on postcolonialism, critical methodologies, global-local feminisms, Internet activism, ethnic and national conflicts, women's narratives of violence and war, sex in the military, queer theory, migration, and hunger. While feminist issues are still mostly concentrated in FTGS panels and issues of the *IFjP*, they are now visible and do attract an audience beyond feminists in IS. Together, they unsettle the discipline. They suggest new ways of thinking about core issues, including power, security, and the state, and introduce new ones.

2. ask different kinds of questions: looking elsewhere, or differently; revealing habitual absences and structured exclusions. A beginning question, "where are the women?"[9] has proven enormously productive, uncovering women in some unexpected places, or women absent because they are women, or women identified and acting as men. Asking "who are the soldiers?" reveals gender (only men?), sexuality (no gays?), (boy?) children, masculinities, ethnicity, and race. Asking why those working in export-processing zones are overwhelmingly young women and are often racialized as, for example, "Asian" or "immigrant," delivers clues about the international sexual division of labor and the gendered nature of global capital, state transformations, and restructuring strategies.

3. reveal the masculinist assumptions, investments, and strategies of mainstream IS. The soldier, citizen, and state are still often presumed to be male; dominant group men's experiences and interests inform much of the discipline's business and culture. Critique can be labeled as negative, but it is actually productive, disrupting the territory, pushing the boundaries, and clearing a space for feminist reconstruction and revisioning.

4. in the process, widen definitions of the political in the international, too. Women's participation is more likely in liberation movements and social movements than on multinational corporation boards or state councils—clues to the gender of state power and signs to other sites of transnational politics. "Women's issues" have become international political issues, too: the recent *Millennium* special issue celebrating ten years since the first Women and International Relations conference held at the London School of Economics in 1988 included four articles related to international sex work, for example.

5. disrupt or transgress disciplinary boundaries. Feminists in IS often explore other ways of being in the world, bringing ways of thinking and seeing back from other disciplines: critical social theory, cultural studies and postcolonial studies, and especially feminism beyond IS.[10] Increasingly, they also find other kinds of texts and sites for interrogating the construction and representations of gendered identities, including films and other forms of cultural production. These travels lead more conservative IS colleagues to question whether what feminists in IS do is really IS at all, and whether they are capable of displaying the desired levels of disciplinary loyalty to earn recognition.

6. internationalize the account—raising questions about the identity of the discipline, too. How do issues to do with representation play out in the discipline? IS appears predominantly Anglo-North American and especially U.S. dominated in terms of jobs and journals for example.[11] (This may seem an accurate reflection of global power.) First-wave feminist IS insisted on gender difference but initially remained largely within the same geopolitical territory. (I deliberately leave aside questions about the difference it makes being a woman doing IS—and of course not all women in IS are feminist.) While often located in these same IS heartlands, more graduate students and recent Ph.D.'s do come from outside the centers, and may be working on "somewhere else" (though of course the relation between origin and identity and intellectual and political interests is

highly problematic). Exciting new work that might be characterized as second generation has helped push the boundaries further, in terms of locale, subjects, and methodology/theory.[12]

7. gender the account. While "gender" still often functions in IS as a euphemism for women, the constitutive role of gender in world politics is now the subject of keen interrogation. There is an extensive feminist literature on the construction of particular kinds of masculinity and femininity in different international sites, and on gender in IS, too.[13] This literature develops more mobile, nuanced, and political understandings of gender relations—meanings and associations that do not necessarily attach to particular sexed bodies. Gender coding mobilizes particular kinds of roles and obligations, directs us to understand who are the good guys or what it is necessary to do, and rules out possibilities of thinking or acting differently.[14]

8. sex the account. While gender figured from the beginning of feminist intervention in IS, identifying the roles that sex and sexuality, and heterosexism, play in international politics is a more recent concern. This includes the frequent sexualization of the Other and deployment of sexual fears and fantasies in domination relations, and in representations of difference that mark boundaries and binaries in world politics.[15]

Gendering and sexing the account together provide

9. the possibility of an embodied IS. There is now a vibrant accumulation of feminist writings that identify particular kinds of bodies in different international engagements and the privilege or penalty that can flow from being identified as male or female, inside or outside, exotic or "normal," in these exchanges. The body you are in can determine which side of the killing line you are on, how exploitable or sexualized you are, and the kinds of attention that your state and other states pay you. These writings also come closer to measuring the actual body impact of international politics and political economy. This is a reminder of the strangeness of a discipline that so relentlessly disavows women, sex, and gender and yet manifests and utilizes gendered discourse and gender meanings and associations to describe, and do, its intellectual business. It often "misses the body"[16] and the bloody bodily impact of different kinds of international politics, which do occasionally become visible in concern about the domestic political effects of the body bag count, for example.

Sex and bodies might sound new for IS, though they were there all along, in the utilization of body metaphors, for example. But what does emerge from these illustrations is how good feminism is to think with in terms of older and more familiar IS concerns. I was enticed into this field three decades ago by two puzzles—the problem of war and the problem of culture. The first I found centrally located, but with deafening silences and tantalizing glimpses. The second, I found hardly ever mentioned but always practiced (like gender, really). I will conclude this contribution with a brief consideration of the difference feminist questions can make to a study of war; and then with an example from my current research, venturing beyond the Euro-North American heartlands, seeking gender and sex in the politics around the Asian miracle and Asian crisis. I hope to use these to revisit the question of "standards," or how we might assess the usefulness and possibilities of particular perspectives and ways of knowing or seeking to know.

Regarding War

Along with nationalism, war is the subject of much of my writing. Definitive answers elude me. Feminist IS reveals that our (and others') work is always in process and can never be fully completed, that productivity and performance might be better judged by the questions we ask and especially useful in pointing out the kinds of questions that have not been or could not be asked.

I made Waltz's *Man, the State, and War* the center of my international relations course in the late 1960s. When I returned to teaching IS in 1991, feminism gave me more, and more useful, ways of interrogating the kinds of relations that make organized large-scale violence possible. I moved from "man" to men, to asking whether certain kinds of masculinity are more violent than others, to whether state militaries need certain kinds of masculinity. And certain kinds of sexuality, too—debates about gay men in state militaries generate as much heat as do those about women serving in combat positions. As the 1990s progressed, feminist and some new masculinities writings provided more clues about kinds of masculinity constructed in war and other kinds of international relations, too. A significant IS collection was entitled *The "Man" Question in International Relations*,[17] refocusing attention on men, this time qua men—including in IS/A. Issues having to do with whether technology and current forms of warfare require different kinds of military masculinity are receiving attention. However, investigation of questions regarding cultural difference and different state and sub-culture notions of what it takes to be a good (military) man are only beginning.[18]

It is a political, ethical, and intellectual question of immense importance to ask how men (mainly) who would not resort to violence in their personal or social lives can be prevailed upon to use violence against those outside their own state or nation; and how people move from holding multiple and often shifting identities to a primary identity for which they will fight, kill, or die.[19] Feminist interrogations of identity and difference and the politics of boundaries provide insights into nationalist passions and gendered civic obligations, including that of citizen soldiers. They help to denaturalize those popularly held explanations of war that center on "human nature" or ancient hatreds or the inevitability of violence in an anarchic world. They trace the history and politics of particular conflicts and wars, and so bring back the possibility of other kinds of response or intervention. In the process, they reveal the gender dynamics that infuse identities, political subjectivities, and power relations in interstate relations, too.

The Asian Other?

New feminist IS writings trace the extent to which IS is manifest in a gaze from the center/s, overlooking other places and ways of being in the world.[20] "Asia" has long functioned as Other for the worlds and ways of thinking that IS exemplifies. Asia was long constructed as feminine and ripe for conquest or domination by the West in colonial and in cold war times. IS's refusal to take coloniality and post-colonialism seriously reinforces and reproduces the circulation of racialized international identities like the West, Asia, and the Third World, which in turn influence analysis and policy toward Others. State and regional identities are effectively homogenized, essentialized; disguising both differences within these big identities (including gender differences) and the constant and considerable inter-change and mutual constitution that the colonial experience has bequeathed to the contemporary world.

These international identities are themselves constituted through gender as well as race/cultural difference. Changing international power relations signaled through the rise of East Asian states and the Asian miracle were seen as a threat to Western state power and manhood. East Asian triumphalism and the self-confident declaration of Asian values (from Singaporean and Malaysian leaders especially) claimed that a newly dynamic, successful Asia had recovered from its colonial emasculation. Instead, in a kind of gender reversal, "the West" was seen to be faltering, losing the manly qualities of hard work, self-control, competition, and strength, becoming decadent, immoral, obsessed with consumption and pleasure—in short, feminized.

The 1997 Asian crisis ushered in new configurations in gender representations of state power, national identity, and international relations. As usual, gender was mobilized along with and to stand in for "culture." Both Asian miracle and crisis were culturalized: what formerly explained success, in terms of miracle (for example, Confucian capitalism) now explained failure and crisis (for example, crony capitalism, corruption).

These forms of essentializing disguise the gendered, and class, costs of both miracle and crisis. They do so through complicity with IS's notorious statecentrism, discouraging us from looking within and across states, and from asking questions such as Who pays during miracle, and crisis, and who gains? How do particular constructions of family and gender relations help subsidize states and markets through the construction of women's labor as cheap labor? And legitimize privileged elites by mobilizing gendered notions of citizenship and hierarchy that undercut the rights and claims of labor, human rights, and women activists? How do reconstructions of national gender roles feed into interstate identity relations?

My current research on Australia's relations with "Asia" asks what is obscured by the failure of academic and other commentators to take women, gender relations, and feminist writings seriously in analyzing these relations.[21] This failure disguises the gendered impact of miracle and crisis, and the ways women's experiences become the basis for transnational organizing and campaigns that generate a feminist politics of region. But more than that: miracle, crisis, and military intervention (for example in East Timor in 1999) become sites for the gendered reconstruction of state power and interstate relations. Gender and sexuality mark hierarchies and power relations among states, too, and signal contests and changes in these relations.

These illustrations demonstrate the usefulness of using feminist perspectives in explorations of key topics already close to IS: militarization, intensifying globalization and state transformations, national interest, and interstate relations. These are hardly add-ons or special interests. They go to the heart of the discipline, and of contemporary world politics and political economy. Feminism brings to IS more inclusive, indeed better, accounts of the world.

But it's not only how "the world" works that feminism in IS thinks about. We have been forced to think seriously about how *we* work: about the politics of representation and the disciplinary politics behind who is heard or seen as an authority. Feminism is a political project, which removes the possibility of occupying an innocent position in knowledge making. It helps us to address key questions about the discipline: Who is it for? What is at stake in doing IS? Who is listening? Who (if anyone) are we accountable to? How do issues of power and identification play out in IS, too?

Interrogating the politics of our own work, of the discipline, and of knowledge making more broadly removes the possibility of expecting a resolution of our differences, within feminism or with IS. Our debates and views will always be contingent, contested, situated, and in some ways quite particular. We are therefore called to reflect critically upon our own practice. Who do *we* recognize as authorities? Whose experiences do we take seriously and admit as evidence? Who do we talk to, read, and cite? Who do we imagine as our audience? Would the people we write about or those whose lives are directly affected by the processes or events we analyze recognize our accounts? Are those whose experiences we seek to understand in any way present in our work?

The struggles around difference and voice in feminism push us to reflect more on our own practice in research, writing, teaching, supervising, and relating to colleagues and to the discipline more broadly. (Which is not to say that only feminists—or all feminists— do this. There are other, critical collaborators, those who work from different political and intellectual terrain to make complementary demands, including some represented in this collection.) Nor have these issues been resolved; but they are now part of our conversations and examples of emerging good practice.[22]

Looking for (a) Home?

It is a cause for celebration that feminism is now well into critical mass in IS. Clearly, however, feminists are (not yet?) at home in IS. Our relations with the father/master discipline remain difficult, and will continue to be so, for feminist IS is disruptive, and hopefully transformative—and therefore rightly perceived as a threat by those who currently exercise disciplinary power and execute border patrols. And for a discipline that has an ongoing fascination with the workings of power, IS remains remarkably incurious (or resistant?) about its own power relations and conditions. For many feminists, the FTGS section and women's caucus offer a home or at least a safe visiting and recovery place while within the IS orbit. There is a tension between a wish to remain at home, to present one's work to colleagues who, however robust the exchanges, form an affinity grouping. Yet staying close to home might reinforce the borders and foreclose possible conversations that some feminists in IS still wish to pursue. And, as usual, home is not always safe—not all feminists feel at home in FTGS. Issues of diversity and difference within feminism are present within feminist IS, too.

Feminism in IS is becoming more international and more representative. Indeed, it is broad and rich enough to raise questions about its own centers and margins. There are important questions here about who "we" are, including in terms of background, generation, and current location, both geographic and institutional (each shorthand for very complicated feminist identity politics). This range, diversity, and at times discomfort provide the context within which we ask what it means to read, write, converse, and organize as feminists, in and around IS. These questions are especially pertinent in terms of building a critical feminist community around the ISA, FTGS, and *IFjP*, which was conceived and initially developed within the FTGS community.

IFjP went to launch in mid-1999. It is located at the intersection of international studies, politics, and women's studies. Its first two volumes illustrate something of the range of contemporary international feminist engagements. It includes articles on girls in war zones, nationalism as heterosexism, travel, feminist nongovernmental organizations and UN conferences, the "temp" industry, and citizenship in these global times. It highlights feminist politics and analysis in amongst others Zimbabwe, Kuwait, Venezuela, Israel, Russia, and France. The "Conversations" section includes fascinating reflections on teaching, commentaries on films like *GI Jane* and *Saving Private Ryan*, and interviews with international activists. The book review section showcases the current state of feminist international studies, including through review essays and reflections on what ought to be taught in IS. The journal appears to be flourishing; though whether it is having any effect on the wider IS community has yet to be tested.

Concluding, then: feminist IS is a new field, and one in which postgraduate work figures largely. Its recent development follows no fixed plan and is not easy to map. Like the real world, it is messy, jumpy, sometimes cumulative, sometimes contradictory or doubling back. Its double view, both feminist and international, is understood and pursued through very different disciplinary, politicogeographic, and cultural lenses. It is not possible, then, to propose a future research agenda. For my own interests, though, I am especially interested in the move to internationalize the agenda, to generate more feminist accounts from outside the usual centers of power, and to do so in ways that combine big questions around globalization and international power relations with careful tracing of the gendered, cross-cultural, and lived experiences of the everyday. These can never be constrained entirely within the discipline; they will continue to be enriched by travels beyond its boundaries.

Notes

1. Though see Christine Sylvester on this problematic, and contested, notion.
2. For a sample copy, send an e-mail message to SARA@tandf.co.uk with the word *info* in the body of the message.
3. Jindy Pettman, "Gendering Australia's Foreign Policy," in *Issues in International Relations for the Twentieth Century: An Australian Perspective*, ed. W. Tow and M. Hanson (Sydney, Australia: Oxford University Press, 2001).
4. For example, Sandra Whitworth, *Feminism and International Relations* (New York: St Martin's Press, 1994); L. H. M. Ling, "Feminist International Relations: From Critique to Reconstruction," *Journal of International Communications* 3, no. 1 (1996): 26–41.
5. J. Ann Tickner in this volume.
6. Exceptions include Philip Darby, ed., *At the Edge of International Relations: Postcolonialism, Gender, and Dependency* (London: Pinter, 1997).
7. V. S. Peterson, "Reframing the Politics of Identity: Democracy, Globalisation, and Gender," *Political Expressions* 1, no. 1 (1995): 1–16.
8. For my take on feminist international studies to the mid-1990s, see *Worlding Women: A Feminist International Politics* (New York: Routledge, 1996). For recent writings see V. S. Peterson, "Feminisms and International Relations," *Gender and History* 10, no. 3 (1998): 581–89; Terrell Carver, "Gendering International Relations," *Millennium* 27, no. 2 (1998): 343–51; recent ISA programs and issues of *IFjP*.
9. Cynthia Enloe's groundbreaking text *Bananas, Bases, and Beaches: Making Feminist Sense of International Politics* (London: Pandora, 1990).

10. J. Ann Tickner in this volume.

11. Robert Crawford and Darryl Jarvis, eds., *International Relations—Still an American Social Science?* (New York: State University of New York Press, 2001). While considering feminist IS, we might add Still a Social Science? See J. Ann Tickner in this volume.

12. J. Ann Tickner's contribution refers to the work of Katherine Moon and Christine Chin in this context; see also Lily Ling's work.

13. Marysia Zalewski and Jane Parpart, eds., *The "Man" Question in International Relations* (Boulder, Colo.: Westview, 1998); Carver, "Gendering International Relations."

14. For example, Carol Cohn, "Wars, Wimps, and Women: Talking Gender and Thinking War," in *Gendering War Talk,* ed. M. Cooke and A. Wollacott (Princeton, N.J.: Princeton University Press, 1993).

15. V. S. Peterson, "Sexing Political Identities/Nationalism as Heterosexism," *International Feminist Journal of Politics* 1, no. 1 (1999): 34–65; Cohn, "Wars, Wimps, and Women"; Cynthia Weber, *Faking It: U.S. Hegemony in a Post-Phallic Era* (Minneapolis: University of Minnesota Press, 1999).

16. Jan Jindy Pettman, "Writing the Body: Transnational Sex," in *Political Economy, Power, and the Body: Global Perspectives,* ed. G. Youngs (London: Macmillan, 2000).

17. Zalewski and Parpart, *The "Man" Question in International Relations.*

18. But see Cynthia Enloe's writings, including *Maneuvers: The International Politics of Militarizing Women's Lives* (Berkeley: University of California Press, 2000).

19. Jan Jindy Pettman, "Theorizing Gendered Violence" (paper presented at the annual conference of the International Studies Association, Washington, D.C., February 16–20, 1999); Jan Jindy Pettman, "Sukupuoli ja vakivalta rauhantutkimuksessa" (Theorizing gendered violence), *Kosmopolis* (special issue on gender and political violence) 30, no. 1 (2000).

20. Lily Ling and Christine Sylvester in this volume.

21. "A Feminist Perspective on 'Australia in Asia,'" in *Race, Colour, and Identity in Australia and New Zealand,* ed. J. Docker and G. Fischer (Sydney, Australia: University of New South Wales Press, 2000); "Identity and Security in Australia–Southeast Asia Relations," in *Security, Community, and Emancipation,* ed. K. Booth (Boulder, Colo.: Lynne Rienner, 2002).

22. For example, the "Forum on Teaching: Globalising Women's Studies" in *International Feminist Journal of Politics* 1, no. 2 (1999): 256–98.

"Progress" as Feminist International Relations

Christine Sylvester

One of the questions put to us by the organizers of the millennial panels at the 2000 International Studies Association (ISA) conference concerns progress: what might we, from our particular positions within a field, say about the progress of international relations (IR) in general? As it happens, I have been ruminating about progress lately, quite independently of this particular query from the ISA. I have done so mostly in the context of productions of women and progress in Zimbabwe[1] but also with respect to feminist IR and whether it has brought us—and who is that?—progress. "Progress" is an odd thing. It twists my head around. Feminists require "it" for the advancement of "women." Much of IR tries to reach "it" cumulatively, using the right methods harnessed to the right research programs—now neorealism, now neoliberal institutionalism, now constructivism, now rationalism, now . . . I delight in feminist IR as a sign of an avant-garde movement making waves and making a certain type of progress in the IR field possible. Simultaneously, knowing that some avant-gardes have been described as working to extricate themselves from the distractions of women,[2] the double edges of avant-garde progress also come into view.

Indeed, progress is a cre(a)p and a leap, a jump, and a crawl. It strives for and against, thrusts, moves, makes a crumble, flows. It is a fact, a sorrow, a make-believe, a virtuality, a compromise, a cynicism. Progress advances. It stands us still. It writhes. It invites nostalgia. It is at once a common notion, easily grasped by the modern mind, and something difficult to understand, make happen, or repudiate. Progressive deterioration even bespeaks progress. Tatters talk. Yet there *is* movement in life and in theory—around and back, in new circles. Certainly there is process, rhythm, and change, the unfolding of potential and intent, simultaneous destruction and renewal. For some, there is steady or at least erratic improvement in their lives, which we often think of as progress: the advance toward more promise for tomorrow than exists today or was possible yesterday. For others, progress is someone else's news today, yesterday, and tomorrow.

Consider a few shades of "progress." A "miracle" precipitously lifts standards of living in some parts of the world, prompting predictions of an upcoming Asian century. In 1997 the lift deflates somewhat, and we ask ourselves how long miracle progress sustains. At the other end of things, only a miracle could bring recognizable progress to certain territories of intractable conflict. In Angola, surviving is a form of advance. A circuitous route to the status quo ante can also mark progress. A Haitian pays the last bit of money for passage to Miami—to the city of progress—but the rickety vessel is intercepted and turned back. The traveler manages to elude arrest and to survive the seas, and progress occurs in the simple fact that s/he has not died. In another case, people adjust to someone else's sense of progress when development feminists turn up at the village toting a water pump (the local women would prefer a school building). And then, of course, there is progress on a Hollywood/Washington scale: Toni Morrison has it that Bill Clinton was the first black president of the United States (and after that an election produces No-body as president of the United States). Now we're really getting somewhere?

Life is ever in progress. Whether it progresses in positive or negative or in-between ways, when, where, and how is an enormous issue. The term eludes definitional clarity. The jury, it seems, is still out. We face a new millennium without a name for "it," or with a name that is everywhere known and there/not there. Is it not rather risky, therefore, to talk about progress . . . in IR?

Elshtain and Enloe Progress IR

Feminist international relations poses an unfinished journey (some progress in progress, you might say) around and about the field of IR.[3] The voyagers set off in earnest in the 1980s, when feminism was in some quandary about Marxist, radical, liberal, and socialist women questions and pitched to new queries around the existence, meaning, discourse, and variety of "women."[4] In that decade, IR came under the influence of Hedley Bull's *The Anarchical Society: A Study of Order in World Politics* and Kenneth Waltz's *Theory of International Politics.* Both tomes put emphasis on anarchies, norms, and modes of conflict and cooperation over agents of them rather than people.[5] Toward the end of the 1980s, feminism and IR made a linkup around Cynthia Enloe's *Bananas, Beaches, and Bases: Making Feminist Sense of International Relations* and Jean Bethke Elshtain's *Women and War.*[6] Then, with rapid progress, came the lively Feminist Theory and Gender Studies section of the ISA in 1990 and an ever-diversifying set of topics defining the feminist IR genre. For the most part, conventional IR did not seize the moment to tie itself to feminism in a field-defining or field-debating way, which is not to say that there was no progress observed.

Elshtain and Enloe certainly did their best to advance "our field." They established themselves as innovators inclined toward framing questions of international relations around feminist concerns rather than around IR agendas. What a difference a starting point would make! Feminists generally begin with gender, bodies, sexuality, difference, voice, patriarchy, subjectivity, representation, and/or travel theory.[7] Enloe wonders where women are in a world that keeps maneuvering patriarchy to the fore.[8] Elshtain finds narratives of soldierly and motherly bodies intriguing points of entry into the puzzle of war and its sexed stories; she is also on about citizenship and civic virtue and the ways America needs to reflect on itself better in order to better engage the world.[9] Meanwhile, conventional IR still typically begins with states, war, trade, regimes, anarchy, and/or rationality. It maps relations of force, power, decision, threat, and agreement. Much of it endeavors these days to sort out the rationalities, construct the codeterminations, find the elusive international society, demarcate globalization, or map the ethics. Working late into the night on such topics, there are inevitable spills of cold coffee on a world atlas that is already stained with burger droppings. There goes Bhutan. The Maldives and Bangladesh smudge, their cities becoming illegible. No worries for IR the Abstract. No power is at stake in those places anyway.

Such spills do not go unnoticed by feminists interested in international relations; indeed, some among them can purposefully cause IR to go missing in the mop up. Elshtain and Enloe write of wars and bases, which (unlike bananas and beaches) are items of interest in IR.

Yet they nearly ignore IR as they journey, which means that they rarely work from its frameworks or systematically critique its myopias. Both pick a few IR themes—for Enloe it is power and for Elshtain, realism—needle the field about the flaws in its preoccupations, and then advance their own ideas with dispatch. The results startlingly recompose the world as a question mark in the study of "women." Here is a form of scholarly progress that takes back the people-alienating night of IR.

As they venture into that abyss, feminists tarry at atypical sites of IR research. Elshtain enters Mrs. Von Clausewitz's parlor in the evening light, where confessions of an unknown wife publishing her husband's work enliven the atmosphere. Enloe takes us to the night laundry of a Jamaican tourist hotel or runs the track telling stories about the gendered history of sneakers. In such IR-estranged places feminists locate events, histories, forms of agency, and people far from great-power concerns that nonetheless have the audacity to contribute to (and therefore have place within) international relations. Hans Morgenthau famously declared autonomy from non-realist standards of sociality. Enloe relies on those "other standards" to spotlight women at the center of certain realms of international relations. She spies Carmen Miranda, for example—the showgirl with all those exotic fruits on her head—as an international actor linked to corporate marketing strategies, to America's Good Neighbor Policy of yesteryear, and to issues of land reform in Latin America. Starting from one glamorous but hardly heroic woman of the world from south of the North, Enloe unravels a series of relations international that IR misses. She and others refuse grandiose sweeps of the world, ignore Waltz's caution about the importance of remaining above the state level of analysis on a systems footing, and typically do not think about strategic games that no particular body plays.[10]

Enloe and Elshtain are unique—they are the innovators who first brought IR questions to feminism.[11] Not all feminists thereafter roaming international relations have taken up their feminist-first agenda. Some prefer starting with a recognizable IR topic and bringing to it new gender-highlighting questions,[12] which lately telescope feminist angles on international political economy, foreign policy, war, peace, globalization, the state, nationalism, trade, and so forth.[13] Nonetheless, most feminists engaged with international relations share interest in ethnographic and anthropological methods of analysis, with human geography replacing geopolitics and bottom-up research transplanting abstractions. Quantitative analysis, formal modeling, gaming—there are few followers of these approaches in the feminist corner of "our field." Feminists explore the lower-than-low politics that comprise, write, and enact relations international alongside the heroics. Such research maneuvers provincialize IR, to borrow an out-of-context thought from Dipesh Chakrabarty,[14] by making the usual field concerns a stage on which other actors perform compelling and salient plays. A brief change of (mise-en-) scene illustrates the types of performances that feminists observe, enact, and bring into being.

Interlude

We are standing at a painting, oil on board, framed. Unlike Helen Brocklehurst's painting of IR,[15] the one that eyes me is very small. It is also abstract and seemingly an anarchy of blacks on black, like Robert Ryman does whites. In the corner is a drip of yellow. Imagine that Deborah Moggach writes a novel around this painting and calls it *Power Fever*.[16] Imagine that her story starts something like this: "I am seated across the table from a man who has spinach caught between his teeth, but who does not know the meaning of embarrassment. He fills the entire dining room with his smoke and fire and words. He neither notices that I am noticing nor assesses himself before standing and solemnly progressing to the heavy front door. He is going out to discuss the small black painting (yellow edging) with important colleagues. None of them will mention the spinach, I know, so I rush forward to spare him from the embarrassment I realize he is not capable of mustering. He smiles at me benignly and bows out. The spinach I have tried to dislodge has been jostled but holds stubbornly, crookedly to its place. The man arrives at the club and takes his seat among others like himself. No one notices his spinach because all have a bit of it caught in their own teeth." Intervention by this field-guarding feminist is foiled by patronizing phantoms of sophistication.

The stage set changes to Langelinie Harbour. A bronze woman's bare back is barely visible among the rocks. "She" is bent away from all the industrial and military installations across the water, turned against ferries that ply waters to Malmo and that also bring visitors to take a look at her. An electric train travels in the background, humming. She does not hum back. She does not look at us looking, does not appear to hear the din or to record the significance of herself. Yet she pulls us toward her as though she knows us and our sounds.

"She" is tiny and young and dignified and odd and not modern and a study in postmodern nostalgia. Her eyes downcast, her body pawed at, leaned against, photo-opped, she evades the myth of her docility; for it is clear that she commands the harbor and its spectators, installations, ferries, and international visitors. She is what people come to see as Copenhagen, no matter that local art critics and some feminists decry her old-fashioned style, her docile image of woman, her crass popularity. Gentle she is and unwavering, even with her head chopped off now and then. She is there winter after summer in unheroic pose and nonmonumental leadership. She, the creature, has achieved a divorce from creators Edvard Eriksen and Hans Christian Andersen. She has been written/has written herself as determined vulnerability rather than Jeanne D'Arc bravery or ladylike weakness.

They say she wants a soul. That's why she is made to sit there with her smooth body in the land of man. Won't some nice young man marry her and thereby give her a soul? That would be progress in a story that has it that soul is a man's to give and that it makes a girl a true human. Yet it is she who is there long after the man passes by, or drools over her, or dresses like her, or whatever it is he does there. Soul passes round, and she is doing the passing. Who has it, who wants it, and who gives it to whom? And who says? Who says! That is one bunch of devilish queries that a keeper of untidy questions of international relations in feminism can ask but that the feminist questioner of IR might not wish to ask or be ignored for asking/answering by an audience that suffers power fever.

More Progress Ahead

As we gaze at mermaid we notice that she has no clothes for the impending Danish winter. She is not fussed, though, because her world persists whether others choose to notice her and help her out or not. In fact, we who gaze at her are the ones written by her authorial capacity to command our attention. Outlined in an unlikely place, national symbolism inclined against the panorama of ships and tanks, buskers, and lookers, mermaid is a living sculptural story of complex gender shaping the world. Surely she is an international relation of ours in that veritable carnival where she dwells—out in the spectacle of beasts, sorcerers, and average people. Mermaid and entourage bring that carnival to feminist-minded readers who journey to ask questions and to read spectacular interpretations.[17]

Where else can we go to relations international that have been neglected in IR? Myself, I like to take to the field for close-up sightings. By "field" I mean not only the usual destinations of IR case studies—Russia, France, the International Monetary Fund (IMF), the State Department—where handmaids may lurk uncited in power.[18] I also mean the fields we currently fence off and call the Humanities. I recommend forays into novels, choreography, drama, poetry, music, and visual arts. These places of fiction, expression, and emotion assist those of us trained in IR to escape narrow vision in order to see other international actors, interactions, products, exchanges, and dramatizations. If we work inside the usual IR frameworks all the time, we may find it difficult to imagine worlds beyond or within the one IR has imagined for us. Call it avant-garde or call it finding lost "data," the advantages of reassigning the arts to social science fieldwork—as vehicles for training in-sight—could be immense. Entering different worlds than those of IR, we might see prisoners, children, mothers, the global goods, petty tyrannies, and murderous attitudes that threaten the relations of many in the world. We will surely stumble onto women and men and transsexuals and texts and terrorism, to say nothing of hyphenators, resisters, laborers, oozers, seepers, and lackers of Phallic access. We will note that the stuff of international relations gets done by women who shoot bullets or women who sew seams for Banana Republic. In rare cases, she is Al(l)bright or Merle Laderman Ukeles, the latter known to wash the floors of a museum of fine arts in a performance of the international-domestic "arts" of women.[19]

If we keep journeying, we might sight signs put up by the Gorilla Girl movement asking: Do Women Have to be Naked to Enter the Metropolitan Museum of Art? We can then more easily picture ourselves entering and performing a different script at the ISA than the one we all know so well.[20] We can imagine the signs we could install there asking the passerby: Must Feminists Do IR in Order to Do International Relations? Fields of vision might widen even more if we enter archives of the Museum of Modern Art to research Georgia O'Keeffe's pineapple paintings for the Dole Corporation, talk to sex workers in Bangkok about their German clients, hold children of Kosovar refugees in Tasmania, kick up our tourist skirts at the Moulin Rouge, stand among women villagers in Java as they worry about forests burning nearby, or ask women microentrepreneurs in Pusan, Korea, why they advertised IMF sales in 1998.[21] It is progress of some sort to find that "women" and the relations of gender that shape international relations come in statistical form, in verse, in camp, in camps, in comics, in mass graves, in frames, in shops, in the World Bank. They hang on the wall, paint the wall, bloody the wall, and line the walls of diplomatic parties.[22] As more of us get better at sighting the habitations of international relations, our "findings" will yield heteroskedasticities that "our field" may come to consider its artful central tendency.

The Theory End

But. While participating in and applauding such sightings as progressive, I am also thinking about how progress can be gauged at the end of a day in the brothel, on the streets of the export zones, after reading the last paragraph of a feminist IR article, while wondering one more time why Lee Krasner's paintings were so thoroughly backseated to Jackson Pollock's internationally enamored work. My particular worry conjures up old ghosts: Where is, where should be, theory at the end of our travails? Should IR questions in feminism lead us to new feminist theories of international relations? Has it done this? Should research on feminist questions in IR contribute new IR theories: has it done this? Do feminists need to find recurring patterns, as, for example, Enloe's extended work on militarism seems to do vis-à-vis masculinity; or do we work best highlighting anomalies?

More questions now. Is the very idea of building feminist IR theory archaic or is it "not yet," as distinct from "now"—to use terms I like when I hear Chakrabarty using them? Is it that a certain progress is being written by what we do and say more than it is the case that we are consciously writing a field theoretically? Is critical theory (small c) where the IR questions in feminism and feminist questions in IR should be? Might it be that whatever we theorize eludes definitional clarity once we mix up the disciplines—literary and art theory, postcolonial studies, cultural studies, psychoanalysis, women's studies—to become (feminist) IR?

Life is ever in progress, and thus so is the theory side of life. Yet as feminist IR/IR feminist articles accumulate, feminist international relations theories go missing. Feminist IR, impressive as it is, has not capitalized sufficiently on its progressive tendencies by theorizing the connective tissues that bind the genre. It paints more and more pictures that possibly chase away (from) theory—as a thing purposively, progressfully, perhaps, to avoid.[23] IR, by contrast, has invested heavily in theory, but of a sort that produces too few pictures of salience to much of the world. Certainly it has failed to cotton onto the sites of gender and women over the years, for reasons, in part, of its chosen locations for seeing the international. Needed is an exercise of theorizing around a millennial question: of what does theory consist at the fulcrum of international relations and feminism? Theory need not be lawlike. It need not be problem solving. What should it, can it, be in this context? If we do not want to do theory or believe we are theorizing in what we are doing—either way, the assumptions must become clearer and subject to more debate. Feminists cannot afford to toss theory to the rationalist and constructivist wings of IR, or to international society traditions that fail to get all the occupants of society counted. We can no longer duck the theory question by hedging it.

In taking up a theory challenge we will want to avoid some common errors of avant-gardism, like seeing ourselves as the saviors of international relations, or as progressively more progressive than foremothers like Elshtain and Enloe—thus forgetting where we have been. Feminists will want to say something mermaidenly memorable and mermaidenly elegant in the midst of the theory talk and steer clear of self-celebratory posturing as a stand-in for progress. There are many cautions, many advances, and many lessons about feminist IR/IR feminism that the humble may weep over and the overconfident regret not heeding. Such is the "nature" of progress. We might keep that bit of spinach and that Langelinie mermaid in our sights as the signifying power of differently positioned theory. And then perhaps we can state the unstated. Or will theory power give us self-induced fever—to ask nothing of whether Angolan villagers and Haitian boaters will survive while more progressive moments of a thing called IR unfold?

Notes

1. See, for example, Christine Sylvester, "'Progress' in Zimbabwe: Is 'It' a 'Woman'?" *International Feminist Journal of Politics* 1, no. 1 (1999): 89–90; and Christine Sylvester, *Producing Women and Progress in Zimbabwe: Narratives of Identity and Work from the 1980s* (Portsmouth, New Hampshire: Heinemann, 2000).
2. John Docker, *Postmodernism and Popular Culture: A Cultural History* (Cambridge: Cambridge University Press, 1994).
3. Christine Sylvester, *Feminist International Relations: An Unfinished Journey* (Cambridge: Cambridge University Press, 2002).

4. Denise Riley, *"Am I That Name?" Feminism and the Category of "Women" in History* (Minneapolis: University of Minnesota Press, 1988); and Judith Butler, *Gender Trouble: Feminism and the Subversion of Identity* (New York: Routledge, 1990).

5. Hedley Bull, *The Anarchical Society: A Study of Order in World Politics* (New York: Columbia University Press, 1977); and Kenneth Waltz, *Theory of International Politics* (Reading, Mass.: Addison-Wesley, 1979).

6. Cynthia Enloe, *Bananas, Beaches, and Bases: Making Feminist Sense of International Relations* (London: Pandora, 1989); and Jean Bethke Elshtain, *Women and War* (New York: Basic Books, 1987).

7. See Chris Weedon, *Feminism, Theory, and the Politics of Difference* (Oxford, England: Blackwell, 1999); and Sandra Harding, *Is Science Multicultural? Postcolonialisms, Feminisms, and Epistemologies* (Bloomington: Indiana University Press, 1998).

8. Among Cynthia Enloe's feminist IR books are *The Morning After: Sexual Politics at the End of the Cold War* (Berkeley: University of California Press, 1993) and *Maneuvers: The International Politics of Militarizing Women's Lives* (Berkeley: University of California Press, 2000).

9. See Jean Bethke Elshtain, *Real Politics: At the Center of Everyday Life* (Baltimore: Johns Hopkins University Press, 1997); and Jean Bethke Elshtain, *New Wine and Old Bottles: International Politics and Ethical Discourse* (Notre Dame, Ind.: University of Notre Dame Press, 1998).

10. Hans Morgenthau, *Politics among Nations: The Struggle for Power and Peace* (New York: Knopf, 1966); Waltz, *Theory of International Politics*; Robert Keohane, *After Hegemony: Cooperation and Discord in the World Political Economy* (Princeton, N.J.: Princeton University Press, 1984); Robert Axelrod, "The Emergence of Cooperation among Egoists," *American Political Science Review* 25 (1981): 306–18.

11. This phraseology is obviously beholden to Sandra Harding's *The Science Question in Feminism* (Ithaca, N.Y.: Cornell University Press, 1986).

12. J. Ann Tickner's *Gender in International Relations: Feminist Perspectives on Achieving Global Security* (New York: Columbia University Press, 1992) is a classic in this vein.

13. For example: Marieke de Goede, "Mastering 'Lady Credit': Discourses of Financial Credit in Historical Perspective," *International Feminist Journal of Politics* 2, no. 1 (2000): 58–81; Nancy McGlen and Meredith Sarkees, *Women in Foreign Policy: The Insiders* (New York: Routledge, 1993); Carolyn Nordstrom, *Girls and Warzones: Troubling Questions* (Uppsala, Sweden: Life and Peace Institute, 1997); Eleanor Kofman and Gillian Youngs, eds., *Globalization: Theory and Practice* (London: Pinter, 1996); *Gender and International Relations in a Nordic Context*, special issue of *Cooperation and Conflict* 36, no. 2 (2001).

14. Dipesh Chakrabarty, *Provincializing Europe* (Princeton, N.J.: Princeton University Press, 2000); also Dipesh Chakrabarty, "Postcoloniality and the Artifice of History: Who Speaks for 'Indian' Pasts?" *Representations* 37 (winter 1992): 1–26.

15. Helen Brocklehurst, "Painting International Relations," *International Feminist Journal of Politics* 1, no. 2 (1999): 314–23.

16. Deborah Moggach, *Tulip Fever: A Novel* (London: Heinemann, 1999).
17. This is one version of the thesis advanced by Minrose Gwin in "Space-Travel: The Connective Politics of Feminist Reading," *Signs: Journal of Women in Culture and Society* 21, no. 4 (1996): 870–905.
18. Christine Sylvester, "Handmaids' Tales of Washington Power: The Abject and the Real Kennedy White House," *Body and Society* 4, no. 3 (1998): 39–66.
19. For a discussion of Ukeles, see Lucy Lippard, *The Pink Glass Swan: Selected Feminist Essays on Art* (New York: New Press, 1995).
20. In fact, for the Pan European Conference on International Relations held in Canterbury in September 2001, Costas Constantinou organized sessions to perform IR.
21. See the IR-relevant feminist work (albeit not strictly IR feminist work) on these and related subjects by Thanh-Dam Truong, *Sex, Money, and Morality: Prostitution and Tourism in South-East Asia* (London: Zed Press, 1990); Gloria Anzaldua, ed., *Making Face, Making Soul: Haciendo Caras* (San Francisco: Aunt Lute, 1990); Chandra Mohanty, Ann Russo, and Lourdes Torres, eds., *Third World Women and the Politics of Feminism* (Bloomington: Indiana University Press, 1991); Caren Kaplan, Norma Alarcon, and Minoo Moallem, eds., *Between Woman and Nation: Nationalism, Transnational Feminisms, and the State* (Durham, N.C.: Duke University Press, 1999).
22. For some "strange" recent sightings, see for example Lisa Bloom, ed., *With Other Eyes: Looking at Race and Gender in Visual Culture* (Minneapolis: University of Minnesota Press, 1999); and *Poetic International Relations*, special issue of *Alternatives: Humane Governance and Social Transformation* 25, no. 3 (2000).
23. See discussions in Judith Butler and Joan Scott, eds., *Feminists Theorize the Political* (New York: Routledge, 1992); and Anne Phillips, ed., *Feminism and Politics* (Oxford: Oxford University Press, 1998).

FEMINIST THEORY AND GENDER STUDIES

Reflections for the Millennium

J. Ann Tickner

A forty-year retrospect is a difficult challenge for feminist theory and gender studies. For thirty of those years there was almost total silence on gender issues in international relations (IR); women were barely visible as scholars and foreign policy practitioners, as well as in the subject matter of the discipline. The invisibility in the discipline was not because gender was, and for some still is, irrelevant but because international relations, in both its theory and practice, was so thoroughly gendered that, in Cynthia Enloe's words, no one noticed that women were missing.[1] So clearly, feminist approaches to IR have come a long way since the late 1980s when, after several conferences at which feminist and IR scholars began to talk together about these issues, feminist IR research began to appear.[2] Probably the most significant accomplishments have been the enormous productivity of a relatively small group of scholars and their success in creating a supportive space within the International Studies Association (ISA) within which this type of work is being pursued.[3] Besides an impressive list of publications and a growing number of panels at the ISA, we have recently witnessed the inauguration of the *International Feminist Journal of Politics*. There has been a genuine attempt to recognize a diversity of voices and approaches on feminist ISA panels. And a volume reflecting the state of the discipline at the millennium that acknowledges this work is clearly an enormous step for a discipline that has had trouble understanding why gender should be relevant to its scholarly concerns.

My first thought on being asked to write these reflections was how difficult a critical assessment of such a young field would be. While there are differences amongst IR feminists, engaging in self-criticism seems premature as feminist approaches still struggle to be heard in a discipline that has not been particularly open to gender approaches. I have also been struggling with a more fundamental problem as I attempt to formulate responses to the questions posed to the partic-ipants in this millennium project—namely that these questions are not ones that many feminists would ask when engaging in self-evaluation. Words such as "state of the art" and "cumulation," as well as the selection of certain scholars to speak on behalf of the rest, are in tension with an approach that celebrates diversity in terms of its subject matters, normative focus, and methodologies. Asking contributors to compare feminist approaches with realism, for ex-ample, is like asking for a comparison of a whole array of theoretical and methodological approaches that cross the disciplines, from the humanities to the social sciences, with one IR approach that, for the most part, has been located within the discipline of political science. Nevertheless, I welcome this opportunity to elaborate on some "pro-gressive" paths in IR feminism and to identify some of the important research questions that have guided feminist scholars in the past and will probably continue to do so in the future. I will also engage in some self-criticism; to this end I will conclude by raising some issues relating to methodological differences amongst IR feminists.

First, some comments on the questions themselves. We have been asked to assess the degree of "integration" and "cumulation" in our field, as well as to decide which core research questions might be the most promising for the future. Such an assessment is framed in terms suited to a social scientific discipline that strives to emulate the universalistic theory-based knowledge cumulation model of the natural sciences. Since many of those who identify themselves as IR feminists do not use social scientific methodologies, preferring in-stead methodologies more compatible with hermeneutic, interpre-tive epistemological traditions, they would be unlikely to use these standards of evaluation. It also assumes a particular definition of the meaning of theory.

Marysia Zalewski has identified three types of theory: theory as a tool for understanding the world; theory as critique, or understand-ing how the world got to be as it is so that it can be changed; and theory as practice in which people engage as they go about their everyday life.[4] Conventional IR theorists, by which I mean scholars who conform to positivist methodologies broadly defined, usually employ theory in the first sense, as a tool to develop explanations for the political and economic behavior of states in the international system. For those who define theory in this sense, its separation from political practice and, as far as possible, from the values of the researcher are thought to be important goals. The reflections and evaluation we have been asked to undertake are quite appropriate ones for those who use theory as a tool to develop better explanations. Feminist approaches, however, are more likely to define theory in Zalewski's second or third sense, which means that they would be likely to use different standards of evaluation.

For many feminist theorists, knowledge construction is explicitly linked to emancipatory political practice, primarily that of transforming the unequal power relationships between women and men. Sandra Whitworth has claimed that contemporary feminism has its roots in social movements; feminism is a politics of protest directed at transforming the unequal power relationships between women and men.[5] Therefore, a key goal for IR feminist theory used in this sense is to understand how the existing social order, one many feminists believe is marked by discrimination and oppression, came into being and how this knowledge can be used to work toward its transformation. For many IR feminists, therefore, knowledge is practical and explicitly normative. Christine Chin has claimed that these emancipatory concerns suggest the need for restructuring the ways in which we conceive and execute research problems; she argues for undoing received disciplinary and epistemological boundaries that segregate the pursuit of knowledge.[6]

Claiming that the kind of practical knowledge they seek emerges from political practice, many feminists do not believe in, nor see knowledge as requiring or benefiting from, the separation between theory and practice. Theory as practice, Zalewski's third definition of theory, means that we need to take into account many more human activities than would be thought necessary by those who use theory as a tool. The goal of this type of practical knowledge is not the improvement of theory but of practice; thus, it requires different standards of evaluation. Explicitly rejecting the separation between observers and observed, considered desirable by practitioners of the first definition of theory, practical knowledge is intended to yield greater understanding of people's everyday lives in order to improve them. Given these very different views of both the meaning and goals of theory, it is unlikely that feminists would use "scientific" criteria, such as integration and cumulation, to evaluate them.

Hilary Charlesworth has described feminist methodology as an "archaeological dig" where different methods are appropriate at different levels of excavation.[7] She claims that no single method is sufficient for analyzing complex social phenomena. Since feminists are using tools that are rarely included in a standard IR methodological training, their methodologies tend to be eclectic. There is a sense that research should be grounded, whether it is in people's everyday activities or in the close reading of texts that can offer interpretations about how people construct their world and, therefore, act upon it. While it is important to do research that is linked to concrete historical cases, it is also important to rethink the theoretical assumptions that led to consideration of these cases in the first place.

Defining gender as a social construction of inequality and preferring critically interpretive, hermeneutic epistemologies and a variety of related research strategies, such as ethnography and discourse analysis, for discovering these structures of inequality makes it difficult to assess feminist theoretical approaches primarily in terms of explanatory power. As mentioned before, most feminists celebrate difference and resist synthesis, positions that are more acceptable in the humanities than in the social sciences. Comparing feminist IR with other IR approaches that share a single set of assumptions and methodological tools is also difficult. IR feminists have drawn on a variety of feminist theoretical approaches variously described as liberal, radical, psychoanalytic, socialist, postmodern, and postcolonial. Besides seeking better understanding of women's subordination, most of these approaches see themselves as politically engaged in the practical tasks of improving women's lives. While liberal feminists have generally relied on empiricist methodologies, other approaches have questioned these positivist methodologies. Arguing from standpoint or postmodern epistemological positions, they claim that "scientific" theories that admit to the possibility of neutrality of facts and a universalist objectivity hide an epistemological tradition that is gendered and built on knowledge mostly about men. These different feminist approaches range across the disciplines, from the natural to the social sciences and the humanities. Forging these transdisciplinary bonds and respecting and using different methodologies is a position to which many feminist scholars aspire.

The editors' assessment of international studies at the millennium speaks of clusters of separable identifiable research questions such as globalization, international institutions, security policy, and gender and international relations as one of the few, but inadequate, signs of cumulation in the discipline. Feminists would probably question the labeling of gender and international relations in these terms; rather than identifying gender and international relations as a separable (and potentially cumulative) research program, a better measure of success would be when those studying each of these realms of activity recognize gender as intrinsic to their subject matter. Rather than defining itself as a separable body of research, feminist IR has ranged across all these research domains (and others) asking how gender as a category of analysis can improve our understanding of them. Feminists have suggested that gender considerations are vital to how we understand security, the construction of international institutions, economic globalization, human rights, democratization, and many other issues in international relations. To this end, feminists point to gender *in* international relations rather than gender *and* international relations.

In spite of my reservations about the adequacy of these questions for evaluating feminist research, I have found them useful in reflecting on some of the accomplishments and limitations of feminist IR. First, there has been progress although defined in rather a different way. To assess this progress, I prefer to draw on the work of Peggy McIntosh, who outlines five phases of curriculum change necessary for introducing gender into the scholarly disciplines.[8] The first phase is what McIntosh describes as a womanless world; this type of analysis describes only the activities of those holding high positions of power, usually in dominant states; much IR literature is still at this stage. Phase two notes the absence of women and adds the "famous few," such as Margaret Thatcher and Madeleine Albright, to the curriculum; several IR textbooks have begun to do this. While the addition of the "famous few" provides role models for women, it does nothing to change the discipline in ways that acknowledge that anything different can be learned from women's experiences. In phase three, the absence of women is seen as a problem as we begin to understand the politics implicit in a curriculum constructed without the inclusion of women's experiences; in this phase, women are typically seen as victims. Moving to phase four involves seeing women as valid human beings whose various life experiences have shaped the world in which we live, even though their contributions involve tasks that are often unacknowledged. The final phase of McIntosh's curriculum development brings us to the point where the subject matter of the discipline genuinely includes the experiences of all individuals regardless of race, culture, class, and gender. Such a discipline, which includes us all, would require a radical redrawing of the boundaries of its subject matter.

While phase five has not yet been realized and while much of international relations scholarship remains at stages one and two, feminist IR has generally progressed to stages three and four. Scholarly progress in feminist IR has involved moving from studies, informed by a liberal empiricist approach, that try to fit women into existing paradigms and frameworks to work that acknowledges the centrality of gender as a category of analysis for explaining, among other things, why women have so often been invisible in international politics. There has also been much more attention paid to race, class, and geographical and historical location, issues that have not received much attention in the discipline as conventionally defined. Challenging a discipline that was, for so long, silent about women, feminist IR has evolved, as has feminist theory more generally, from early studies of women *and* development and women *and* the military to more recent empirical studies that situate women *within* gendered structures of power.

For example, Kathy Moon has challenged us to recognize the plight of prostitutes serving the U.S. military in Korea and to understand how their lives are embedded within the broader framework of U.S.-Korean security relations.[9] In her study of prostitution around U.S. military bases in South Korea in the 1970s, Moon shows how these people-to-people relations were actually matters of security at the international level. Cleanup of prostitution camps by the South Korean government was part of its attempt to prevent withdrawal of American troops that had begun under the Nixon Doctrine of 1969. Crossing levels of analysis, Moon demonstrates how weakness of the Korean state in terms of influencing the U.S. government resulted in authoritarian sexist control at the domestic level. In other words, national security translated into social insecurity for these women. Moon describes her methodology as ethnographic; her interviews are not intended to offer statistical evidence but "to give voice to people who most Koreans and Americans have never considered as having anything important to say."[10] Moon's stories help us locate women in places not normally considered relevant to IR and to link their experiences to wider gendered processes and hierarchical structures of power from the local to the international levels.

Likewise, Christine Chin has demonstrated how overseas domestic workers in Malaysia are supporting the Malaysian state and the political economy of the East Asian region to the detriment of their own security.[11] The Malaysian state has needed Malaysian women to fill labor shortages in the industrial sector; thus, foreign workers are being used in the home for family-related tasks, and modernization is being achieved at the expense of the working poor, many of whom are immigrants left unprotected and often working under extremely harsh conditions. Describing her research as ethnographic, Chin rejects the survey method because it oversimplifies the complexities of life, which, she claims, cannot be distilled in a series of hypotheses to be tested. She describes her work as multi-method ethnographic research and offers field note quotations as evidence that allows her subjects to use their own words and the right to speak about any issue they pleased. Chin describes her analysis of her interviews as a study of narrativity or how we come to construct our identities by locating ourselves within our life stories.

Narrative is a method sometimes used by feminists to further their goal of constructing practical knowledge that comes out of people's everyday life experiences. Such work grows out of multiple sites and multiple perspectives. In other words, feminist scholars are challenging us to look at IR from the margins, to ask questions not normally thought to be relevant to the discipline, and to use different methodologies to answer them. Frequently, investigations begin at the level of the individual, or level one, and move up to levels two and three, the state and the international system. IR feminists believe that such investigations can also help us to understand that IR's levels of analysis are not discrete concepts but mutually constituted.

Using theory in Zalewski's third sense, Jane Mansbridge has claimed that if good theory evolves from practice and from seeing with a feminist eye, then it will never be possible to predict the most important future issues in feminist theory.[12] Nevertheless, we can identify some broad research questions that have motivated IR feminists over the past ten years and that will probably continue to do so in the future. As mentioned before, they are questions that cross issue areas and perspectives. One question with which feminists often begin is "where are the women?" Finding women involves looking in places not usually investigated in international relations. Acknowledging that we need to look in unconventional places not normally considered within the boundaries of IR, Cynthia Enloe has asked whether women's roles, as secretaries, clerical workers, domestic servants, and diplomats' wives, are relevant to the business of international politics.[13]

Moon, Chin, Enloe, and many others have demonstrated that women in their various roles as domestic servants, prostitutes, and homeworkers are relevant and vital to the business of international politics. Locating women must include placing them within gendered structures. Typically, feminist research questions have to do with investigating how the international system and the global economy contribute to the subordination of women and other subjugated groups. IR feminists ask what kind of evidence might further the claim that the practices of international politics are gendered. Through what mechanisms are the types of power necessary to keep unequal gender structures in place perpetuated? To fully understand the role of gender and other social hierarchies, questions about men and masculinity are also beginning to be asked. For example, does it make any difference to states' behavior that their foreign and security policies are so often legitimated through appeals to various types of hegemonic masculinity? It is important to emphasize that these feminist questions are often investigated with emancipatory goals in mind and with the understanding that the choice of questions we ask is never neutral. Feminists will continue to push the boundaries of the discipline, question our understanding of "common sense," and hypothesize a world that could be otherwise. Questioning the way we have come to understand the world as well as the forms of power necessary to sustain dominant forms of interpretation demands quite different methodologies from those generally used by conventional IR. Recovering the experiences of subjugated people demands methods more typical of anthropology and sociology than political science.

Given these goals, typically these and other feminist questions are investigated using critical rather than social scientific methodologies; many IR feminists, myself included, have claimed that positivist methodologies are inadequate for building a body of knowledge that takes gender identity and hierarchical social relations as its central framework and that acknowledges the mutual constitution of theory and practice. However, while many IR feminists have rejected social scientific methodologies, the introduction of feminist approaches into the discipline has also stimulated a growing body of research on women in international politics that draws on these more conventional methodologies. Indeed, there is a long tradition of this type of research in American politics, dealing with issues such as voting, public opinion, and the advancement of women in different arenas of public and private life. An important (and uncomfortable) question for many IR feminists is whether our tolerance (and celebration) of difference can extend to this type of work.

In international relations, feminists writing from a social scientific perspective have investigated the role of gender in foreign policy, particularly the evidence for a fairly substantial gender gap, in the United States at least, in attitudes about war and peace. Women in the United States have consistently shown less support for forceful means of pursuing foreign policy goals than men, and this gender gap continues to grow.[14] This leads to questions that are also being asked as to whether the presence of more women in elite foreign policy–making positions would make any difference in the conduct of foreign policy. For example, Mary Caprioli has quantitatively tested the relationship between state militarism and domestic gender equality; her study shows that domestic gender equality has a pacifying effect on state behavior on the international level.[15] Another study that uses public opinion data on attitudes toward the Arab-Israeli conflict found a strong positive correlation between attitudes toward support for equality of women and support for diplomacy and compromise.[16] The literature on the democratic peace has made these questions particularly compelling for scholars working on these issues.

Lisa Brandes, a scholar who does empirical research on the gender gap in popular attitudes, has suggested that I, amongst others, have dismissed these types of research questions largely on methodological grounds.[17] She argues that rather than dismissing a research program out of hand, it is incumbent upon IR feminist scholars to do the hard investigative work to find out what the results will be, before making claims about their likely value. Yet, since women do not come close to parity in any state in terms of occupying positions of power in foreign policy–making, I remain skeptical of efforts to explain the foreign policy orientations of liberal states in these terms. Given the pitfalls of McIntosh's stage two analysis discussed earlier, I am also suspicious of attempting to understand gender hierarchies by adding women to existing paradigms and research traditions. Nevertheless, I do think that IR feminists in postpositivist traditions should consider how to engage more seriously with this type of work. While bridging the methodological divide between scientific traditions of explaining and hermeneutic traditions of practical understanding is difficult and, according to some, impossible, feminists need to talk more, albeit acknowledging their differences, across these theoretical divides.[18]

In a relatively short span of ten years, feminists have challenged the gendered foundations of IR; they have introduced new issues and brought new questions into a discipline in which women were largely absent. In order to answer their questions, many IR feminists have ranged far from the discipline as conventionally defined and drawn on methodologies unfamiliar to many in IR. They have challenged disciplinary boundaries and methods that, they believe, impose limitations on the kinds of questions that can be asked and the ways in which they can be answered. However, these transdisciplinary excursions and methodological innovations have consequences. Most graduate education in IR, at least in the United States, still occurs within political science departments where training in the kind of critical methodologies used by many feminists may not exist. Moreover, power differences between conventional and critical approaches, which often play out by drawing disciplinary boundaries around subject matter and methods, will continue to render judgment of feminist approaches as less than adequate.

Nevertheless, feminists must continue to challenge and critique a discipline that has been quite ethnocentric both in terms of its subject matter and its methodology. At the same time, those who have gone outside the discipline of political science to find tools for understanding global politics must converse with those feminists more conventionally trained. Since a basic assumption of postpositivist feminist IR has been the inadequacy of conventional methodologies for understanding the issues with which it is concerned, can (or should) we be truly tolerant when fundamental questions about epistemologies are at stake? These are difficult questions both for IR feminists and for a discipline much of which judges itself in terms of social scientific standards. At the end of a century that has witnessed the founding and institutionalization of this IR discipline, as well as a great deal of conflict and injustice, much remains to be done. Could we not all agree on the additional, even more pressing need to measure the progress of feminist scholarship in terms of its contributions to the betterment of the lives of women and men?

Notes

1. Cynthia Enloe, *Bananas, Beaches, and Bases: Making Feminist Sense of International Politics* (Berkeley: University of California Press, 1989).

2. Much of the early work in feminist IR was generated by a series of conferences in the United States and the United Kingdom. Conferences were held at the London School of Economics (LSE) in 1988, the University of Southern California in 1989, and Wellesley College in 1990. Grant and Newland's *Gender and International Relations* and Peterson's *Gendered States* were the products of the LSE and Wellesley conferences respectively. Rebecca Grant and Kathleen Newland, eds., *Gender and International Relations* (Bloomington: Indiana University Press, 1991); V. Spike Peterson, ed., *Gendered States: Feminist (Re)Visions of International Relations Theory* (Boulder, Colo.: Lynne Rienner, 1992).

3. Some of the early texts include Enloe, *Bananas, Beaches, and Bases;* Grant and Newland, *Gender and International Relations;* Peterson, *Gendered States;* Christine Sylvester, *Feminist Theory and International Relations in a Postmodern Era* (Cambridge: Cambridge University Press, 1994); J. Ann Tickner, *Gender in International Relations: Feminist Perspectives on Achieving Global Security* (New York: Columbia University Press, 1992); Sandra Whitworth, *Feminism and International Relations* (New York: St. Martin's Press, 1994).

4. Marysia Zalewski, "All These Theories Yet the Bodies Keep Piling Up," in Steve Smith, Ken Booth, and Marysia Zalewski, eds., *International Theory: Positivism and Beyond* (Cambridge: Cambridge University Press, 1996).

5. Sandra Whitworth, "Gender in the Inter-Paradigm Debate," *Millennium: Journal of International Studies* 18, no. 2 (1989): 265–72.

6. Christine Chin, *In Service and Servitude: Foreign Female Domestic Workers and the Malaysian "Modernization" Project* (New York: Columbia University Press, 1998).

7. Hilary Charlesworth, "Feminist Critiques of International Law and Their Critics," *Third World Legal Studies* (1994–95): 1–16.

8. See Peggy McIntosh, "Interactive Phases of Curriculum Re-Vision: A Feminist Perspective" (Wellesley College Center for Research on Women, Wellesley, Mass., 1983). McIntosh is using history as her example, but her analysis could equally well be applied to the discipline of international relations.

9. Katharine Moon, *Sex among Allies: Military Prostitution in U.S.–Korean Relations* (New York: Columbia University Press, 1997).

10. Ibid., 15.

11. Chin, *In Service and Servitude.*

12. Jane Mansbridge, "Frontier Research and Crucial Questions for Research in Feminist Theory" (paper presented at the Frontiers of Women and Politics Research Workshop, APSA Women and Politics Seminar, Harvard University, 1998).

13. Enloe, *Bananas, Beaches, and Bases,* 8.

14. Nancy Gallagher, "The Gender Gap in Popular Attitudes toward the Use of Force," in *Women and the Use of Military Force,* ed. Ruth Howes and Michael Stevenson (Boulder, Colo.: Lynne Rienner, 1993), 29.

15. Mary Caprioli, "Gendered Conflict," *Journal of Peace Research* 37, no. 1 (2000): 51–68.

16. Mark Tessler and Ina Warriner, "Gender, Feminism, and Attitudes to-
    ward International Conflict: Exploring Relationships with Survey Data
    from the Middle East," *World Politics* 49, no. 2 (1997): 250–81.
17. Lisa Brandes, "Research Frontiers in Gender and the International Or-
    der" (paper presented at the Frontiers of Women and Politics Research
    Workshop, APSA Women and Politics Seminar, Harvard University,
    1998).
18. This issue is discussed in some detail in Martin Hollis and Steve Smith,
    Explaining and Understanding International Relations (Oxford: Oxford
    University Press, 1990). These authors conclude that bridging this divide
    is not possible.

FEMINISM AND/IN INTERNATIONAL RELATIONS

An Exhausted Conversation?

or

FEMINISTS DOING INTERNATIONAL RELATIONS

The Cut(ting) Edge of Contemporary
Critical Theory and Practice?

Marysia Zalewski

Questions about Questions

In common with the other presenters on the millennial reflections feminist theory panel, I found the task at hand something of a challenge. At one level this should not be surprising; writing any academic paper usually is—and should be—a challenge. But there was something about the kinds of questions we were being asked to consider that clearly troubled our group. J. Ann Tickner, for example, suggested that the questions asked were not ones that "feminists would ask when engaging in self-evaluation."[1] Jan Jindy Pettman claimed that "it is a daunting task to respond to the challenges laid down for this panel"[2] and further explained that one of the things feminists do is ask *different* kinds of questions about *different*

I would like to thank the following for conversations about this essay: Helen Brock-lehurst, Cynthia Enloe, Cynthia Weber, Antje Wiener, and the organizers and participants at the seminar organized by the Gender and Women's Studies Seminar series at the University of Bradford in March 2000, especially Ruth Jacobson and Anne Scott. I would also like to thank Michael Brecher and Frank Harvey for organizing this series of panels and the subsequent publication of the papers and to commend them for their patience.

things. L. H. M. Ling, through her tale about the fish and the turtle, implied that "old questions" would not tell us anything about "the new."[3] And Christine Sylvester cautioned us to "mind the easy answers" when asking questions about progress within feminism and IR—or indeed IR in feminism.[4]

Why were the questions we were asked to consider so problematic for us? Surely it makes eminently reasonable intellectual sense to engage in "critical self-reflection" or to "assess where we stand on key debates and address why we have failed to resolve them" or to suggest "what intrasubfield standards we might use to evaluate the significance of feminist theoretical insights"? I think there are at least two main reasons that we found these kinds of questions so problematic. One is that what makes "reasonable intellectual sense" is structurally defined by the traditional or neotraditional center of the discipline, and therefore, by definition, a critical approach such as feminism will have an alternative sense of what counts as reasonable in the realm of the intellectual. A second reason is that we were being asked to make authoritative statements about the impact of the work on feminism and gender in international relations. This is problematic as it relies on the assumption that feminist work in international relations can be fitted into a coherent framework upon which such judgments can then be made. This is not the case as feminism is a vast and sometimes contradictory body of work that makes it therefore difficult (and perhaps inadvisable) to make sweeping and authoritative generalizations about.

But the fact that we had "questions about the questions" did not inevitably make the questions we were asked useless or irrelevant! Indeed, the original questions instigated a plethora of other questions, which, in my view, is a positive intellectual practice. For example, when asked to "look back" at the development or trajectory of feminist work within the discipline of international relations over the last ten or more years: Where do we start? Where will we look? How would we know what "difference" feminisms have made? Or, where do we go in the discipline to find the answer to these questions—whether they are about accomplishments, shortcomings, or where we stand on key debates? How do we know what a *key* debate is anyway? What are the correct answers to all these questions?

Of course, there is no such thing as the "correct answer." It depends on which perspective one starts from and crucially on how one is situated in relation to the core of the discipline. If, for example, one is working in the area of neorealism, the key debates are well defined and indeed well protected. Scholars may disagree over the most appropriate approach to dealing with interstate relationships and have vigorous debates about this. But the value and centrality of the debate itself is well protected by the very self-definition of the discipline. This is not the case for those who work on feminism and gender. By definition, these scholars not only debate amongst themselves—but crucially we are challenging the self-definition of the discipline.

Following from this last point a serious issue needs to be raised that gives some further indication as to one of the reasons we found the questions challenging. This is that the questions asked of the millennial reflections panelists had the potential to consolidate and reinforce *some* areas of debate in the discipline (the mainstream and neomainstream ones) but significantly also had the potential to render *vulnerable* those areas that, by their very nature, challenge the status quo.[5] For example, being self-critical within and amongst the margins is a very different enterprise with very different issues at stake than being self-critical within the established center. No wonder we found these questions problematic. Nevertheless, the challenge was taken up by the participants of the feminist theory and gender panel, but in ways that I believe did *not* facilitate a falling into the very gendered space of *vulnerability* just alluded to.

In my own case I was particularly vexed with the idea of having to tell one "story" about feminism and international relations. But I decided that my propensity to see more than one story at a time was something I should work with. As Irigaray suggests, "don't worry about the 'right' word. There isn't any."[6]

And there isn't any right word or "correct" answer to all the questions asked of us. There isn't any "right" or "truthful" story about feminism and international relations because it depends who speaks the words and who has the authority to decide which voices and which stories are the authentic and legitimate ones. This led me to choose two stories of the many stories that could be told about "feminism and IR."

Story One: An Exhausted Conversation?

As I try and "time travel" back to the late 1980s and "reflect" on my early, formal introductions to the "feminism and IR" debate, two memories demand my attention.

The first is of a graduate student speaking at the 1988 London School of Economics and Political Science (LSE) conference on "Women and IR." She was speaking on the topic of abortion, suggesting that no time limit be imposed on when a woman could have an abortion. There was a stunned silence in the audience. It was clear the student was expecting such a reaction. "Why," she asked, "why wouldn't we trust women enough to make humane and reasonable decisions in this context?" Is the assumption that removing the legal constraint here would result in a deluge of abortions of near-to-full-term babies? Why would we fear this? Why do we think the law is so necessary to contain women's behavior? I can't remember who that graduate student was[7]—but I do remember being both shocked and impressed by what she said.

The second memory is of a paper given by Sarah Brown at the conference.[8] I remember how her paper seemed to sit uneasily alongside many of the other papers at the conference, which were eventually published in a special issue of *Millennium*.[9] Perhaps more pertinently, I recall that Sarah Brown's paper was not included in the follow-up volume edited by Grant and Newland.[10] Maybe one reason Brown's paper "sat uneasily" with many of the others is because it was her view that "a feminist critical theory of International Relations is fundamentally a political act of commitment to understanding the world from the perspective of the socially subjugated."[11] This was quite a radical view at the time (and probably still is) especially as it appeared to be departing from the traditional agenda of international relations in a big way, further, perhaps, than other feminists were prepared to go.

Do these two memories have anything to tell us about the contemporary relationship between feminism and IR? As I asked myself this question, I was reminded of a more recent piece on feminism and international relations by Molly Cochran in which she suggests that "the key to the possibility of real dialogue between feminists and the discipline rests on whether or not IR is prepared to accommodate epistemological doubt."[12]

What would Sarah Brown think of Molly Cochran's suggestion? Perhaps Brown would insist that questions of epistemology necessarily implicate questions of ontology. Maybe she would suggest that if "real dialogue" were possible between feminists and the discipline, IR would have to accommodate not only epistemological doubt but also ontological doubt. But even further, she would probably suggest that what is necessary is more than an *accommodation* and more than simply *doubt*. Only a radical restructuring of many of IR's epistemological, ontological, and political beliefs will do, alongside the commitment to make real and effective changes that would accompany such a restructuring.

But many feminist international relations scholars and international relations scholars then and now have not been willing to embrace the idea or reality of such a radical restructuring. Speaking on behalf of the discipline in 1993, the question I asked of Brown's work was "why would IR scholars want to change the focus of the discipline from war, peace and interstate behaviour and turn their attention solely to issues of gender—thereby reconstructing the starting point of International Relations enquiry?"[13] To start addressing this question we would surely have to know where to start.

And Where Do We Start?

The usual place to start is IR. Consider this encyclopedic entry on feminism and IR:

> International Relations is a paradigmatically male dominated subject. The academic discipline is overwhelmingly male and the conventional practices of international relations are typically associated with men. War is still regarded as the core topic of international relations. The discipline itself originated in 1919, instigated by the carnage of World War One, inspiring the laudable aim to understand wars in an attempt to prevent them. This concern with war leads international relations scholars to be pre-occupied with power, security, international structures, and relations between states especially in the realms of foreign policy and military strategy. A concurrent underlying theme of international relations is a desire to achieve order and stability on a global scale.[14]

As the story unfolds, it might seem that IR conceptualized in this way has little in common with feminism, in all its manifestations. Indeed, feminism appears significantly mismatched with conventional international relations. Feminism's questions about women and domestic/personal politics and interest in disrupting the traditional (patriarchal) order seem inherently incompatible with international relations. As Sandra Whitworth remarks, it is perhaps not surprising that there is such resistance to feminist intrusions into

international relations as feminism and IR appear to be "politically
at odds with one another."[15]

Despite the (political) odds, feminist intrusions have continued.
The encyclopedic entry continues.

There is the classic "add women and stir" approach, influenced
by liberal feminist theory and politics. In the "real world" of
international politics, this is a logical move, especially in the
context of western liberal democracies apparently committed to
equal rights. A brief look around the world's senior politicians
and diplomats, combat soldiers or military commanders reveals
the scarcity of women. However, the ontological move of "adding women" revealed something initially paradoxical; that
women are already in international relations. This did not simply mean some women are in traditionally powerful international roles; but rather that traditional (and therefore invisible)
women's activities ensure the international system works
smoothly and efficiently.

But as we know, there is more to feminism than this.

A second approach, evolving from the liberal inspired one, is
more concerned with epistemology. This has at least two
strands; one linked with radical feminism and standpoint feminism; the second influenced by postmodernism and cultural
studies. The radical feminist focus on the lives and experiences
of women and the standpoint feminist interest in the gendered
construction of knowledge encourages some feminists to investigate how we understand traditional topics in international
relations. Security, for example, is conventionally understood
as militarily defending the state from attack. Feminists studying women's lives ask if this idea about security is a "male"
one, shot through with the typically masculinist belief that
power concerns control rather than empowerment.[16] If women
defined security, the important issues might be different because women are more likely to be attacked by men they know
rather than strangers from other states.

But the feminism and IR story clearly doesn't end there. Beginning
the story of IR with its own self-defined origins and purpose perhaps

makes it more difficult for many within the discipline to understand that "feminist work goes beyond a desire to be included onto the traditional agenda."[17] Feminist insistence on the relevance and importance of women's lives and the significant power of gendered imaginations on the structuring, representation, and acting out of matters international logically goes way beyond a desire to be included onto the traditional agenda and instead moves us into the realm of radical restructuring. If this is the case—what does this mean for feminist interventions in IR?

Then What Happened?

As we know, much has been written in the area of gender, women, feminism, and international relations and continues to be so. But it is abundantly clear that the starting point of international relations inquiry has not been fundamentally reconstructed. In response to one of the questions asked by the panel organizers, does this mean feminists have failed?

For most feminists it's not so much a question of failure—or if it is, one might argue that the failure belongs to the mainstream in IR who resist or indeed refuse to listen.[18] This mainstream and neo-mainstream resistance and refusal has led to a number of feminist calls to work out a better and more successful way to have the conversation with the mainstream in the pursuit of a more constructive dialogue between the "two communities," such as that suggested by Cochran. But still the discipline looks unlikely to be restructured in the ways implied by much feminist work, which begs the question "Is the conversation between feminists and the discipline now an exhausted one?"

For those who leave the discipline, like Sarah Brown, it clearly is an exhausted conversation. Relying on the ideals and practices of liberal humanism in an effort to persuade the mainstream and neomainstream to widen their epistemological and ontological boundaries to take on board feminist insights radically underestimates the relationship between epistemology, ontology, and power.[19] There would appear to be little hope of achieving the separation of epistemology and ontology from power that is necessary to gain the radical restructuring demanded by scholars like Brown.

But should we be disappointed about this? Not necessarily.

Story Two: Feminism in International Relations — The Cut(ting) Edge of Contemporary Critical Theory and Practice?

Caricature and forgetting is the great[er] danger
haunting women's political actions.
— Lynn Segal, Why Feminism?

"Looking back" over the past in the context of the relationship be-tween feminism and IR has led me to ask myself two questions in particular. What did feminists in IR expect would happen, and what does feminist theory do to IR?

As with any revolutionary political movement in the "early" days, there is often a sense of euphoric optimism. Areas that need changing are identified and targeted, which goes along with a willingness to make the changes and a sense of vision that change *will* be achieved. In the context of feminism and IR—what did all of that mean? At a basic level it meant a more equitable inclusion of women both "out there" in the world of international politics as well as "in here" in the institution. But crucially it also meant a legitimate place for femi-nist scholarship in the discipline. Let me concentrate on the latter issue of legitimacy by moving on to my second question asked above: what does feminist theory do?

What Does Feminist Theory Do?

As Patricia Clough puts it, "Feminists have made the academy itself a site of feminist politics."[20] The challenge that the graduate student threw out to the audience at the Women and IR conference at the LSE in 1988 surely gives us a clue as to one of the things "feminism does" and one of the ways in which feminism makes the academy a site of feminist politics. I mean by this that her comment was shock-ing, and additionally it didn't *seem* to have anything to do with IR— the latter being a common reaction to feminist questions in IR. In the "early days" it seemed that people in the discipline were excited about the contributions feminists could make to IR. There was an overall keen interest in hearing what feminists had to say. This did mean that for a short time, feminists could say anything—even the comment made by the unnamed graduate student! Because of this interest alongside a certain "freedom" of speech, it did seem that in the late 1980s there was a sense that feminist scholarship was well on its way to achieving a legitimate place within the discipline.

But legitimacy and subversion are not very compatible! And if feminism is (in large part) about blurring disciplinary boundaries, exposing the hard work that goes into maintaining institutional and hierarchical parameters and privileges, and subverting more traditional academic practices, this makes it an unlikely candidate to be embraced by the discipline as legitimate. For as we know, disciplines have boundaries; institutions have parameters that they jealously guard; the academy has a "purpose" and will resist attempts to subvert it. This suggests that the ways *available* to the discipline of international relations to respond to feminism are actually somewhat limited.

What this means in practice is that since feminists "intruded" in the discipline we have witnessed an incremental resistance to and refusal of this work—or rather the *implications* of this work. This does not mean that many of the more traditional international relations scholars are not genuinely interested in the work that feminists produce. My point is not one about individual motivation—but about how scholars are positioned in relation to the discipline and what this entails for how they will be able to respond to challenges feminist work poses.

Let us consider further what these challenges are in the context of what feminism "does to IR." Think of the millennial reflections panels held at the International Studies Association convention in Los Angeles in March 2000 at which an earlier version of this paper was presented. Does the organization of these panels tell us anything about "feminist effects" and "disciplinary resistances"? The "feminists" were all gathered together on one panel, which certainly appears to divide "feminists" and the "rest of IR" sharply into "two communities."[21] But are we two separate communities—"the feminists" and the rest of IR?

"You? I? That's still saying too much. Dividing too sharply between us: all."[22]

Of course we have *all* been involved in affirming the idea of "two communities"—but one effect arising from this is the idea that dialogue between the two communities is necessary. This also logically leads to another effect in the feminism and IR context—which is that the dialogue between the two communities isn't working very well partly because the communities appear to have very different agendas but also significantly because the two communities are unequally positioned within the hierarchy of the discipline.

My recent move to Queen's University, Belfast, in Northern Ireland has forced me to think more deeply about the notion of two communities and the necessity of dialogue. Having heard many of the "leading actors" speak, it seems that without exception, "dialogue is seen to be key." My intention is to (hopefully) not fall into the trap of drawing inappropriate parallels—rather it is to question what the idea of two communities does, especially in the context of apparently "failed dialogue" and the persistent attempts to improve dialogue.

An initial suggestion about what follows from the construction of two communities—particularly as evidenced by the construction of the millennial reflections panels—is that it gives the impression that feminists are not involved in any of the other debates currently being rehearsed within IR.[23] Is it really the case that no feminist scholars are involved in the neorealist debate or the critical theory/postmodernism debate? This certainly appears to be the case as there were no "out" feminist scholars on any of the other reflections panels. And on the "other side" of that particular coin, there were hardly any women on the other panels either and none on those particular two panels!

Of course these are just panels at a conference—where else might we look for evidence of what "feminism has done to IR" and the implications of thinking of feminist scholars and IR scholars as two separate communities? What about the arena of publishing? A cursory glance at some of the main IR journals will probably show that feminist work is still poorly represented; in the main (and best-selling) textbooks there may be a token page or two—or even chapter or two—but it seems that "IR" is still . . . IR, taking us right back to the idea that there are these "two communities."

What if we abandoned the idea of having to create and sustain a functioning dialogue with the discipline of IR? This might mean that instead of looking at what "feminism has done to IR"—we might want to look at how feminists "do" IR. Let's take the example of teaching. What is happening there?

It can be difficult, in the first instance, getting students to think about the effects and impact of gender. One has to find something—some example—that will grab their attention. One thing that always really grabs my students' attention is the image of a mainstream political theory or IR theory module on which the vast majority of the authors are female. I usually tell them I have taught on many undergraduate core political theory modules that have included a number of authors such as Plato, Aristotle, Schopenhauer, J. S. Mill, Kant, Marx, Weber, Rousseau, Rawls, and so on. And I would come in and give the Mary Wollstonecraft lecture somewhere near the end of the course. Now of course the students see that there is possibly an issue of male dominance and the invisibility of women at stake here. But the move that really gets them to start understanding what gender does is one in which I suggest the whole mainstream module might instead be based on female authors—maybe with one token lecture on a male author. Looking at their incredulous faces, the questions I then ask them are—wouldn't it feel *so* biased? Wouldn't it seem ridiculous at some level? Doesn't this tell us something about the "naturalness" of the visibility of "things masculine" and the naturalness of the invisibility of "things feminine"? (One might try the same thought experiment about the reflections panels at the ISA. An all-female "realist" or "alternative" panel perhaps?)

This "moment" of destabilization takes us right back to the un-named graduate student's challenge at the LSE in 1988. And I think it demonstrates one of the most exciting and important things that feminist work does—particularly at the level of teaching. *It can destabilize what we think we already know and how we know it.* In the context of the contemporary academy this destabilization may not appear to be the most appropriate or best thing to do! Of course students have assignments to do, essays to complete, exams to sit, and degrees to get, and we need to help them succeed in that. But I maintain that a vastly important part of a university education is to destabilize established knowledges about how things work and to emphasize the relationship between how we think and what we do and what happens to us outside in the real world. *Because of this I would argue that feminist work is at the cut(ting) edge of contemporary critical theory and practice within international relations.*

What I mean by cut(ting) is that feminisms are "cut" (or attempts to cut are made) from what is counted as the "real," the "important," the "significant," the "relevant" in international relations. But one of the reasons so many attempts are made to cut feminisms out or pare feminisms down is precisely because this work *is* so cutting edge. And I say this work is cutting edge because "[feminist] studies alters the very subject of knowledge by calling into question what is considered knowledge in any discipline."[24]

By asking the question "who is woman, what is woman, how is woman?," which is where much feminist work starts—we are set

off on a veritable avalanche of deconstructive and destabilizing processes and practices that have the potential to radically shake up
conventional ideas about subjectivity, epistemology, ontology,
agency, and political action in international relations. Opening the
doors for other deconstructive theories and practices such as critical
theory, postmodernism, poststructuralism, and queer theory, feminist work is one of the most upsetting things to have happened to
international relations.

Like the notion of "play" in postmodern approaches, the notion
of "upset" is not used lightly—although I am aware it can be seen
as too negative a strategy. But of course the point is—there is no
choice to be had. Feminist work is inherently upsetting in a number
of ways because it calls into question what constitutes the discipline.

Where Do We Go from Here? . . . To New Conversations?

When initially working on this paper, my first conclusion about the
current state of feminism and IR led me to the first story told in this
chapter—one in which the relationship between feminism and international relations could be characterized as an "exhausted conversation." Perhaps I reached this conclusion as I was too concerned
with thinking about the notion of "two communities" and the presumed necessity and/or impossibility of dialogue between the two
in the context of exploring and expanding feminist questions. Having
spent much time thinking about and working on these issues and
having numerous conversations with friends and colleagues working
in this area, I have come to the conclusion that if we think about
feminists and IR as two separate communities we are necessarily
drawn toward the conclusion that the conversation between these
two communities is not going to go very far because of their very
different agendas and positionings.

But if we shift how we think about the positionings of the so-
called communities we can tell a different story. For example, if we
begin to see feminist scholars as IR scholars, then we can look at the
conversation within this community and come up with a story,
which tells us that this conversation is actually doing rather well.
The two stories I have told in this paper may both be "true" (or not),
but I think much more momentum and energy is to be found by
starting with the feminist IR community (in all its guises) than by
starting with what we traditionally think of as IR. Additionally it is

interesting to think about where some of our most fruitful and innovative conversations occur.

In my and many of my colleagues' experience, the students who choose to do feminist work or who are genuinely curious about it generally love this work—and courses are highly popular. This is surely a wonderful sign of success. Additionally, I think we have started a trend in "backpack" books—by which I mean the books that some of our number writes are actually to be seen being read by people going on holiday! I'm thinking in particular here of Cynthia Enloe's *Bananas, Beaches, and Bases*[25] (and I am sure there are many more). This must surely imply that this work is reaching a wider audience than just university students and thus must be entering into any number of everyday conversations. How many more conventional or neoconventional IR books can we say this about?

And staying with the idea of "conversations," the new journal that all of us who presented papers on the millennial reflections panel are involved with, the *International Feminist Journal of Politics,* has a section called "Conversations." I wonder if Sarah Brown would write a piece for this section as this is a space where we hope all manner of radical and innovative and unusual voices might be heard.

Returning to the Questions and Questions about Questions

I want to return to the original questions asked of us, specifically the request by the organizers of the reflections panels that we include in our revised conference papers a consideration of what we thought would be a fair measure of success or failure in our own field and then to assess the extent to which "core objectives" have or have not been met and why.

In this chapter I have suggested that we could think about two of the initial objectives of feminist work in IR as to increase the numbers of women in the realms of international relations and international politics and to find a legitimate place for feminist scholarship in the discipline. Have these objectives been met? How can we find out? And what would the answers to these questions tell us about the successes or failures of feminist work in IR?

There probably are more women now in the public world of international politics and the academic world of international relations. But it is still the case that most of these women are clustered at the lower and middle levels of the hierarchies. Does this mean feminists have failed in their objectives? Or does this mean that the institutions have failed feminists?

With regard to the legitimacy of feminist scholarship—it clearly depends where one goes to find the criteria of legitimacy. As I have intimated in this chapter, if we judge feminist work by the standards of conventional and neoconventional IR, much feminist work would probably fail the test of legitimacy. However, if we use feminist criteria of legitimacy—a different story can be told. Of course feminists do not all agree with each other, and some feminists will find some feminist work inappropriate. But that the debate *itself* is legitimate and centrally important is unlikely to be in doubt. And this makes a lot of difference.

At the end of the day—or more accurately, at the beginning of a new millennium—as I see it, the task for scholars like myself is *not* to identify "intrasubfield consensus," yet I do not see this as a cause for lament. Indeed, if after a decade and more of feminist international relations scholarship there was a synergy of interests, concerns, and approaches between feminists and the mainstream and neomainstream of the discipline—this would indeed be a cause for lament; we would have lost the battle. This, I know, sounds paradoxical. Wasn't feminism supposed to change IR into something "feminist friendly," "gender sensitive," even "emancipatory"? Possibly.

Of course the questions we were asked were problematic. It is the traditional practice of an institution like IR to try and secure itself against radical change. Indeed, IR's task in terms of "reflection" is to see itself reflected back. However, I share Jenny Edkins's view that the role of the critical IR theorist—feminist or otherwise (though I happen to think feminists do it better . . .)—is *not* to secure the discipline from theoretical danger but indeed quite the opposite.[26] This can be quite a risky practice and may not be one agreed upon by all the presenters on the panel from which these chapters are a result. This is not surprising, as there are many differences between feminists! But it is a practice that feminists continue to engage in because despite the differences between us, my guess is that we all still believe "it matters." That is, whatever we think feminism is, there is a sense that injustices continue, hierarchies persist, and people are consistently harmed. Therefore "it matters" to continue to be involved in the practice of insecuring the discipline and to not only provide "answers" but to question what it is we are to provide "answers" to.

Notes

1. J. A. Tickner, "Feminist Theory and Gender Studies: Reflections for the Millennium," in this volume.
2. J. J. Pettman, "Critical Paradigms in International Studies: Bringing It All Back Home?," in this volume.
3. L. H. M. Ling, "The Fish and the Turtle: Multiple Worlds as Method," in this volume.
4. C. Sylvester, "'Progress' as Feminist International Relations," in this volume.
5. This potential is a function of the structure of the discipline and not the intentions of the organizers.
6. L. Irigaray, *This Sex Which Is Not One* (Ithaca, N.Y.: Cornell University Press, 1985), 213.
7. I apologize for not being able to name her—perhaps this tells a story in itself.
8. S. Brown, "Feminism, International Theory, and International Relations of Gender Equality," *Millennium* 17, no. 3 (1988): 461–76. I believe that Sarah Brown was a graduate student at Sussex University at the time of the LSE conference. She has since left the profession.
9. R. Grant and David Long, eds., *Women and International Relations,* special issue of *Millennium* 17, no. 3 (1988).
10. R. Grant and K. Newland, *Gender and International Relations* (Milton Keynes, England: Open University Press, 1991).
11. Brown, "Feminism, International Theory, and International Relations of Gender Equality," 472.
12. M. Cochran, "Talking with Feminists about What We Can Know in IR," *Cambridge Review of International Affairs* 12, no. 2 (1999): 46–56, 51.
13. M. Zalewski, "Feminist Theory and International Relations," in *From Cold War to Collapse: Theory and World Politics in the 1980s,* ed. M. Bowker and R. Brown (Cambridge: Cambridge University Press, 1993), 128. I would not ask this kind of question now.
14. M. Zalewski, entry on "Feminism and International Relations," in *The Encyclopaedia of Feminist Theory,* ed. Lorraine Code (New York: Routledge, 2000).
15. S. Whitworth, *Feminism and International Relations* (London: Macmillan, 1994), ix.
16. J. A. Tickner, *Gender and International Relations* (New York: Columbia University Press, 1992).
17. C. Sylvester, *Feminist Theory and International Relations in a Postmodern Era* (Cambridge: Cambridge University Press, 1994), 134.
18. M. Zalewski, "Where Is Woman in International Relations? To Return as a Woman and Be Heard," *Millennium* 27, no. 4 (1999): 847–67.
19. M. Zalewski, "Playing Like a Girl: A Response to Molly Cochran," *Cambridge Review of International Affairs* 12, no. 2 (1999): 57–60, 59.
20. P. T. Clough, *Feminist Thought* (Oxford, England: Basil Blackwell, 1994), 2.
21. My point is not to imply that the organizers of the panels intended to marginalize feminist work. Indeed, the inclusion of this panel indicated

precisely the opposite. My aim is rather to peruse the effects of the categorizing practices we are all involved with.

22. Irigaray, *This Sex Which Is Not One*, 218.
23. See note 21.
24. J. Gallop, *Reading Lacan* (Ithaca, N.Y.: Cornell University Press, 1985), 18.
25. C. Enloe, *Bananas, Beaches, and Bases: Making Feminist Sense of International Politics* (London: Pandora, 1989).
26. J. Edkins, *Poststructuralism and International Relations: Bringing the Political Back In* (Boulder, Colo.: Lynne Rienner, 1999), 142.

About the Contributors

Michael Brecher

Michael Brecher is the R. B. Angus Professor of Political Science at McGill University. Educated at McGill and Yale (Ph.D., 1953), he is the author or coauthor of eighteen books and eighty-five articles on India–South Asia, international systems, foreign policy theory and analysis, international crises, conflict and war, and the Indo-Pakistani and Arab-Israel protracted conflicts. Since 1975, he has been director of the International Crisis Behavior Project.

His most recent books are *Crises in World Politics* (1993) and *A Study of Crisis* (1997, 2000, with Jonathan Wilkenfeld). He has received two book awards: the Watumull Prize of the American Historical Association in 1960 for *Nehru: A Political Biography* (1959) and the Woodrow Wilson Award of the American Political Science Association in 1973 for *The Foreign Policy System of Israel: Setting, Images, Process* (1972). Among his other awards are the Fieldhouse Award for Distinguished Teaching, McGill (1986); the Distinguished Scholar Award of the International Studies Association (1995); the Leon-Gerin Prix du Québec for the human sciences (2000); and the Award for High Distinction in Research, McGill (2000). He has been a fellow of the Royal Society of Canada since 1976 and has held fellowships from the Nuffield, Rockefeller, and John Simon Guggenheim foundations. He has been a visiting professor at the University of Chicago, the Hebrew University of Jerusalem, University of California, Berkeley, and Stanford University. In 1999–2000 he served as president of the International Studies Association.

Michael Cox

Professor Cox is currently editor of the *Review of International Studies*. He is an associate fellow of the Royal Institute of International Affairs in London and an executive member of the National Committee for the Study of International Affairs at the Royal Irish Academy in Dublin. The author, editor, and coeditor of more than twelve books, his most recent publications include *Rethinking the Soviet Collapse* (1998); *The Interregnum: Controversies in World Politics, 1989–1999* (1999); *E. H. Carr: A Critical Appraisal* (2000); and *American Democracy Promotion* (2000).

Robert W. Cox

Robert W. Cox is a professor emeritus of political science at York University, Toronto, Ontario. He is author of *Production, Power, and World Order: Social Forces in the Making of History* (1987) and *Approaches to World Order* (1996, with Timothy J. Sinclair). His recent work has been about civilizations.

Ernst B. Haas

Ernst B. Haas is Robson Research Professor of Government Emeritus at the University of California, Berkeley, where he is also a professor in the graduate school. His most recent publication is the two-volume study *Nationalism, Liberalism, and Progress* (1997, 2000). His current research is concerned with the institutionalization of international norms.

Peter M. Haas

Peter M. Haas is a professor of political science at the University of Massachusetts at Amherst. He received a Ph.D. in political science from the Massachusetts Institute of Technology. He has published widely on international environmental subjects, including pollution control in the Mediterranean, pollution control in the Baltic and North Seas, UNEP's regional seas programs, stratospheric ozone protection, and international environmental institutions. He has also published works on international relations theory, focusing on the interplay between knowledge and power in international policy co-ordination.

His recent work has focused on the interplay between international institutions and scientific involvement in the creation and enforcement of international regimes addressing transboundary and global environmental risks. He is writing a book on the evolution of multilateral environmental governance since 1972.

He is the author of *Saving the Mediterranean: The Politics of International Environmental Cooperation* (1990), editor of *Knowledge, Power, and International Policy Coordination* (1997), and coeditor of *Institutions for the Earth: Sources of Effective International Environmental Protection* (1993). He has written thirteen articles published in journals such as *International Organization, Millennium, Global Governance, Environment, Environmental Conservation,* and *Global Environmental Change* and fourteen chapters appearing in eleven edited volumes.

He has consulted for the Commission on Global Governance, the United Nations Environment Programme, the U.S. Department of State, the U.S. Environmental Protection Agency, the U.S. National Academy of Sciences, the American Association for the Advancement of Science, and the World Resources Institute. He has received grants from the National Science Foundation, German Marshall Fund, Rockefeller Brothers Fund, Institute for the Study of World Politics, and the Gallatin Foundation.

Frank P. Harvey

Frank P. Harvey is director of the Centre for Foreign Policy Studies at Dalhousie University. He is also a professor of political science at Dalhousie. His current research interests include ethnic conflict in the former Yugoslavia, NATO military strategy and peacekeeping, and national missile defense.

His books include *The Future's Back: Nuclear Rivalry, Deterrence Theory, and Crisis Stability after the Cold War* (1997); *Conflict in World Politics: Advances in the Study of Crisis, War, and Peace* (1998, coedited with Ben Mor); and *Using Force to Prevent Ethnic Violence: An Evaluation of Theory and Evidence* (2000, with David Carment). He has published widely on nuclear and conventional deterrence, coercive diplomacy, crisis decision making, and protracted ethnic conflict in such periodicals as *International Studies Quarterly, Journal of Conflict Resolution, Journal of Politics, Interna-*

tional Journal, Security Studies, International Political Science Review, Conflict Management and Peace Science, Canadian Journal of Political Science, and several others. Professor Harvey is currently working on his next book, *Coercive Diplomacy and the Management of Intrastate Ethnic Conflict.*

Yosef Lapid

Yosef Lapid is a professor of government at New Mexico State University. His research interests include international relations theory, culture and identity, and border studies. He is coeditor of *The Return of Culture and Identity in International Relations* (1996, with F. Kratochwil) and *Identities, Borders, Orders: Rethinking International Relations Theory* (2001, with M. Albert and D. Jacobson).

L. H. M. Ling

L. H. M. Ling is a senior lecturer in international studies at the Institute of Social Studies, The Hague. Her work applies a postcolonial-constructivist model of international relations to a wide range of issues: democratization, globalization, media images, urban design, peace and conflict studies, development and politics in East Asia, and transnational scholarship in the Western academy. Dr. Ling is the author of *Postcolonial IR: Conquest and Desire between Asia and the West* (2001).

V. Spike Peterson

V. Spike Peterson is an associate professor in the Department of Political Science with courtesy appointments in women's studies, comparative cultural and literary studies, and international studies at the University of Arizona, Tucson. She has held research fellowships at the Australian National University, University of Bristol, and Goteborg University. She is a past recipient of the MacArthur Foundation Research and Writing Grant and the author of numerous chapters and journal articles on the topics of feminist international relations theory, global political economy, nationalism, and critical postmodernist and feminist theory.

She is the coauthor of *Global Gender Issues* (1993, with Anne Sisson Runyan) and editor of *Gendered States: Feminist (Re)Visions of International Relations Theory* (1992, 1999). She has published articles in *Millennium, Women's Studies International Forum,* and

International Feminist Journal of Politics and numerous chapters in edited volumes. She is currently working on a book-length project, tentatively titled *Rewriting (Global) Political Economy as Reproductive, Productive, and Virtual (Foucauldian) Economies.*

Jan Jindy Pettman

Jan Jindy Pettman is a professor of international relations at Australian National University and director of the Women's Studies Centre. She is coeditor of the *International Feminist Journal of Politics.* She is the author of *Worlding Women: A Feminist International Politics.* She writes extensively on international domestic work, sex work, and globalization in Southeast Asia. Her current research project is "A Feminist Perspective on 'Australia in Asia.'"

James N. Rosenau

James N. Rosenau holds the distinguished rank of university professor of international affairs at the George Washington University. Professor Rosenau has held a Guggenheim Foundation Fellowship and is a former president of the International Studies Association.

His scholarship has focused on globalization, the dynamics of change in world politics, and the overlap of domestic and foreign affairs, resulting in more than thirty-five books and 150 articles. Some of his recent publications include *Thinking Theory Thoroughly: Coherent Approaches to an Incoherent World* (1995, 2000); *Stability, Stasis, and Security: Reflections on Superpower Leadership* (2000); *Along the Domestic-Foreign Frontier: Exploring Governance in a Turbulent World* (1997); *Global Voices* (1993); *Governance without Government* (1991); and *Turbulence in World Politics: A Theory of Change and Continuity* (1990).

Steve Smith

Steve Smith is pro vice chancellor (academic affairs) and professor of international politics at the University of Wales, Aberystwyth, which he joined in 1992. He was previously a professor of international relations at the University of East Anglia and has also taught at the State University of New York, Albany.

Since 1986 he has been the founding editor of the Cambridge University Press Studies in International Relations series. From 1995 to 2000 he was a member of the SSRC/MacArthur Committee on International Peace and Security. He has been a member of the executive committee of the British International Studies Association since 1980 and has served on the executive committee (1991–92) and was then vice president (1992–93) of the International Studies Association (United States). He has recently been appointed to the governing council of the American Political Science Association section on International Politics and International History. In 1999 he was awarded the Susan Strange Award by the International Studies Association for his contribution to intellectual diversity in the study of international relations.

He is the author of some eighty academic papers and chapters in major international journals and edited collections, and he is the author/editor of thirteen books, including *Explaining and Understanding International Relations* (1990, with Martin Hollis); *International Relations Theory Today* (1995, edited with Ken Booth); *International Theory: Positivism and Beyond* (1996, edited with Ken Booth and Marysia Zalewski); and *The Globalization of World Politics* (1997, edited with John Baylis 2001). His research interests involve the theory of security studies, contemporary international theory, and foreign policy analysis.

Christine Sylvester

Christine Sylvester is a professor at the Institute of Social Studies in The Hague. Her books include the forthcoming *Feminist International Relations: An Unfinished Journey* and *Feminist Theory and International Relations in a Postmodern Era*. Recent articles appear in *Alternatives*, *Third World Quarterly*, *International Feminist Journal of Politics*, *Body and Society*, and a variety of Africanist journals.

J. Ann Tickner

J. Ann Tickner is a professor of international relations and director of the Center for International Studies at the University of Southern California. She is the author of *Self-Reliance versus Power Politics: The American and Indian Experiences in Building Nation States* (1987); *Gender in International Relations: Feminist Perspectives on Achieving Global Security* (1992); and *Gendering World Politics: Issues and Approaches in the Post–Cold War Era* (2001); as well as numerous articles and book chapters on feminist international theory.

R. B. J. Walker

R. B. J. (Rob) Walker is a professor in the School of Politics, International Relations, and the Environment at Keele University in the United Kingdom. He has written widely on the implications of contemporary global transformations for modern accounts of sovereignty, subjectivity, and political practice. He is best known for his work *Inside/Outside: International Relations as Political Theory* (1993), and he is currently completing a new book, *After the Globe/Before the World* (2003). He is editor of the journal *Alternatives: Global, Local, Political*.

Marysia Zalewski

Dr. Marysia Zalewski joined the Centre for Women's Studies at Queen's University of Belfast in September 1999. Her teaching and research interests include feminist theory, international relations theory, the politics of theory (particularly as related to practice), reproductive technologies, and masculinity studies. She has published widely in the area of gender and international relations. Her most recent book is *Feminisms after Postmodernism: Theorising through Practice* (2000).